Start Drawing Landscapes

Basic Principles, Design and Exercises

by Markus S. Agerer

Imprint

Start Drawing Landscapes
Basic Principles, Composition and Exercises

ISBN: 9798612822158

Original Texts: Markus S. Agerer
Illustrations: Markus S. Agerer
Cover Design: Markus S. Agerer
Translation: Paul Ronning

Copyright: © 2020 Markus S. Agerer

Bürgermeister-Haidacher-Straße 1
82140 Olching
Deutschland

email: markus-agerer@web.de
web: www.markus-agerer.de

Printed in Germany by Amazon Distribution GmbH, Leipzig

This book, sections thereof as well as the pictorial material – if not otherwise noted – are protected by copyright. It may not be used or exploited in any manner divergent from the law without authorization from the creator.

The author/illustrator has produced all contents with the utmost care; nevertheless, liability of any kind can not be assumed for errors and the direct or indirect consequences thereof.

This book contains links (also via QR code) to external third-party websites, on whose content the author of this book has no influence. Therefore, no liability can be assumed for this external content. The linked pages were checked for possible legal violations at the time the link was created. A permanent control of the content of the linked pages is not reasonable without concrete evidence of an infringement.

QR codes: The QR codes in this book contain links to various websites. This expands the content of the book. No guarantee can be given for the continued existence of this online content. It should also be noted that the websites linked in this way may contain advertising, affiliate links etc. The terms of use and the data protection declaration of the respective website must be observed.

Table of Contents

1 INTRODUCTION – LANDSCAPES	**6**
2 BASIC PRINCIPLES OF DRAWING	**12**
3 ELEMENTS OF A LANDSCAPE DRAWING	**40**
4 REPRESENTATION OF SPACE AND PERSPECTIVE	**76**
5 PICTURE DESIGN AND COMPOSITION	**104**
6 STUDIES – DRAWING LANDSCAPES	**128**
7 CLOSING REMARKS	**160**

Introduction – Landscapes

» All beginnings are light-hearted; the threshold is the place of anticipation. «

- Johann Wolfgang von Goethe -

1 Introduction – Landscapes

1.1 Preface

I'm glad you chose this book. So you want to learn to draw landscapes and learn more about landscape images? This book will accompany you on your way. Besides the basic principles of drawing, you will also learn more about the history of landscape representation (drawing & painting). This is knowledge that is valuable for the development of your own skills, since you can become acquainted during the process with further aspects of landscape drawing.

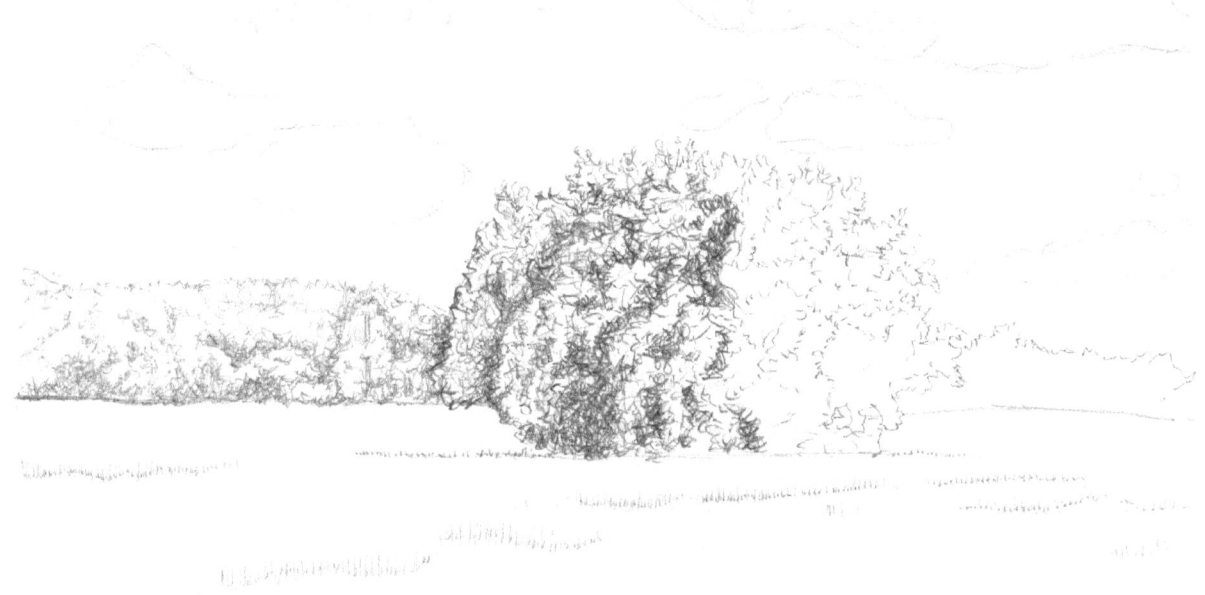

So that you can quickly and directly get into the topic of landscape drawing, in this book you will find the most important basic knowledge about drawing techniques, perspective drawing and image design. This means you don't have to buy a stack of books - you can find it all here. After looking at the basics of drawing, we will look at the various elements that can be found in a landscape and learn how to draw them. In the following chapters you will learn more about perspective as well as image composition. The new skills that you can develop with this book will ultimately be tested in step-by-step instructions for complete landscape drawings. In addition, historical details on the development of landscape drawing and painting will also be included, since you can learn directly from the old masters in this manner.

1.2 What is a Landscape Drawing?

The term landscape image is used when an extract from the space determined by nature or man is depicted. Concrete and idealized natural landscapes can be depicted. Typical landscape pictures show mountain landscapes, hilly country, forests, seascapes, coastlines, rivers, lakes and more. But also cities, architecture, gardens, park landscapes and factory landscapes belong to the field of landscape drawing and painting. In these cases we are talking about so-called cultural landscapes - i.e. landscapes that have been permanently shaped by man.

Landscape depictions are a genre of representational art alongside historical paintings, portraits, genre paintings and still lifes. The great significance of this genre can be seen in the depictions of scenic motifs in paintings from ancient Egypt, from antiquity to the present. In China and Japan, the depiction of landscapes also represents an important branch of the visual arts.

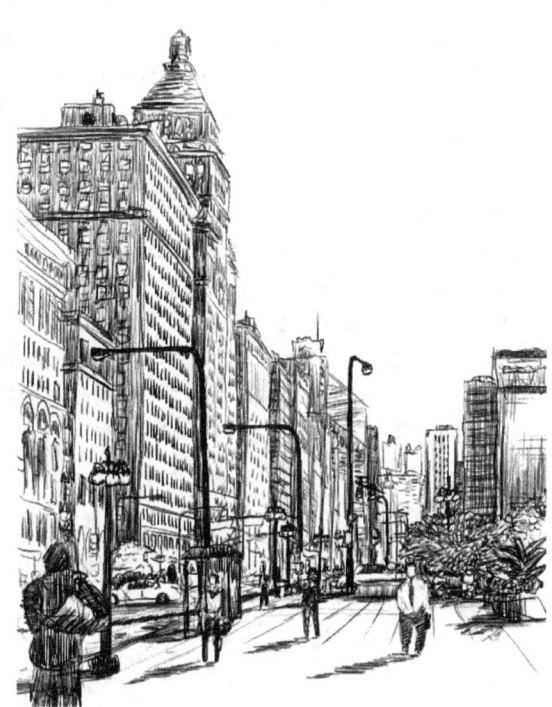

Cityscape – street in Chicago

Landscape Representation in the Course of History

The art of landscape representation looks back on a long history. Written records of landscape paintings from the time of **Greek antiquity** are the earliest evidence of this. Furthermore, at least portions of frescoes of the Cretan-Mycenaean culture have been preserved. In the Rome of antiquity, landscapes were converted into wall paintings.

During the **Middle Ages**, the area of landscape representation lay fallow, so to speak. It was not until the end of the Middle Ages, with the transition to the Renaissance, that the depiction of landscape emerged as the background for a pictorial narrative in the Netherlands.

The **Renaissance** represented a new beginning for landscape painting. Driven by a shift towards scientific exploration of the world and a new appropriation of antiquity, techniques such as linear perspective and aerial perspective were studied by artists such as Filippo Brunelleschi and Leonardo da Vinci. Landscapes could thus be staged even more effectively.

The first flowering of landscape painting began in the middle of the **16th century** in the Netherlands. Famous artists from this period included Joachim Patinir, Gerard David, Hieronymus Bosch and Pieter Brueghel.

Development continued and with the turn of the **17th century**, depiction of landscapes became a theme in its own right. While the landscape was until then only the scene of mythological or historical scenes in paintings (i.e. mainly background), from then on landscapes could be admired as the central motif in pictures. This was due to social changes during the Golden Age of the Netherlands, as a result of which bourgeois classes were now able to acquire paintings for private use. Due to its great popularity, the depiction of landscapes was divided into a multitude of themes, such as forest landscapes, mountain landscapes, river landscapes, fantasy landscapes, Italianizing landscapes, coastal and seascapes, topographical landscapes, winter scenes, etc.

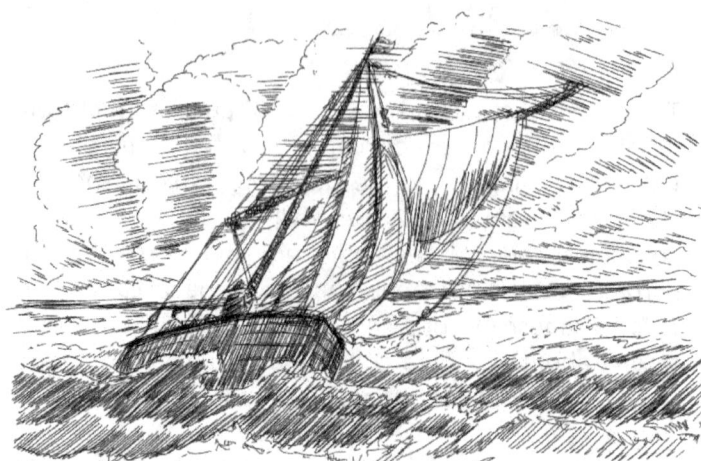

Indian-ink drawing after the work "Stormy Sea with sailboat" by Jacob van Ruisdael

In the **18th century**, the focus was more on the topographically exact representation of certain places, while the demand for arbitrary landscapes declined.

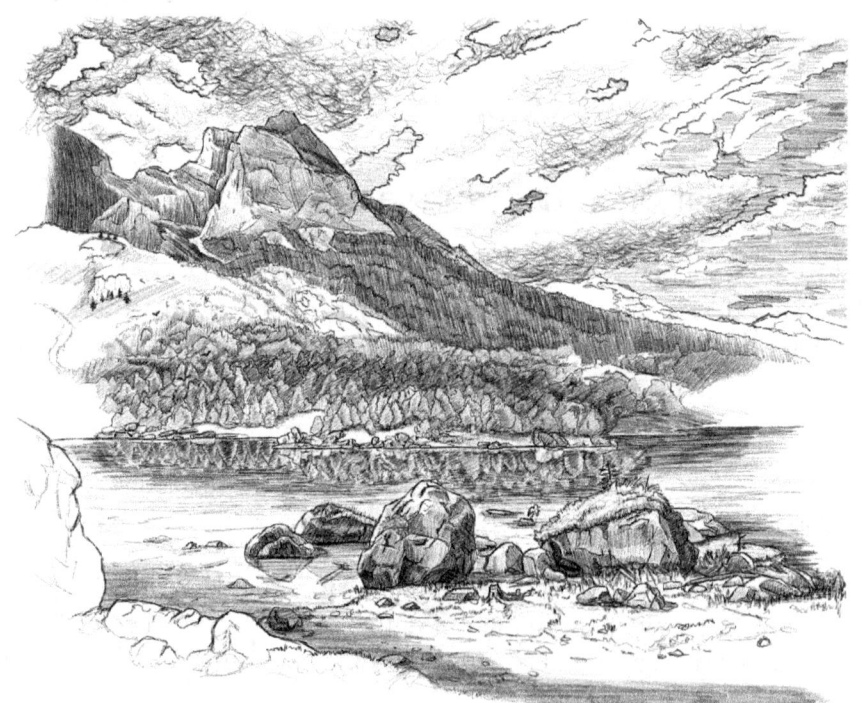

Landscape drawing according to the prototype of Carl Rottmann

At the beginning of the **19th century**, the era of Romanticism dominated landscape painting. For some art enthusiasts, the paintings created in this period even represent the epitome of landscape painting. Caspar David Friedrich was one of the best known and most important painters of his time.

But landscape painting experienced an even greater development in the same century. A new state of mind emerged in the field of fine art, which manifested itself in a subjective perception of the world. Great attention was no longer paid primarily to the motif, but increasingly to the style of painting. It was all about the personal handwriting of the artist. Thus the Impressionist artists played very vigorously with the effect of light and let colors merge smoothly into one another.

Landscape depiction of the **20th century** is particularly multi-facedted and can be seen in paintings, drawings, photographs as well as direct interventions in the existing natural or cultural landscape. A great influence on the way the landscape is treated in the visual arts of the 20th century is the turn to science, which led to a kind of alienation between man and nature.

Landscape in Asian Art

Landscapes were also of great importance in the art history of Asia. In the **8th century**, Chinese landscape painting experienced a climax. A further development took place in the **11th and 12th centuries**, whereby it was above all a matter of realistic reproduction. After that, the main focus was on literary painting.

In Japan landscape depictions arose between the **8th and 11th centuries**, which had their origin in Buddhist painting. Landscape painting did not become an independent art movement until the end of the 16th century.

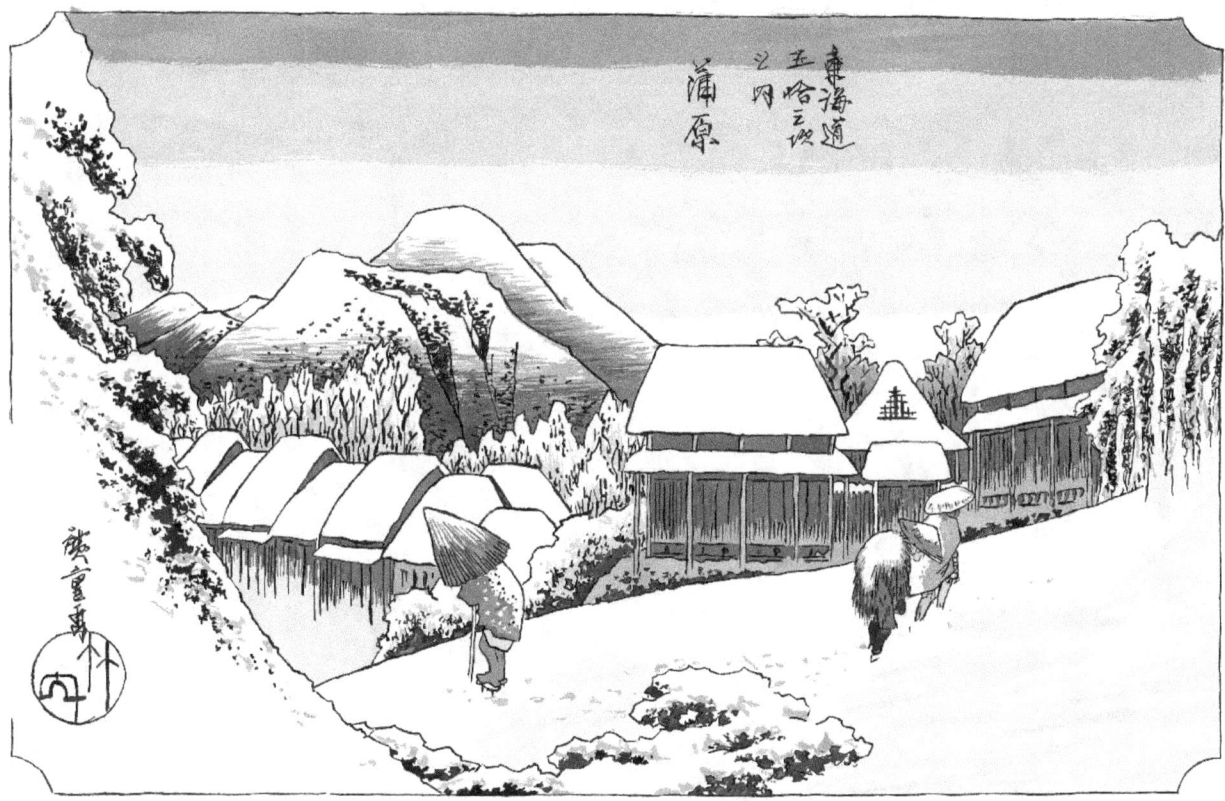

Replica of a Japanese woodblock print: "Station Kambara" taken from the series "The 53 Stations of Tōkaidō"
Original: Utagawa Hiroshige

Basic Principles of Drawing

» Drawing is the art of taking lines for a walk. «

- Paul Klee -

2 Basic Principles of Drawing

Simple drawing exercises form the basis for the first steps. Get to know your drawing tool and develop an initial understanding of drawing techniques and the illustration of forms.

The basics of drawing also include knowledge of the artist's design tools.

2.1 Drawing Design Tools

The term drawing design tools can be understood primarily as the point and the line, while structure, surface, and light-dark differentiation must also be included here. At least one of these means of design can be found in every drawing - but in most cases there are several.

The point is the smallest and most inconspicuous element in a drawing. The line starts at the point and can be used in different ways: as the outline of a body, as traces of movement, to describe forms and much more.

By drawing points or lines on the paper you can create surfaces, light-dark differentiations, hatching and structures. You can control this through the flow, distribution and density of points or lines.

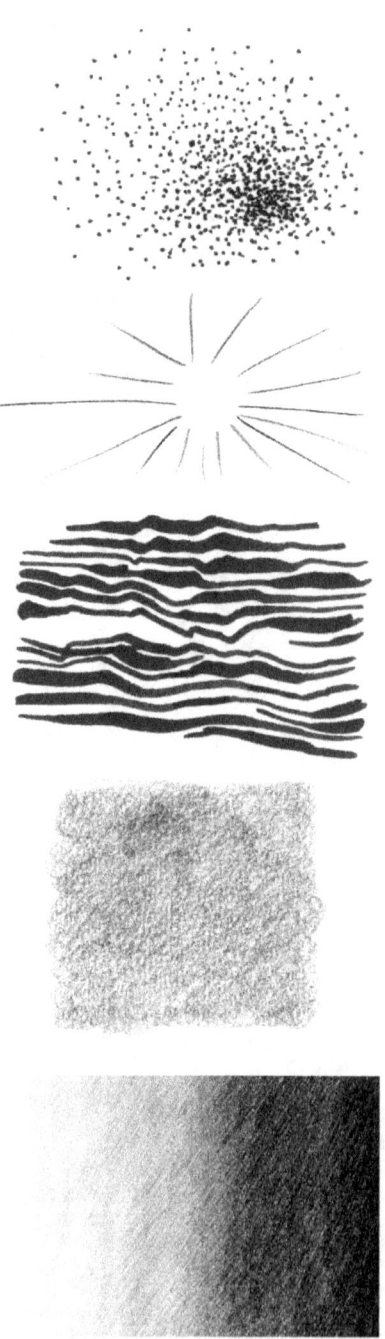

Drawing design tools: point, line, structure, surface and light-dark differentiation

Basic Principles of Drawing

Exercise for drawing design tools

Line

In a few simple exercises, try to use the design tools of the illustrator (artist). We start with the line. So draw lines in different shapes and different dynamics: straight lines, curved lines, lines carefully drawn or with temperament - anything is allowed.

These simple exercises are especially interesting for beginners and will loosen you up a bit. But the lesson also makes sense for more experienced illustrators, because it is about basic skills.

Lines drawn in a radiant pattern

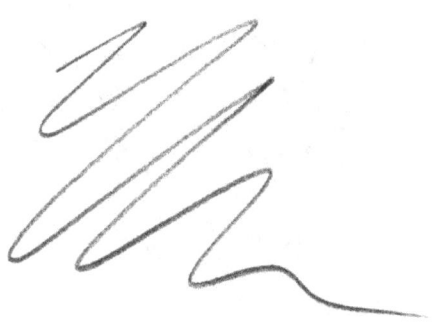

Swiftly drawn scribble line

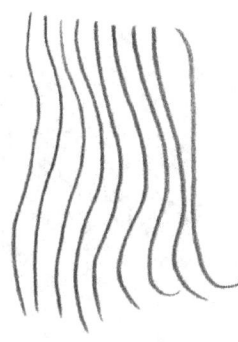

Wavy lines next to one another

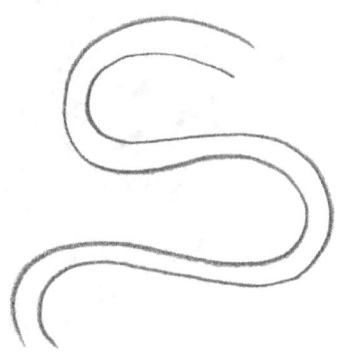

Parallel serpentine lines

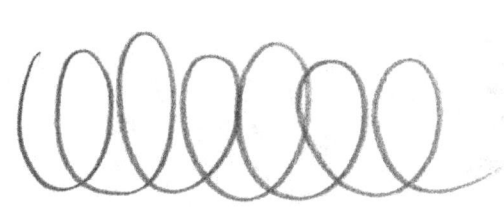

Spring-shaped line

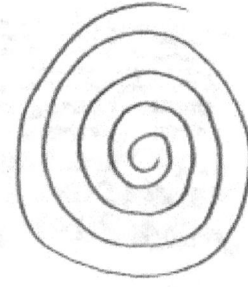

Spiral line

Structure

Structures can also be represented with lines. Structures must be differentiated from hatchings, since structures are usually not uniform. Each line of a structure can differ in shape, direction, line width and length. Even within a single line, these properties can change. The lines in a structure do not have to have the same distance from one another. Structures are therefore a creative means with which one can also represent a certain rhythm. This allows you to create tension in an image and add effects that are particularly interesting.

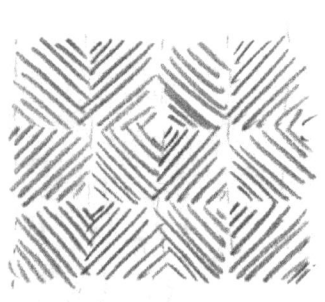

Chessboard structure with lines at a 45°-angle

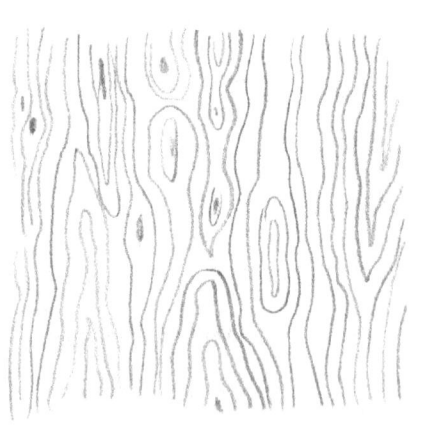

Structure with a series of irregular lines

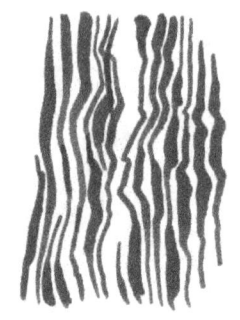

Tree bark-like structure

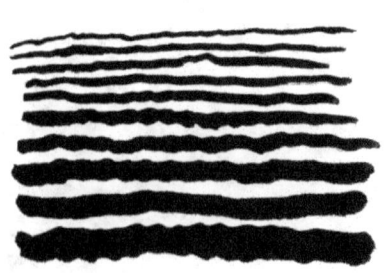

Structure with increasingly thinner lines

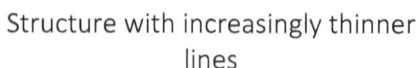

Wood-like structure

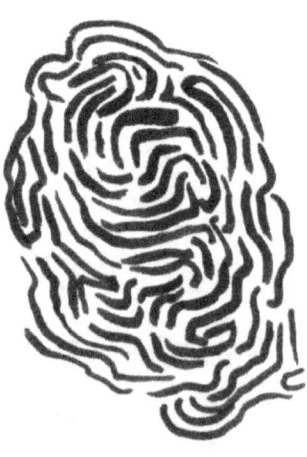

Natural-looking structure

Surfaces

Surfaces are a medium for graphic (drawing) design in which a certain drawing technique must inevitably be selected. Drawing techniques for flat-surface working are hatching, shading, wiping and washing. When hatching, the surface is sometimes prepared with a level structure. Additionally, the representation of several surfaces automatically results in the use of the "light-dark" design medium, since several surfaces are formed by different tonal values.

Level surface

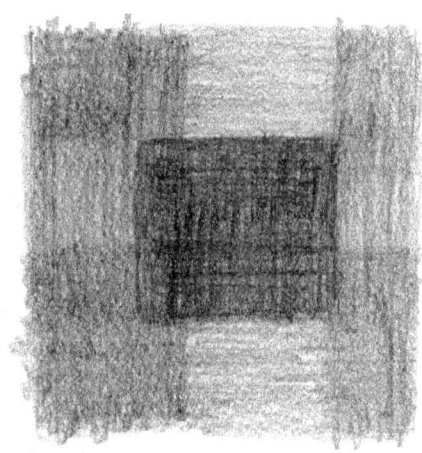

Contrasted surface

Distributed surfaces

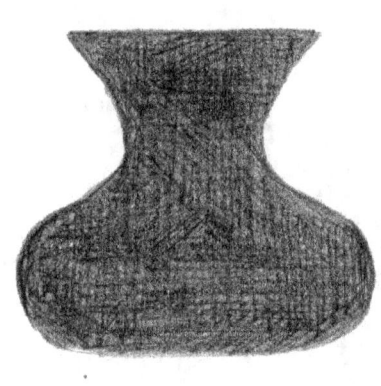

Shaped surface

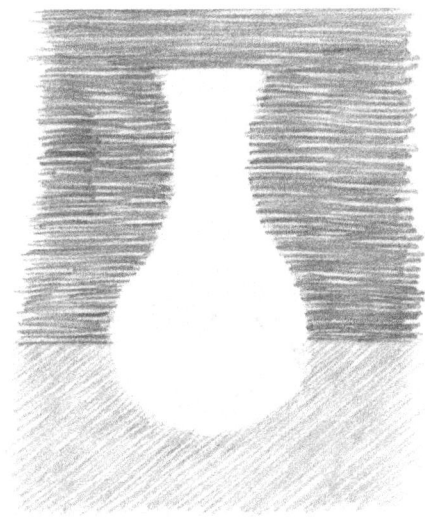

Negative drawing of a surface

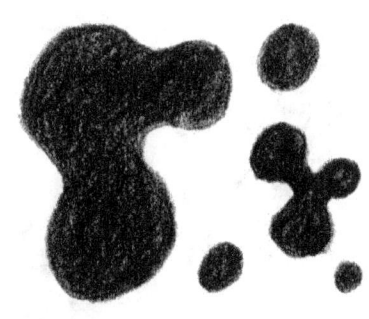

Drop-like surfaces

Examples in images

The following image examples illustrate the possibilities which one has with the use of simple graphic design means. Without using more elaborate techniques, such as light-dark gradients using hatching, it is possible to create quite expressive drawings.

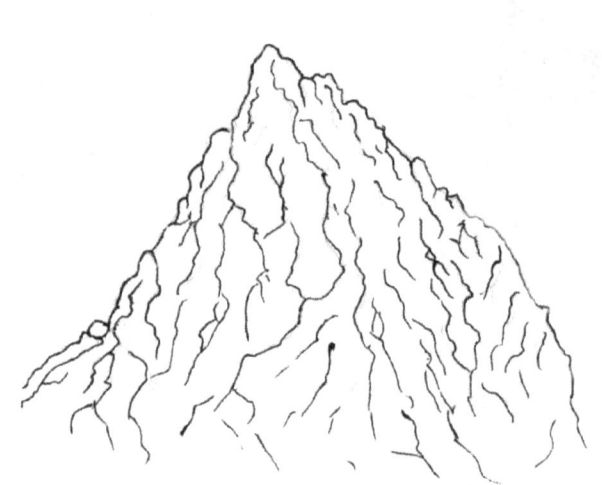
Line drawing of a mountain

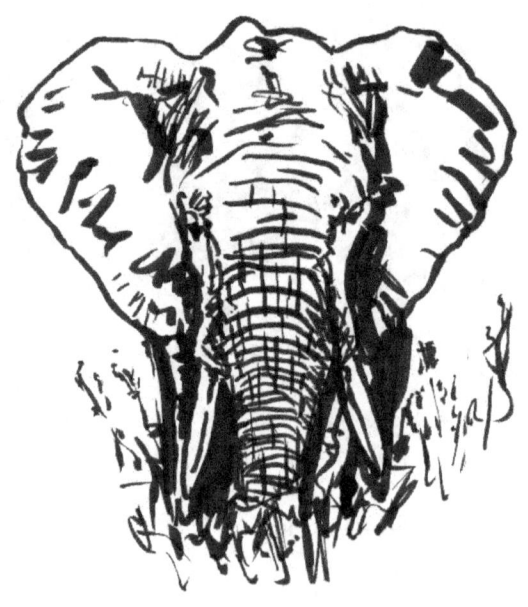
Elephant drawn with lines, surfaces and structure

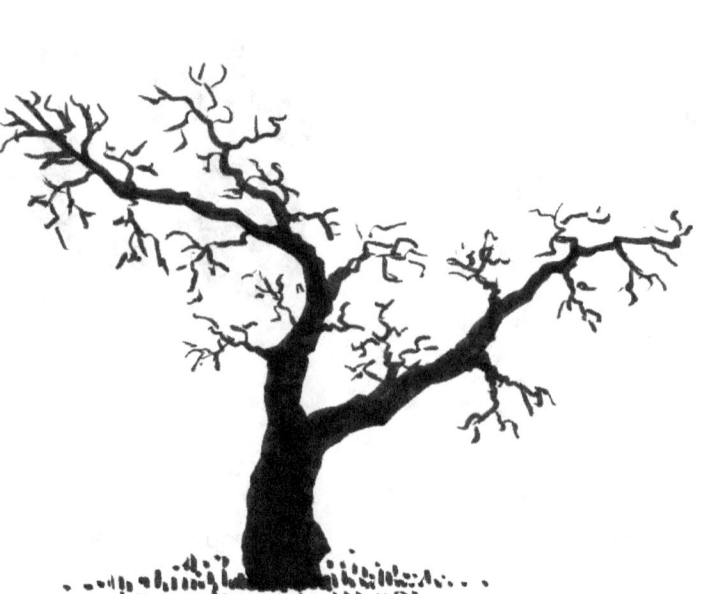
Leafless tree drawn by deploying surface and line

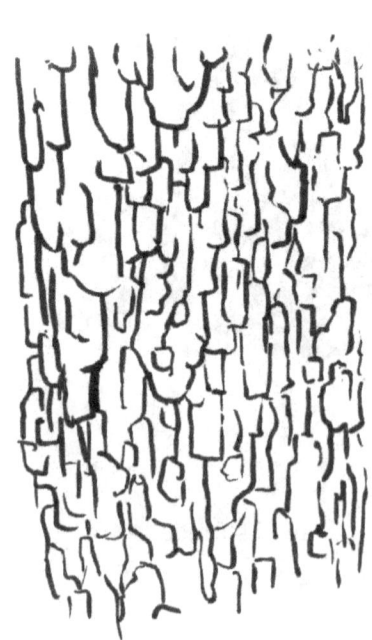
Structure-drawing used to represent tree bark

2.2 Drawing Simple Forms

Another good exercise is to sketch basic shapes. This refers to simple geometric figures that are only two-dimensional. In the pictures below you will find examples to trace or reproduce. You can also create your own shapes and sketch them. It makes sense to practice these basic forms, because you will encounter them again and again while drawing different motifs.

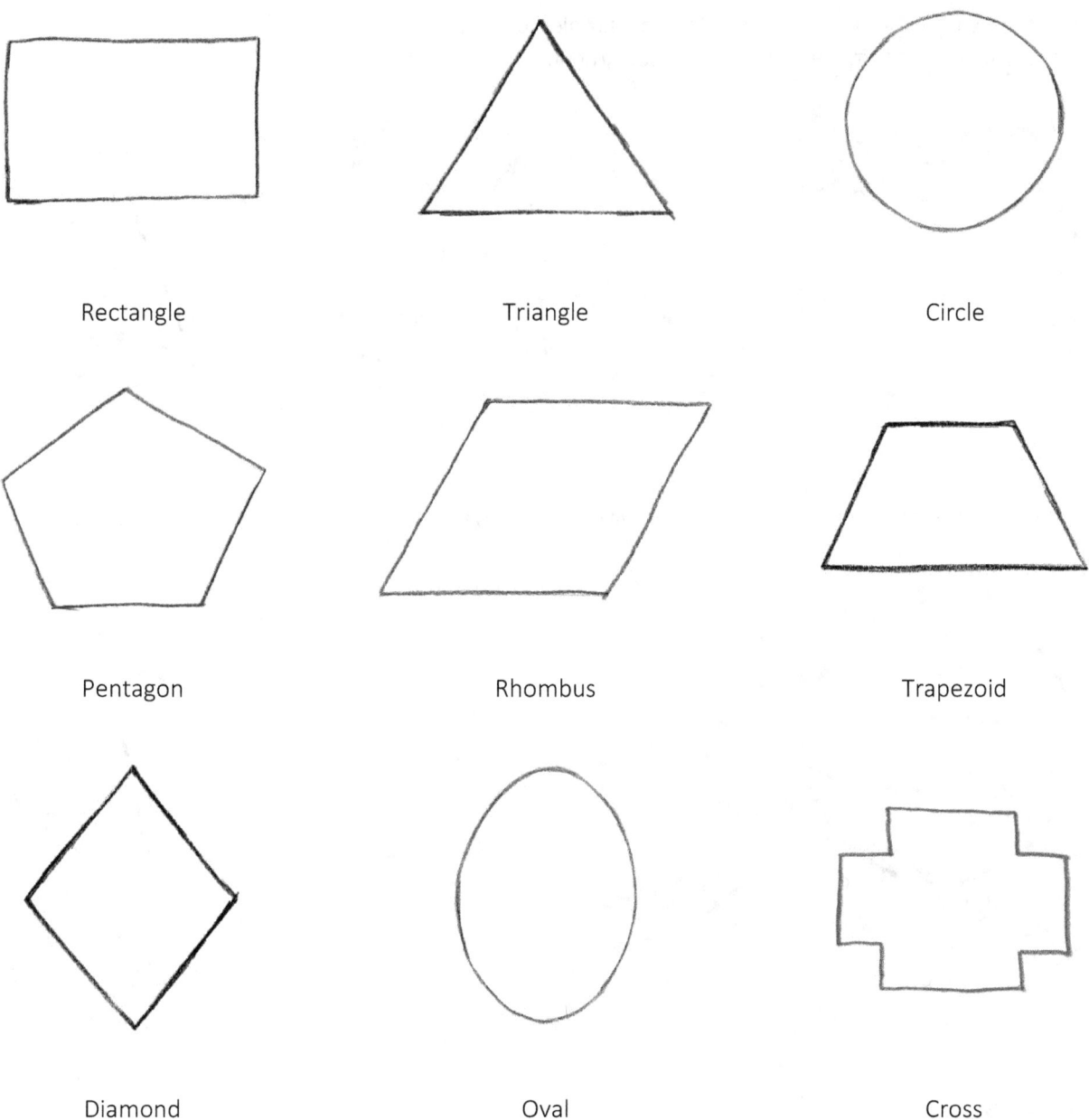

2.3 Representing Three-Dimensional Bodies

In the previous examples and exercises we have limited ourselves to the representation of lines, surfaces and mostly two-dimensional motifs. Space and depth have so far only been represented by surfaces. Now we go one step further and try to depict real bodies.

The term "*body*" refers to a geometric figure that occupies a certain space and is therefore three-dimensional. Drawing a body is much more demanding than sketching two-dimensional forms. For this reason we will start with the simplest objects and slowly improve.

Simple Geometric Bodies

In the following sketches important and simple bodies are depicted, which you can trace or reproduce for practice:

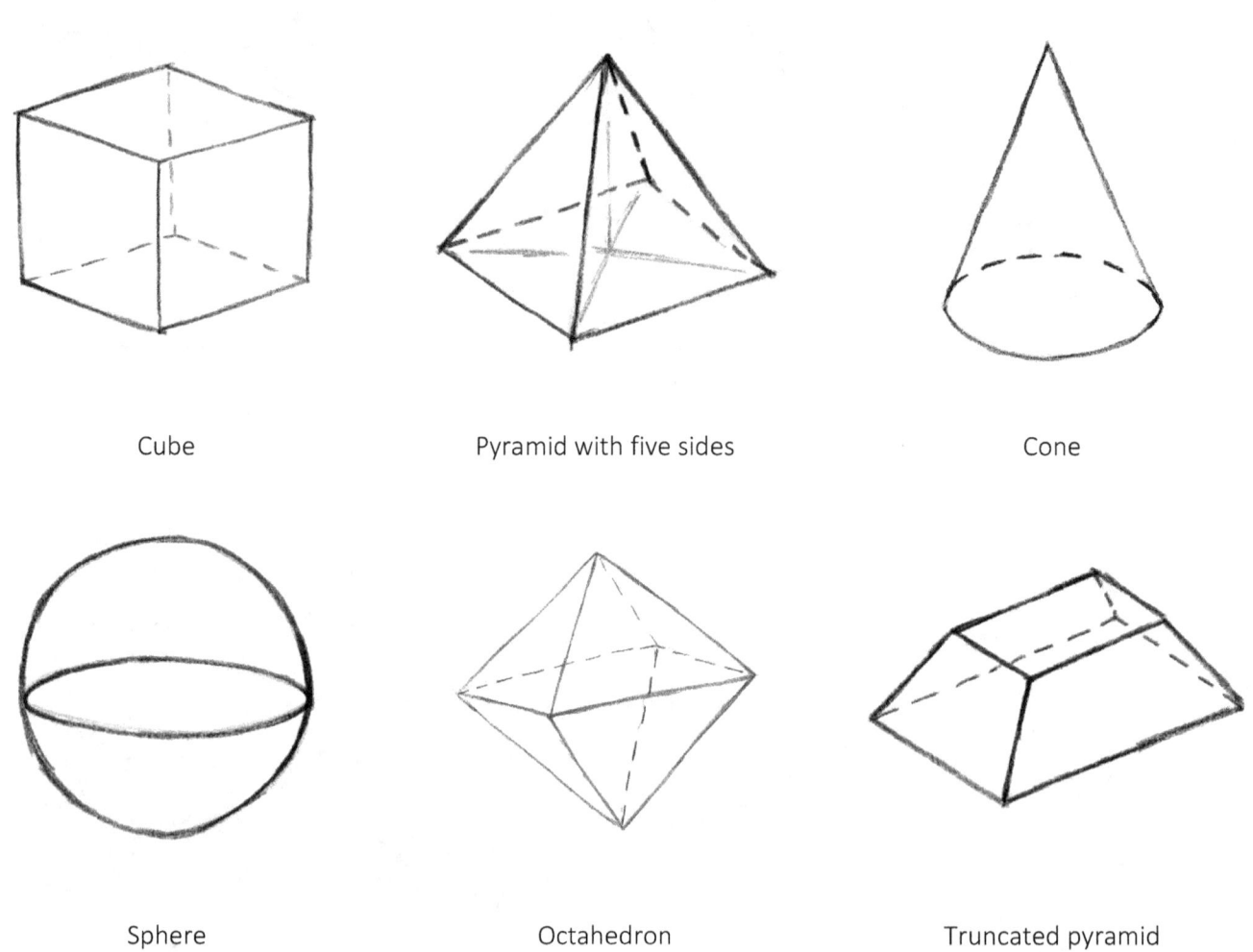

Cube
Pyramid with five sides
Cone

Sphere
Octahedron
Truncated pyramid

Basic Principles of Drawing

Transferring from the Surface into Space

The difference between two-dimensional shapes and three-dimensional bodies has already been described. However, to emphasize the meaning again, a descriptive example follows.

With the following drawings you can understand how a drawing gradually leaves the two-dimensional space and transforms into a completely spatial representation. We use a truck as our motif.

Step 1:
Pure two-dimensional drawing

Step 2:
Simple expansion of the drawing into depth – but only on one side.

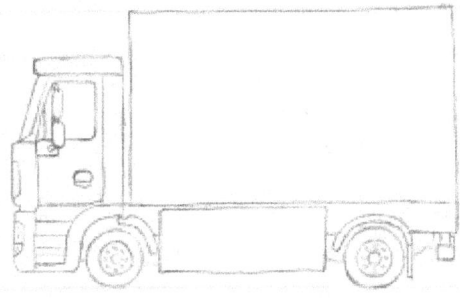

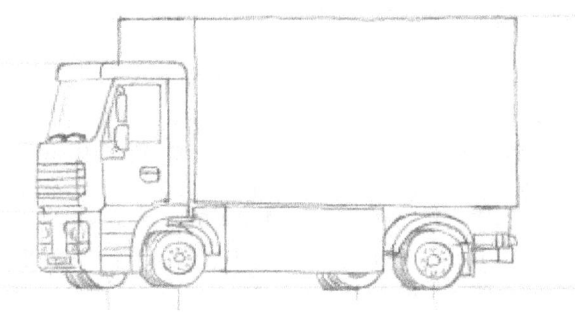

Step 3:
More complex expansion of the representation into depth

Step 4:
Perspective representation from the front oblique perspective

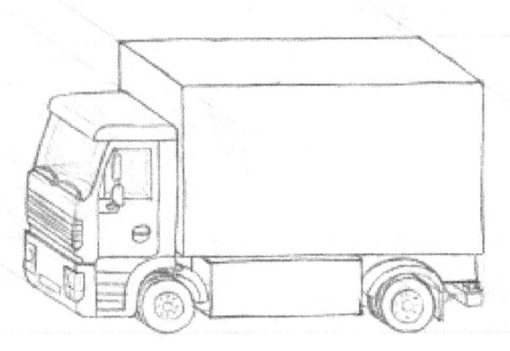

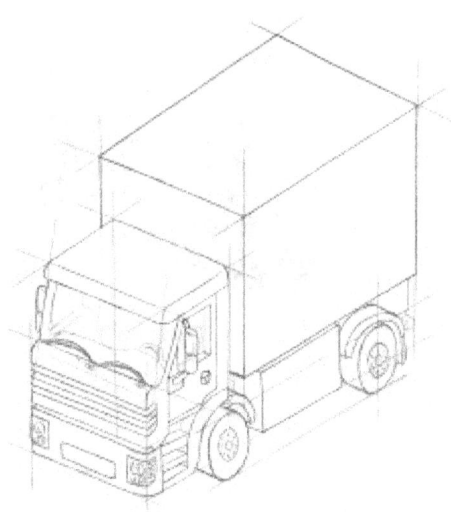

Even more realistic, albeit more complicated, is the three-dimensional representation of objects applying the so-called vanishing-point perspective. Using this method of drawing, the perspective distortion is represented, which we actually perceive in reality.

A drawing of the truck utilizing vanishing-point perspective can be seen here in the following image.

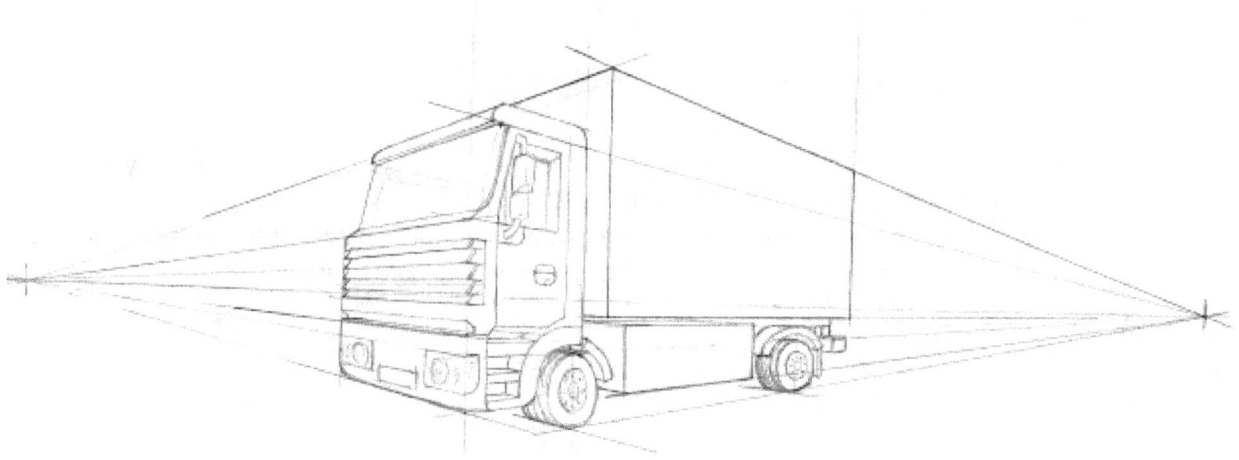

We will take a look at the method of representation using vanishing points in one of the succeeding chapters in this book. In the event that you would like to learn more about this, I recommend my book:
"Drawing Perspective and Space: The Basic Principles of Drawing in Perspective"

The example of the truck demonstrates quite well what it means to illustrate three-dimensional bodies. Knowledge in this area can also be logically applied to landscape representation, since motifs within a landscape are also spatial bodies.

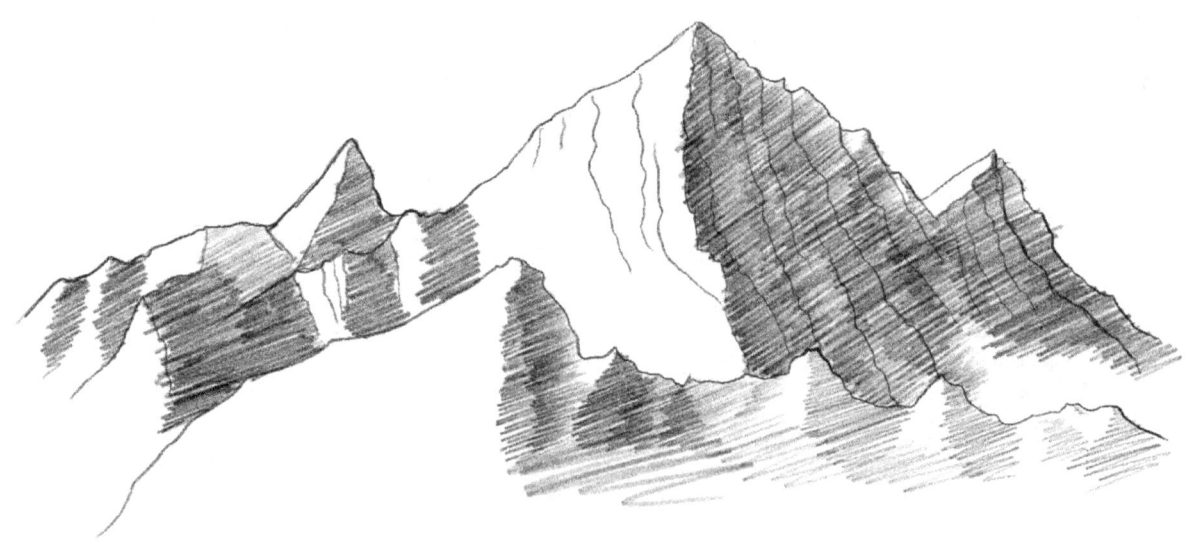

This sketch of a mountain landscape illustrates an example of spatial bodies within a landscape. One can achieve the best three-dimensional effect by including shadows in the image. You can learn how to draw shadows in one of the succeeding chapters in this book.

2.4 Exercise – Simple Motifs

Mini-Landscapes

In this exercise you can practice using initial small motifs. By making use of only a few strategic lines, mini-landscapes can be created as seen here below.

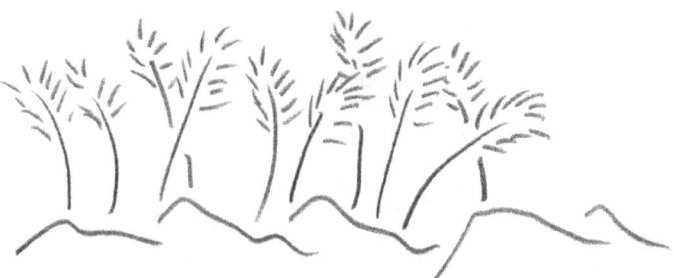

Field with wheat

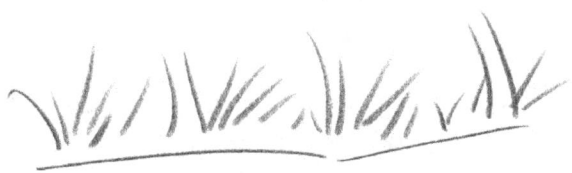

Field with wheat

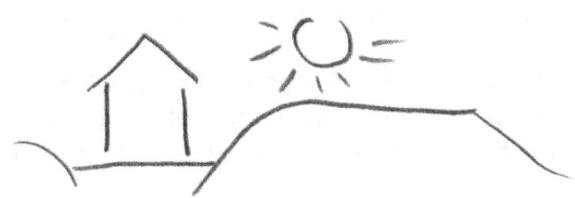

House in a hilly landscape

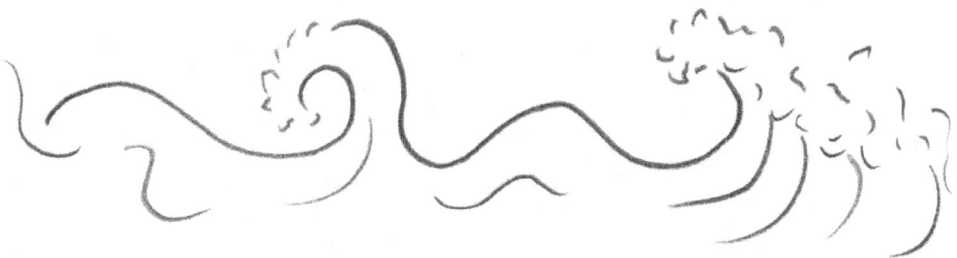

Surging ocean waves

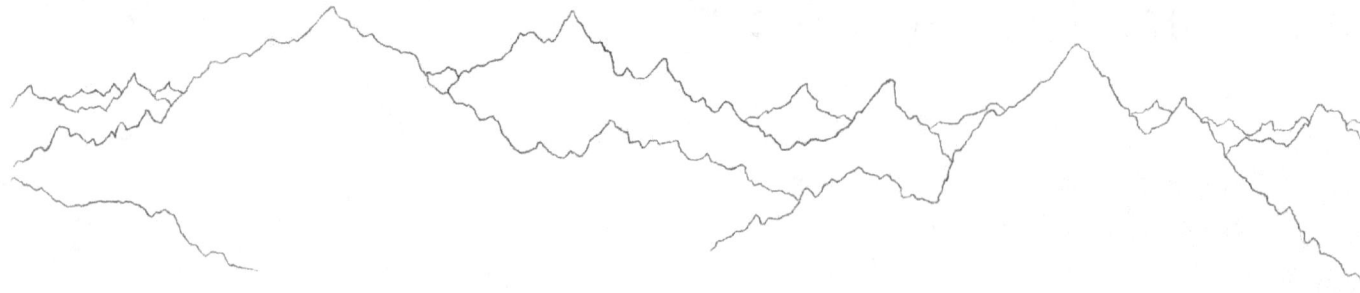

Mountain range

Exercise: Buildings – Constructing Objects in Perspective

And now try drawing a building from a perspective point-of-view. Your goal here is simply the depiction of the contours – and if you like, you can use a ruler to make straight lines. We will proceed in four steps, whereby we first of all make a rough sketch; then we work out the form in two steps and, finally, add a few more details.

Drawing motifs that are geometrically simple and rigidly constructed is an excellent exercise, since you can acquire, in this manner, a better feeling for the representation of space and form. However, these challenges are not meant for everyone, since intuition is rarely required here – this exercise more likely involves a technical approach to drawing.

Basic Principles of Drawing

Step 1:
An initial rough draft of the form

Step 2:
More detailed development of the form

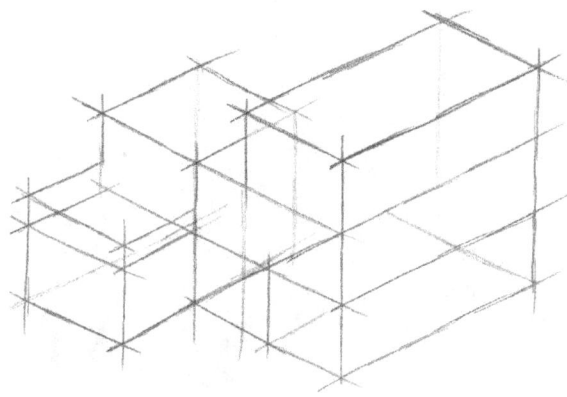

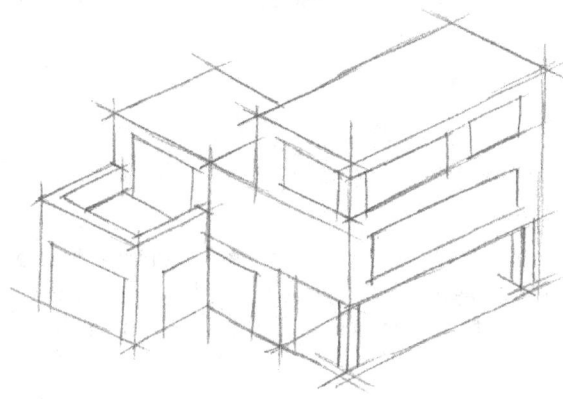

Step 3:
Completion of the geometric body

Step 4:
Detailing and completion of the drawing

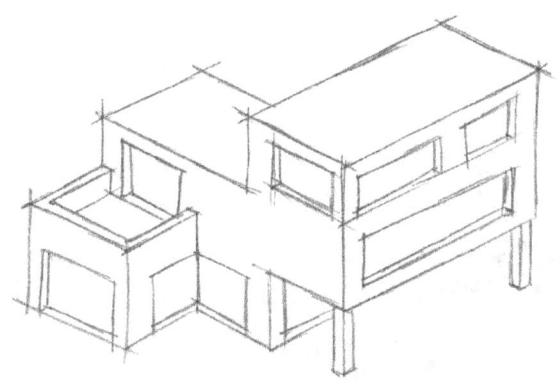

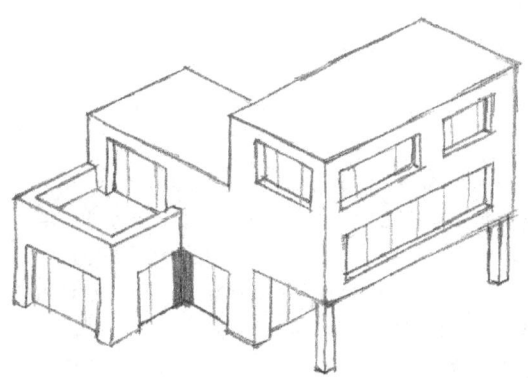

The technique behind three-dimensional drawing is not limited exclusively to geometric representation; illustration of the shadows is also important. Only through shading are motifs able to display their full, spatial effect.

2.5 Drawing Tools

At this point, the various drawing tools will be described. When one is aware of the different material means and their characteristics, it is easier to predict when a certain tool would be most suitable or which ones will be personally more preferable.

Lead Pencil / Graphite Pencil

One of the most important tools for drawing is the "lead", i.e., graphite pencil. The designation lead pencil is historical and false in reality, since a pencil core actually consists of a mixture of graphite, clay and water and not of lead.

Pencils have many advantages: one can draw varyingly strong lines by controlling the hand pressure while drawing, and also erase previously drawn lines. Also, by choosing different degrees of graphite hardness in the pencils, various shades of gray (tonal values) can be achieved.

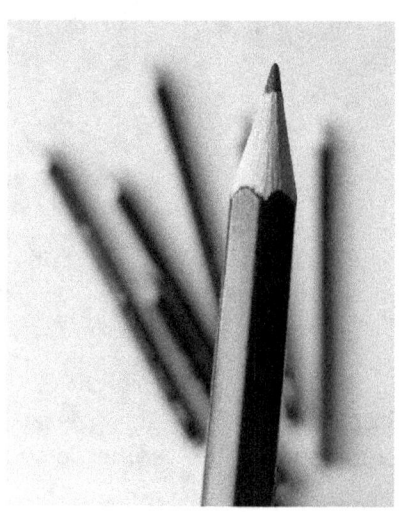

Indian Ink and Ink

When we refer to Indian ink or ink, we are talking about liquid media for drawing. Artists have traditionally drawn with either quill with Indian ink (bottled ink) or they have used pens. The quill has the disadvantage that one has to dip the quill into the bottle again and again, which can easily lead to splashing. With pens we are offered a broad palette of various products. Examples are fiber pens that utilize Indian ink as well as ballpoint pens, fineliners and drawing ink pens.

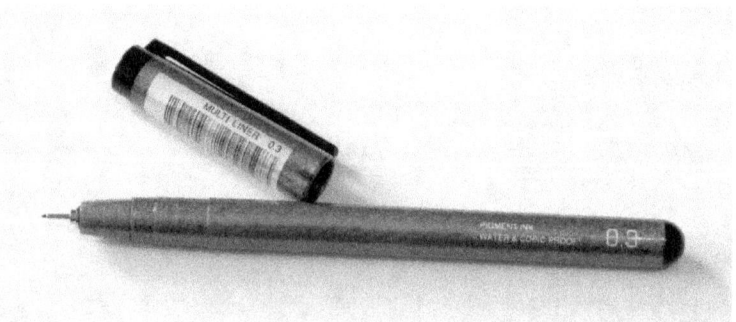

Fineliner with a 0.3mm point

These pens have the advantage that it is not necessary to always refill the India ink or ink by hand, since the drawing medium is contained inside. Once the ink reservoir is empty, it can be exchanged, or a new pen has to be used.

Basic Principles of Drawing

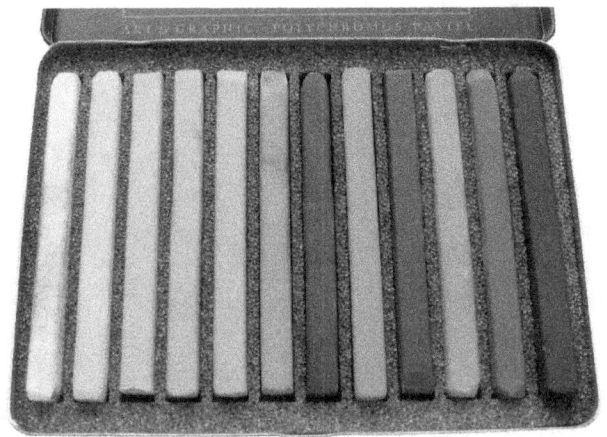

Chalk / Pastel chalk

Pastel chalk is suitable primarily for color drawings and/or paintings with large colored surfaces and soft color gradations. Application of the color can be either soft or robust. Typical for pastel paintings are, however, the soft color gradations. These colors can easily be blurred with a finger or a swiping tool.

Charcoal

We can also draw using charcoal. The so-called drawing charcoal consists of carbonized wood. The drawing charcoal is available in either stick or charcoal pencil form. A considerably robust, dark color application can be achieved here, with which highly expressive and contrast-rich drawings are created. One can draw thin lines and uniform surfaces. It is also well-suited to the technique of smearing, which can be used to draw on a large scale.

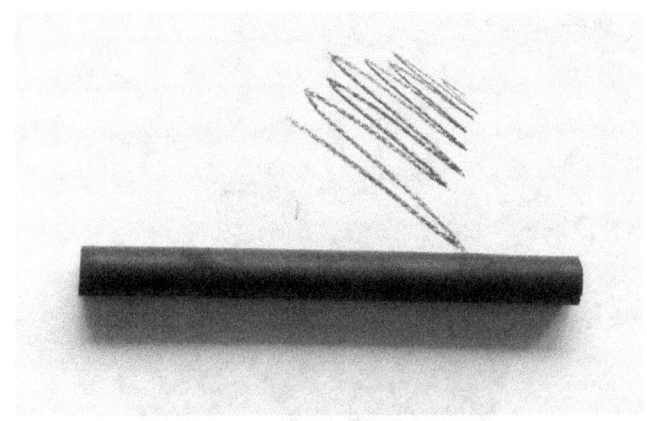

Colored Pencils / Crayons

A colored pencil is a pencil with a colored core which is – as is the case with a lead pencil – encased in wood. The colored core consists of a mixture of colored pigments, fat, wax, a binding agent, talcum and kaolin.

Colored pencils can be qualitatively quite varied. It is better here if one does not necessarily select the cheapest product, since qualitatively inferior working materials can easily diminish the joy of drawing. Furthermore, among artists colored pencils are preferred over crayons because a reference to crayons reminds one of rather low quality materials from primary school.

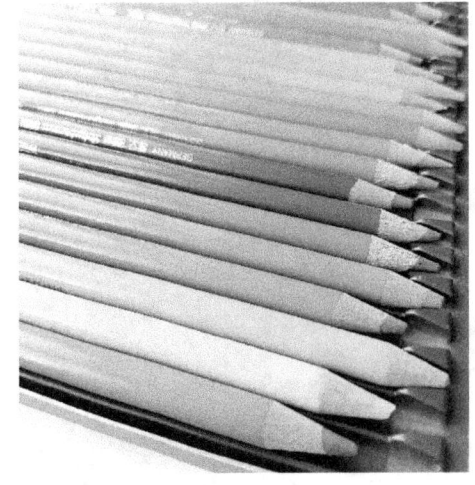

2.6 Further Material for Drawing

Paper

After the pencil, the second most important thing is the drawing surface – that is, the paper or cardboard. The drawing surface is essential for the achievable quality of a drawing.

Important characteristics of a drawing surface are, in addition to the paper format, the roughness and the relative weight (gram per square meter). In reference to the weight it can be said: the higher the better, since the paper becomes thicker and more stable. The roughness of the surface depends on personal preference.

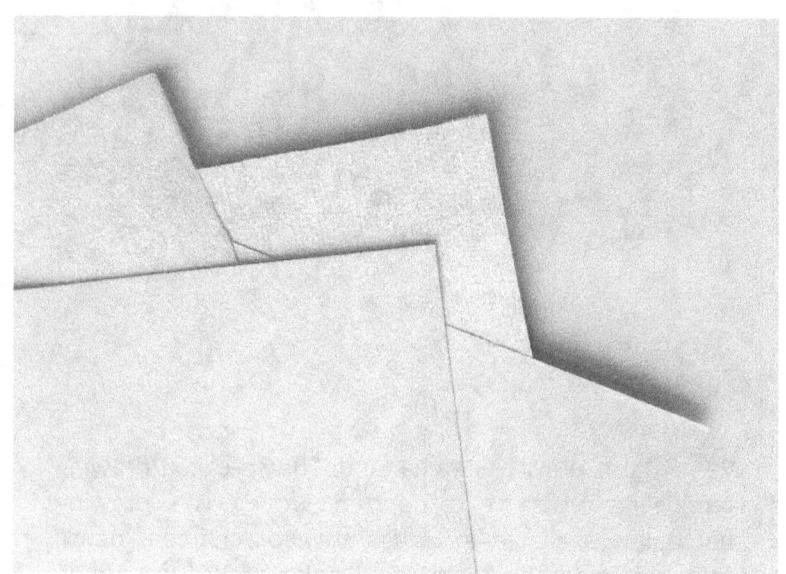

Various forms of drawing paper

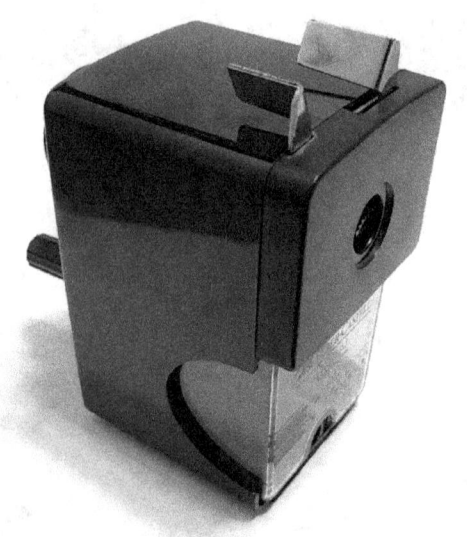

Pencil Sharpener

With the sharpener you can keep pencils and colored pencils pointed and thus draw thin, fine lines. It is available in different versions and sizes.

A hand-operated sharpening machine is recommended for drawing. Working with it is more pleasant than with a normal sharpener. Moreover, it occurs less frequently that, while sharpening the pencil, the point breaks off. Some artists alternatively use a sharp knife to sharpen their points.

Erasers

The eraser is not to be underestimated as a valuable tool for drawing. The function of an eraser is of course to remove lines that have been drawn with a graphite pencil, colored pencil, chalk ,etc.

During the drawing process, an eraser is frequently used specifically to implement small details – for example, small points of light or light-catching contours. Another function in drawing could also be intentional smudging.

The various kinds of erasers are: rubber eraser (hard), vinyl eraser (soft), eraser pencil ("erasil") and kneaded eraser.

Rubber eraser

You can remove strong drawing lines and, in part, Indian ink. It has the advantage of a relatively sharp edge that can be used to erase details. The main problem with a rubber eraser is that it can damage the structure of the paper. It thus becomes difficult to erase on roughened paper. However, the removal of color cannot be achieved so readily.

Vinyl eraser

A vinyl eraser is considerably gentler on paper than the hard variety. A soft eraser is much easier on paper than a hard one. But the removal of color, which can be achieved with the vinyl eraser, is also reduced.

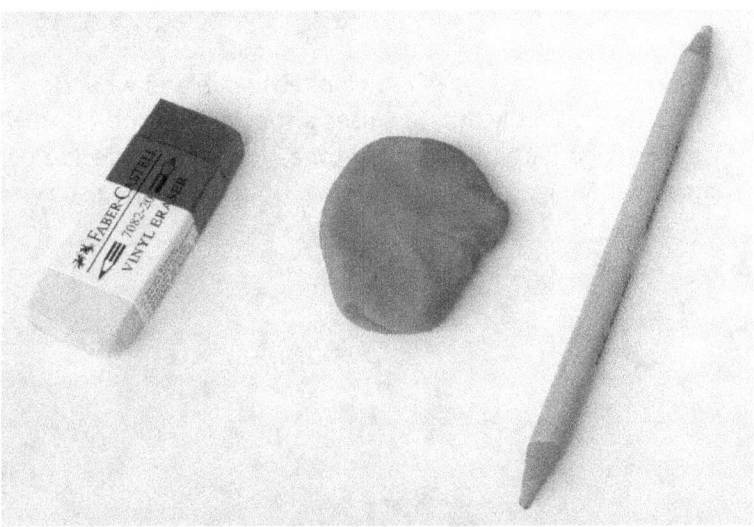

Two-sided eraser (hard & soft), gum eraser & eraser pencil

Eraser pencil

With the eraser pen you can work out fine details in drawings. The eraser pencil can be sharpened. There are pencils with a hard and a soft end. The soft end is also suitable for using the smudging technique.

Kneaded (art) eraser

The unique characteristic of the kneaded eraser its formability. It can remove sections of the drawing by simply being pressed onto the paper. This can best be achieved with loose drawing methods such as charcoal or pastel chalk as well as pencil. The formability is of great advantage here in particular. The kneaded eraser is soft for the paper, but is not able to remove all of the drawing details.

2.7 Drawing Technique Methods

What are the *methods of drawing technique* and what do you need them for? Both questions can be explained in one answer: simply put, one uses a specific method of drawing technique as soon as one begins. Especially if you want to fill an area with a grey tone, you have to decide on a method. You have the choice between techniques such as shading, hatching or wiping. Grey tones are also referred to as tonal values in technical jargon.

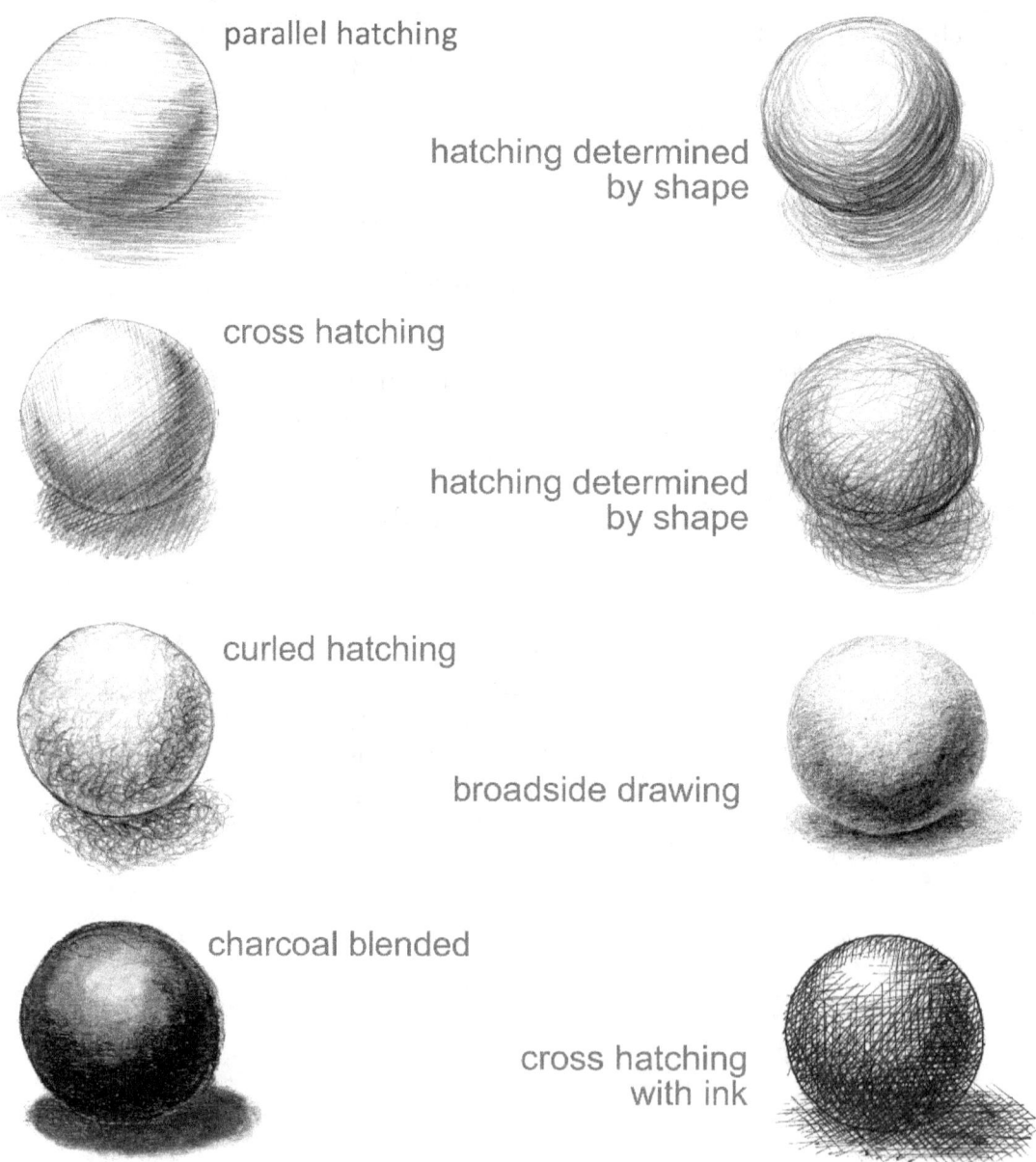

Basic Principles of Drawing

The most important and probably most frequently used drawing technique - besides the line itself - is hatching. In this book we will therefore deal with this drawing technique in particular. Other important drawing techniques you will learn in this book are the following:

- Hatching
- Shading
- Wiping
- Washing

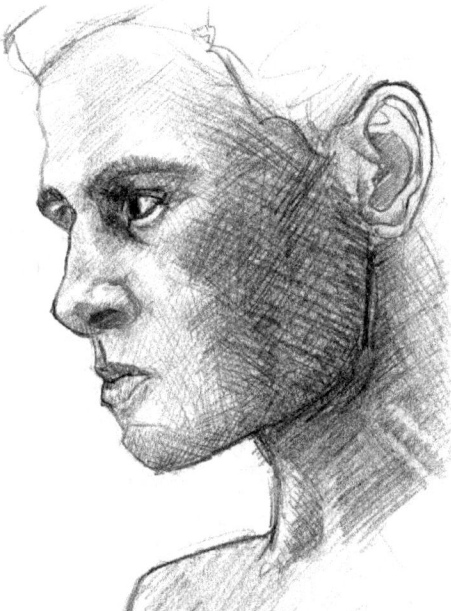

Hatching in a portrait drawing

Drawing Technique 1 – Hatching

In hatching, a row of lines is usually drawn parallel to each other at the same distance apart. It is also possible to draw several hatches at different angles on top of each other. If lines are drawn in only one direction, this is referred to as parallel hatching. If hatches are drawn at least two different angles, this is called cross hatching.

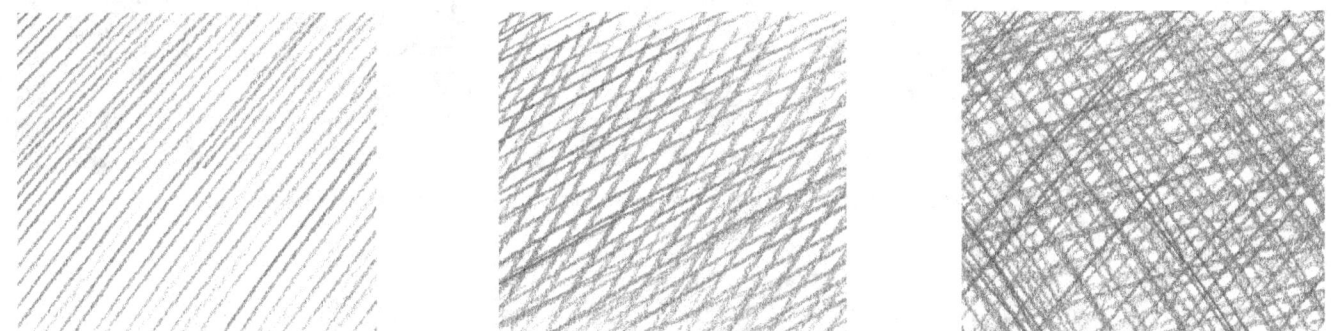

Parallel hatching, cross hatching in two directions, cross hatching in three directions

The aim of hatching is to generate a specific tonal value. The tonal value is obtained by mixing the lines with the white paper that appears between the lines. For the observer, lines and background mix to form a uniform grey tone.

Producing Tonal Values with Hatching

There are different possibilities to draw lighter and darker surfaces using hatching. All methods will be described here in the following.

Method 1: Line density

By compressing the lines of a hatch, the tonal value can be made darker. You can also darken the overall tonal value by overlaying the lines of a hatching with a different orientation. If, on the other hand, you want to make a hatch brighter, you have to draw the lines at a greater distance from each other.

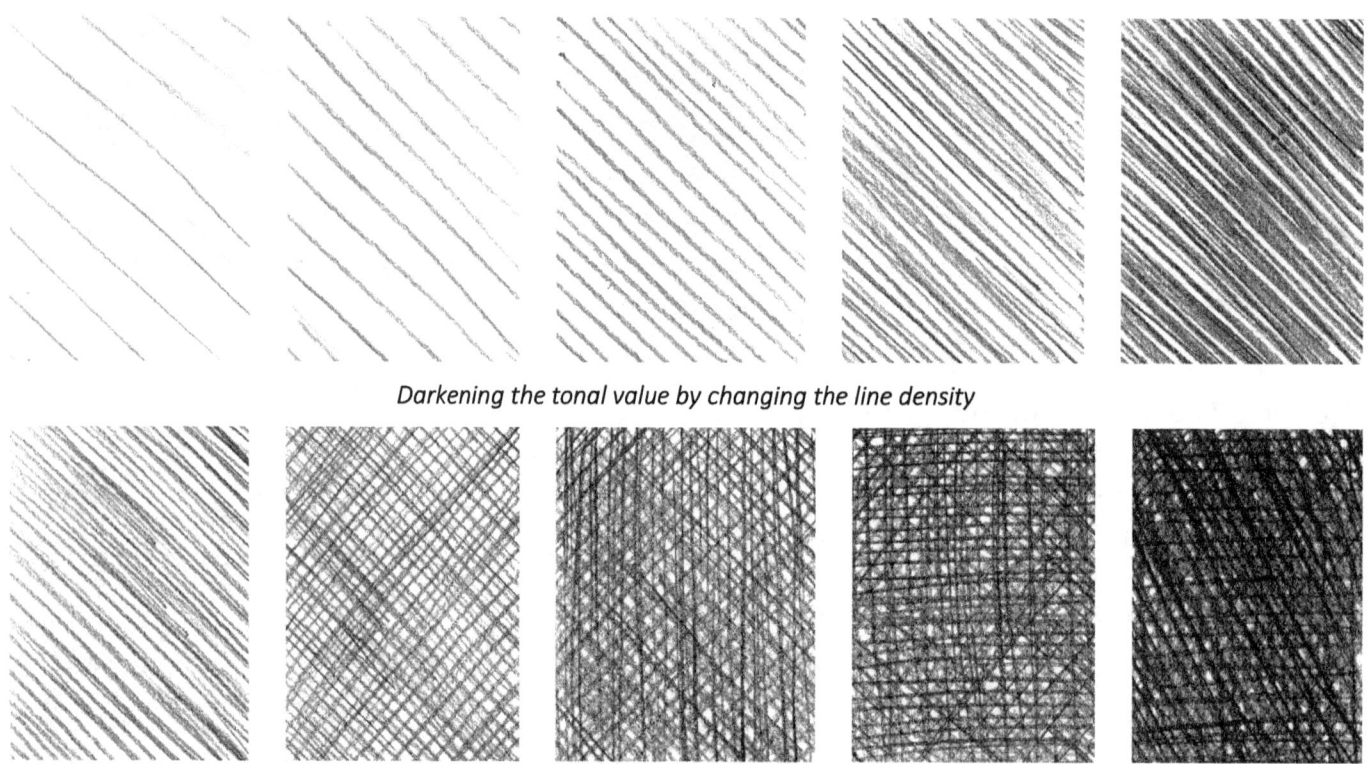

Darkening the tonal value by changing the line density

Darkening the tonal value through additional hatches with a different orientation

If you are drawing with ink, this method is mainly used. The only alternative would be to dilute the ink with water to draw lighter lines.

Method 2: Downforce of the Pencil

If you draw with a pencil, you also have the possibility to control the downforce of the pencil. If you press more strongly, the lines become thicker and darker, which automatically results in a darker tonal value. If, on the other hand, the hatching is drawn with little downforce, the lines become thinner and lighter. In this way, dense hatchings can be drawn that still correspond to a light shade of gray.

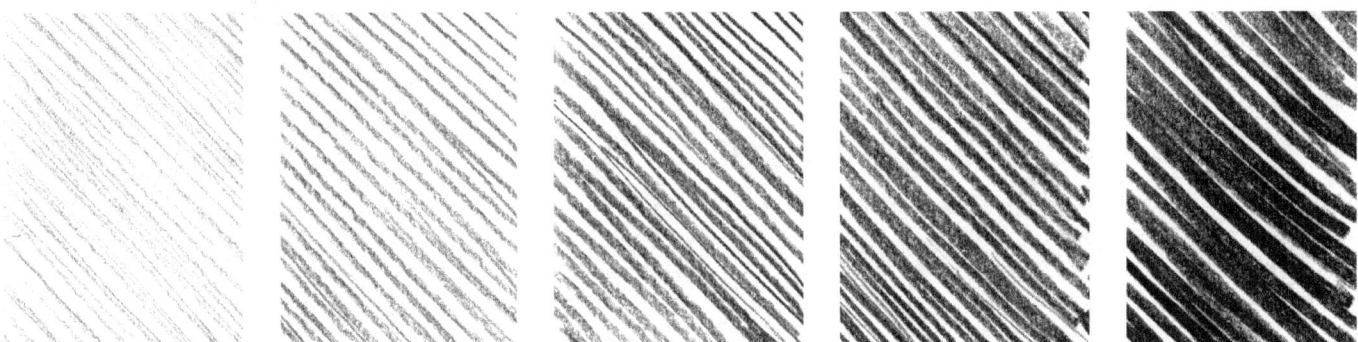

Different hatchings drawn using varied downforce

Method 3: Hardness of the Pencil

You can also use pencils of different hardness to draw lighter and darker hatches. Hard pencils produce a light gray shade, while soft pencils produce a dark gray shade.

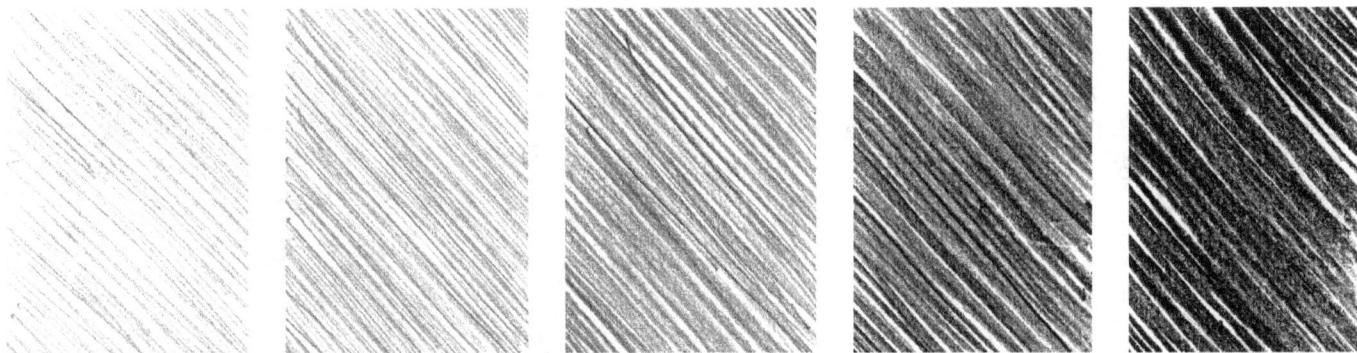

Hatchings generated using the pencil hardnesses 2H, H, HB, 2B and 6B (from left to right)

Special hatchings and Styles

Shape-determined hatchings

The shape of a body can also be made clear by means of hatching. The hatching follows the shape of a body. This so-called shape-determined hatching is particularly suitable for objects with convex or concave geometry.

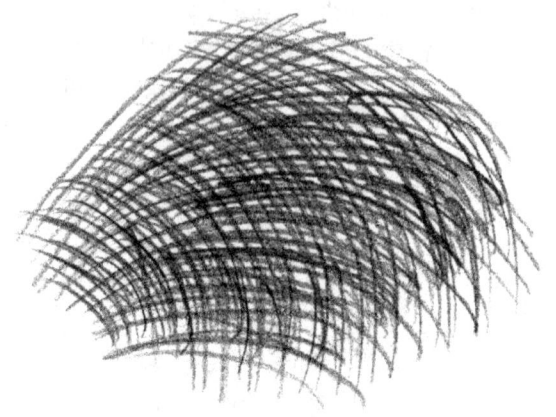

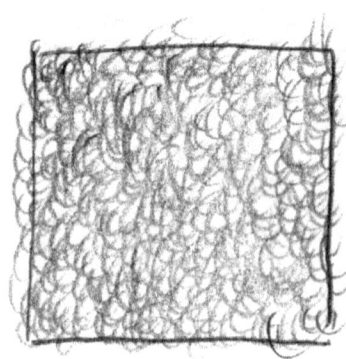

Curled hatching

Another variant is, for example, curled lines, with which a certain structure or surface texture can also be conveyed by hatching.

Hatched groups

Very interesting and lively hatching can be obtained by drawing small groups of parallel lines in different orientations.

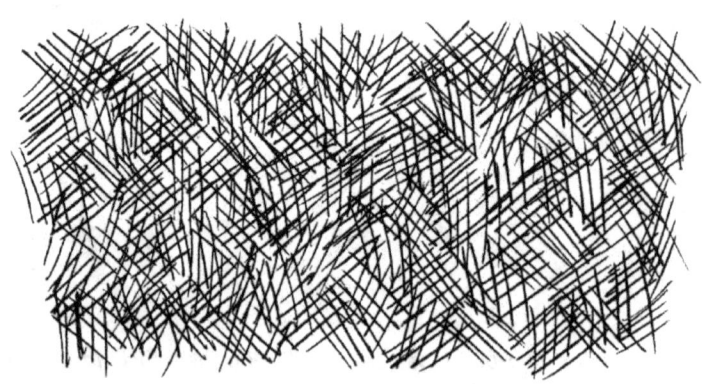

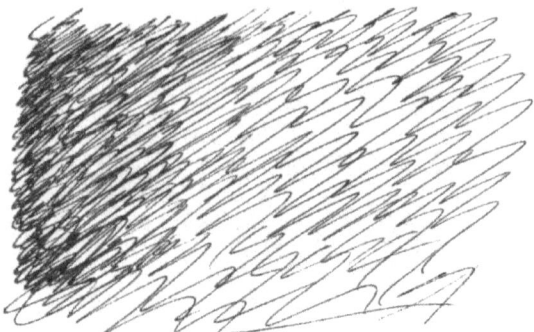

Scribbled lines

A drawing can impart a certain dynamic through scribbled lines. The hatchings appear more spontaneous and disorganized, which makes the respective image particularly unique.

Drawing Technique 2 – Broadside Drawing

When drawing with the broad side of the pen, you work back and forth by holding the pen at a relatively flat angle to the paper. You can use this technique with a pencil/graphite pencil, colored pencil, or charcoal and pastel chalk.

By *broadside drawing* you can quickly and easily fill large areas without having to master a particularly skilled technique. Often this technique is regarded as a rather inexact technique. In addition, this is already a drawing technique in which no strokes or lines are visible, which means that the classic criteria of a drawing are no longer fulfilled.

The optical results of hatching are often more impressive than those of broadside drawing and the characteristic handwriting of the draftsman is more clearly visible.

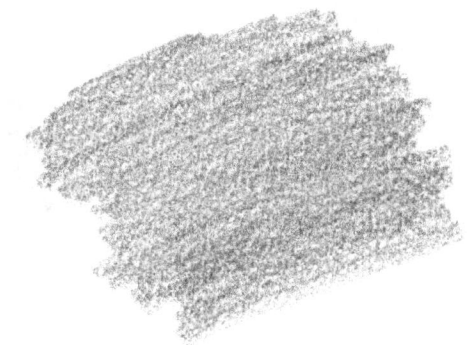

Area drawn with the broad side of the pen

Shaded tone value progression

Drawing Technique 3 – Blending/Smudging

The blending technique can be applied with pencil, colored pencil, chalk and charcoal. Especially the loose drawing media - chalk and charcoal - are excellent for wiping.

In the blend technique, a previously drawn surface is wiped with a finger or a wiping tool. In this way you can quickly fill large areas and create particularly soft light-dark gradients.

Please note: When blending, one is already at the border between drawing and painting, as there are hardly any lines or lines to be seen.

Charcoal hatch blended in the upper right section

The wiping technique proceeds in three steps: First you draw a surface - for example with charcoal. Then you use a wiping tool such as an Estompe to wipe the surface in one direction. In the end you can blur the charcoal even further beyond the drawn surface to create a tone gradient.

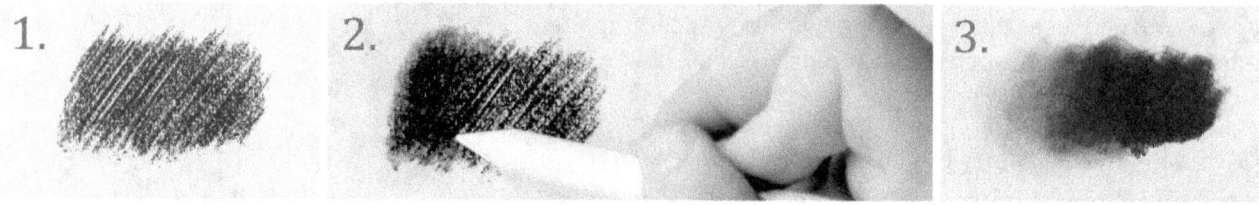

Smudging in three steps

Drawing Technique 4 – Washing

The technique of washing is used in combination with Indian ink and ink. The color is applied with a brush, as in watercolor painting, in order to represent shades and tints. To apply Indian ink or ink transparently, it is mixed with water.

Pen and brush drawings are often combined. In this way, outlines and structures drawn with pen and Indian ink are created, which are then shaded by washing.

Basic Principles of Drawing

2.8 How to Draw Shadows

In the previous chapters we learned how to draw objects spatially. We also learned techniques such as hatching to display tonal values.

By combining this knowledge, we are able to draw motifs with shadows. Through the representation of shadows one can make objects look really three-dimensional.

Light and Shade

A prerequisite for the representation of shadows is the corresponding basic knowledge of the interaction of light and shadow. We all know that shadows are created wherever light does not reach. For example, if the sun shines on a wall, it is brightly lit on one side while it remains dark on the other. But not only the wall itself is dark on one side, also a shadow is cast on the floor by the wall.

The sketch shown describes the different types and areas of shadows using the example of a sphere.

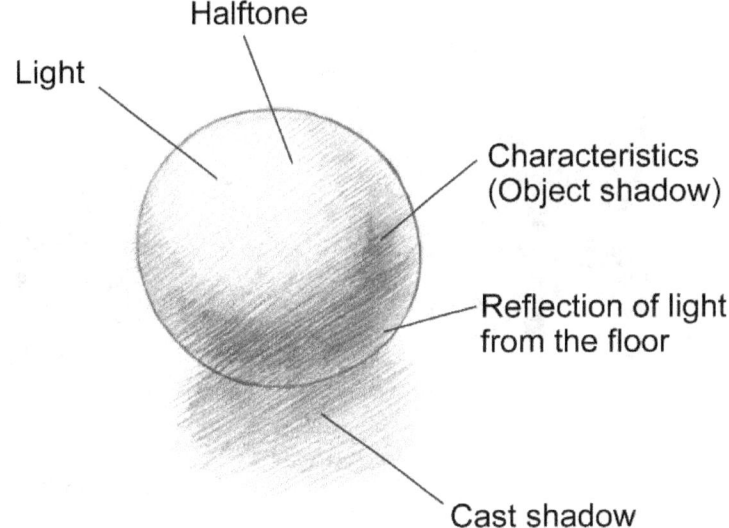

Various Objects

And now you can draw various basic geometric objects in order to practice. First draw the contours and then shade the object. In the following sketches you can find some examples that you can draw.

Tip:

The graphic study of simple geometric bodies is important, because you will find these simple bodies in all complex objects. It is often possible to divide complex shapes into several simple geometric bodies, which is often a great help when drawing.

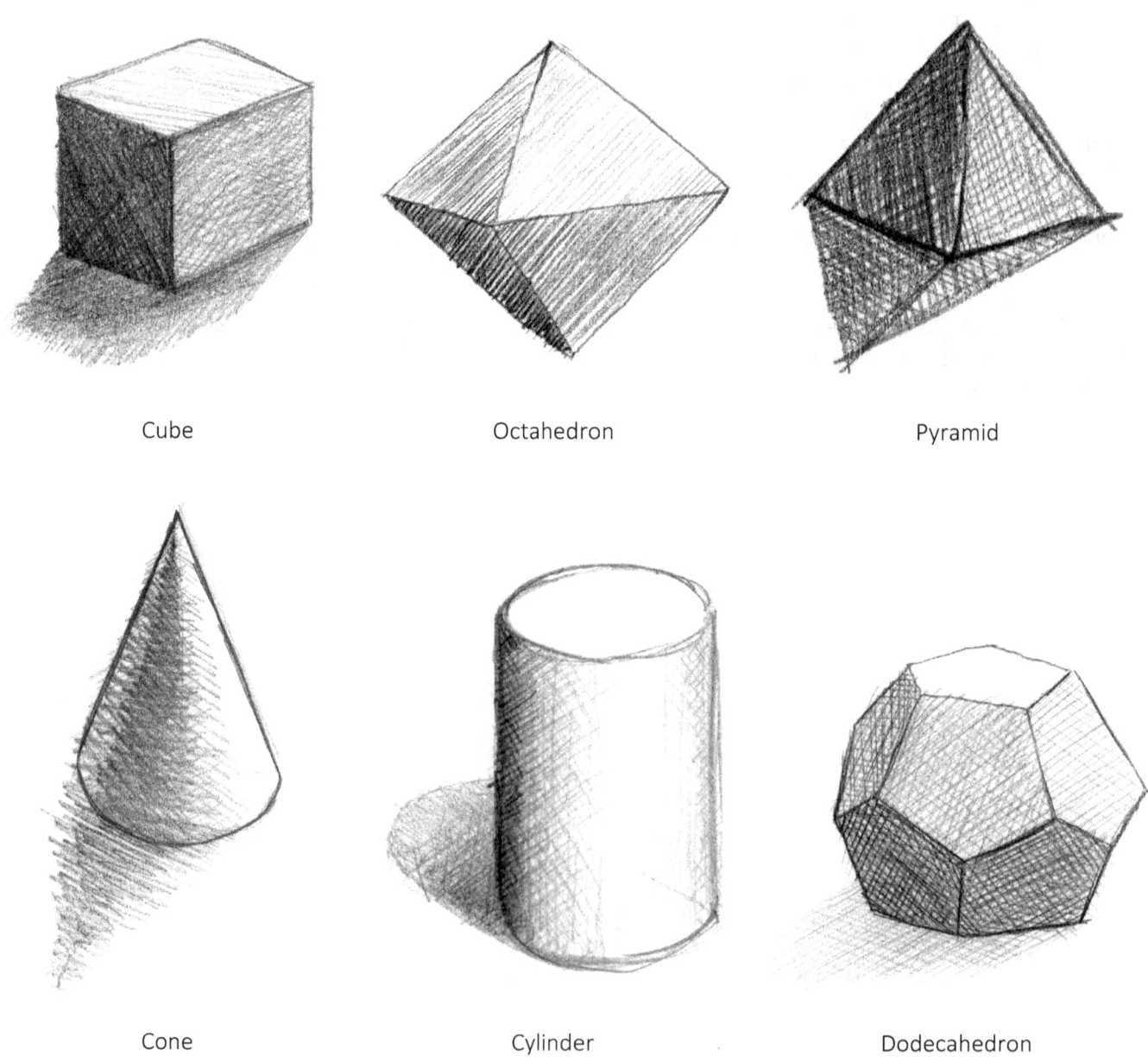

Cube   Octahedron   Pyramid

Cone   Cylinder   Dodecahedron

Drawing Texture and Structure

Textures and structures are important tools for artists and graphic designers, since they use them to represent various materials and surfaces. The possibilities for application are far reaching: wool, scales, gravel, water, skin, grass and countless other things can be illustrated by means of structure or texture.

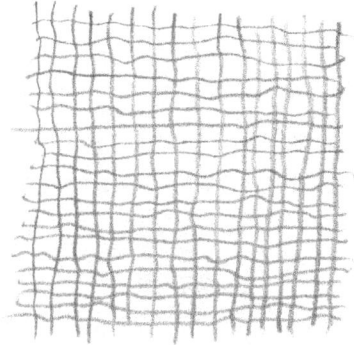

Grid-like lines that recreate a fabric

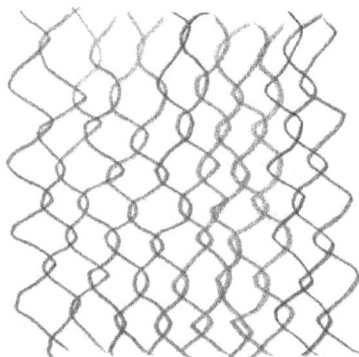

Mesh-like pattern of snake lines

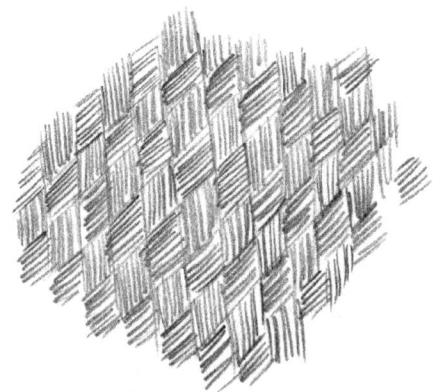

Groups of lines that produce a pattern

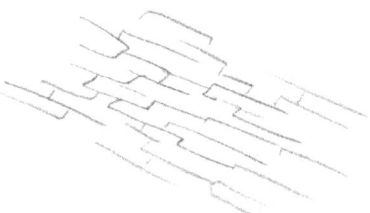

Line structures similar to the wings of a dragonfly

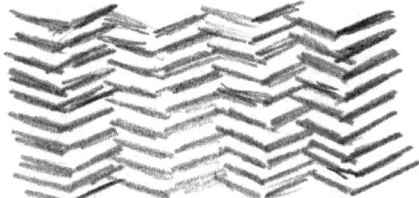

Pattern that recreates the surface of a woven basket

Pattern that looks like a brick wall

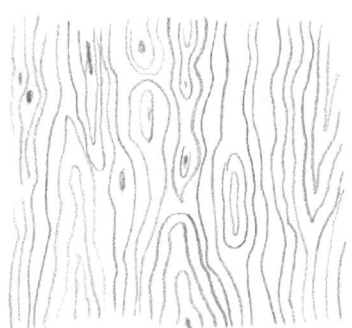

Wood pattern, similar to a board

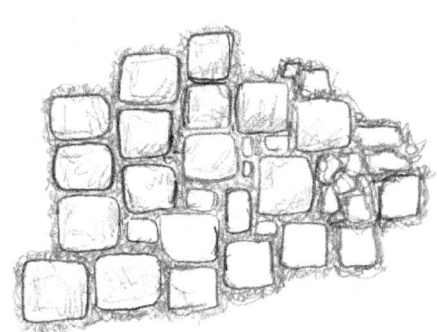

Texture of a stone wall

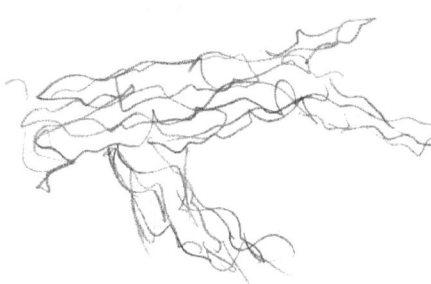

Structure of a branch using scribbled lines

Elements of a Landscape Drawing

» Simplicity is the highest form of sophistication. «

- Leonardo da Vinci -

3 Elements of a Landscape Drawing

Before you start with elaborate landscape drawings, you should first learn to represent the most important elements that typically occur in a landscape. These include trees, clouds, mountains, rocks, rivers and the like. Each of these elements has characteristic properties. If one knows and understands these, the graphic representation is much easier.

3.1 Study Drawings

Whenever you have to draw a motif that you've never attempted before or with which you have little experience, it is advisable to practice with a few studies beforehand. In the visual arts, a graphic (or painted) investigation of an object is known as a study or sketch.

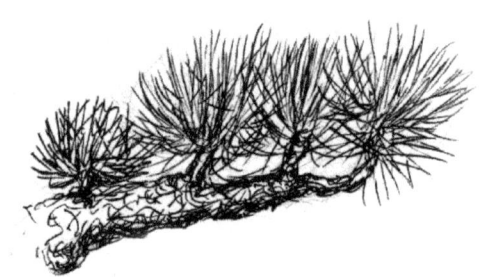

The aim of this investigation is to develop drawing techniques or methods that are particularly well suited to represent the various elements of a motif. These can be shapes and geometries, structures, surfaces, patterns, colors or other properties. So the study is a method of teaching yourself how to draw certain motifs.

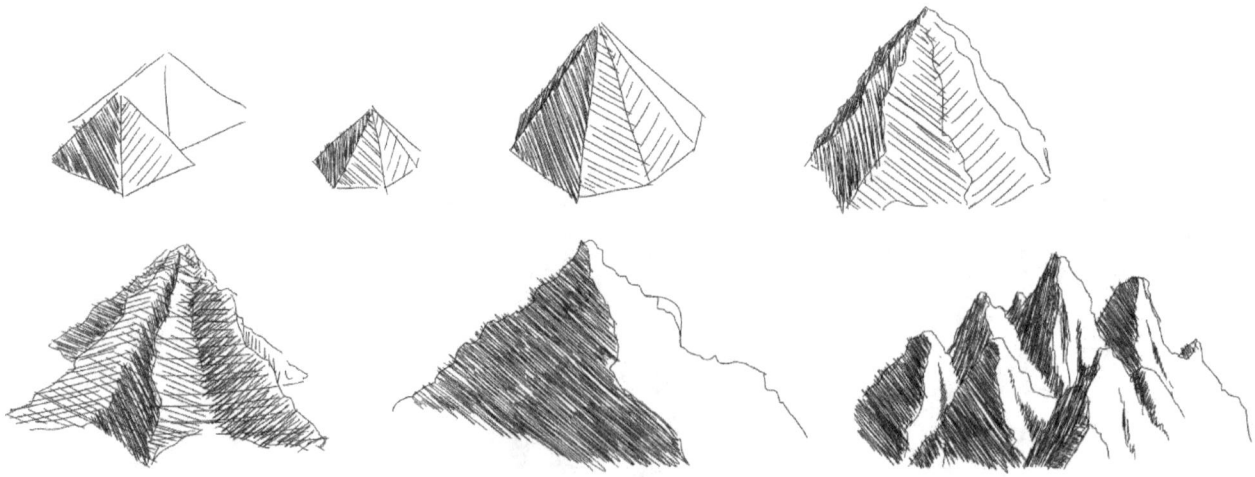

Consequently, if you want to draw landscapes, it makes sense to do studies for objects such as trees, rocks, mountains, rivers, etc. These objects are probably the most common motifs in landscapes. Therefore, this chapter is dedicated to the techniques of representing these important elements of a landscape drawing.

3.2 Trees

Trees are one of the most important image objects when you want to draw landscapes. Presumably they appear in 9 of 10 pictures. So we will look at the techniques for drawing them first.

Simplification

By the way, trees are excellent for describing important methods of drawing. Because an important aspect - especially in landscape drawings - is simplification.

A tree consists of an infinite number of details. However, it makes no sense to depict everything down to the last leaf. This means that you have to simplify the drawing very much and at the same time convey the illusion of richness of detail.

Indicate details in some places here and there. Thus you show the observer what the details look like and give the impression that there are actually many more of them present.

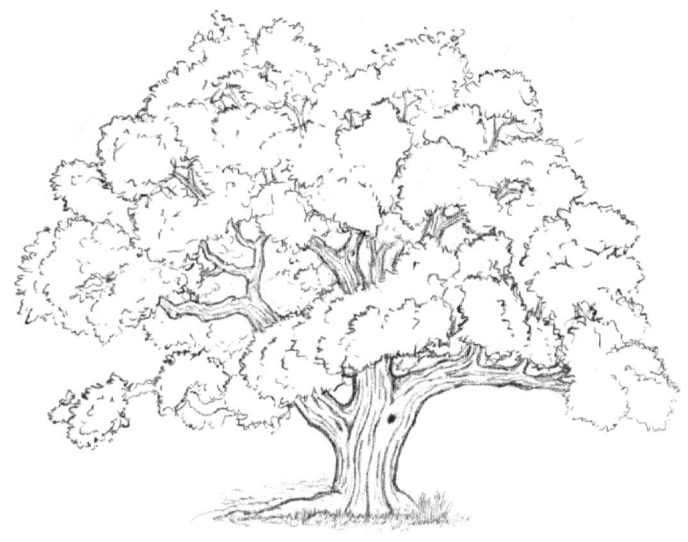

Stroke technique

With different techniques of stroke guidance one can let different varieties of trees develop. Also make sure that your contours don't become too even, as this will look unnatural.

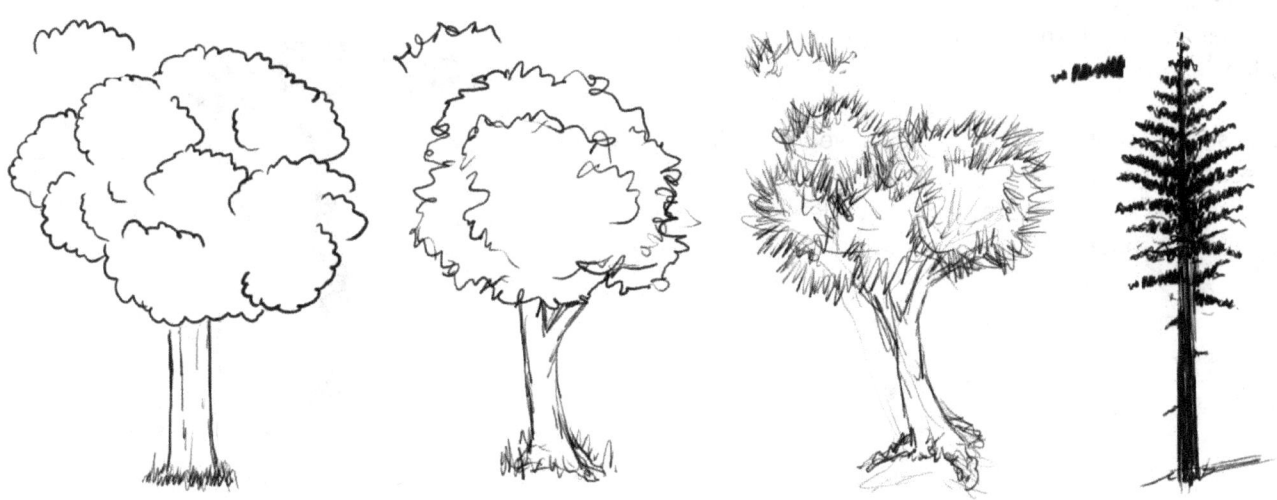

Representation of trees using various stroke techniques

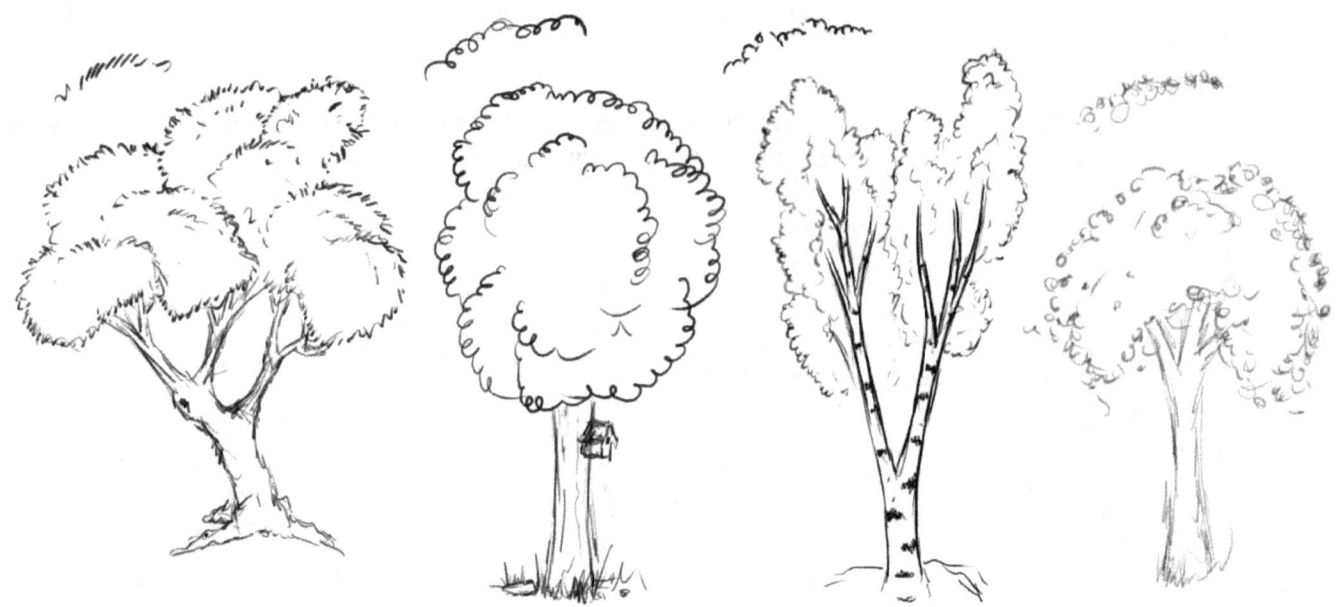

Representation of trees using various stroke techniques

The Tree as a Voluminous Object

Something that can easily be overlooked: Trees form voluminous bodies - also the treetop. Their shape could best be described as a sphere or hemisphere. This superordinate form is particularly important when drawing shadows.

In the sketch shown you will find a very simplified representation of a tree in which the crown of the tree is depicted as a hemisphere. On the underside of the hemisphere a shadow has been created.

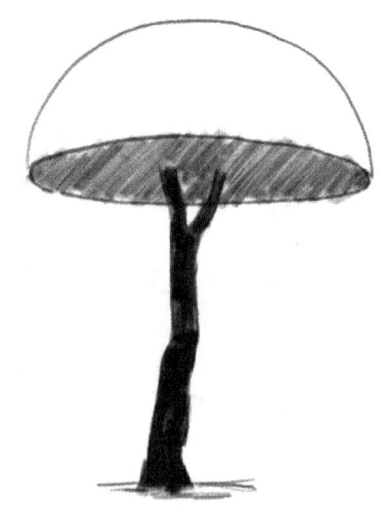

Elements of a Landscape Drawing

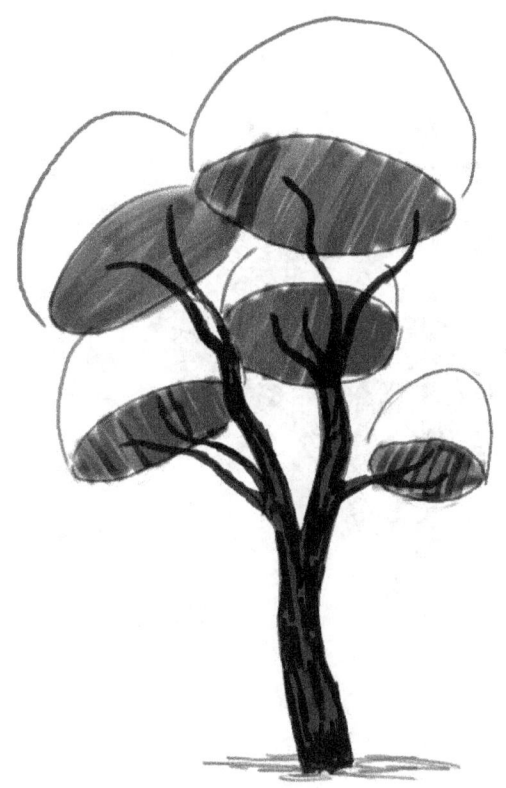

This technique can also be applied to trees whose crown is divided into several smaller crowns. One can imagine several hemispheres that make up the entire foliage.

If you now fill out the crown of the tree graphically, you already get an impressive sketch of a tree.

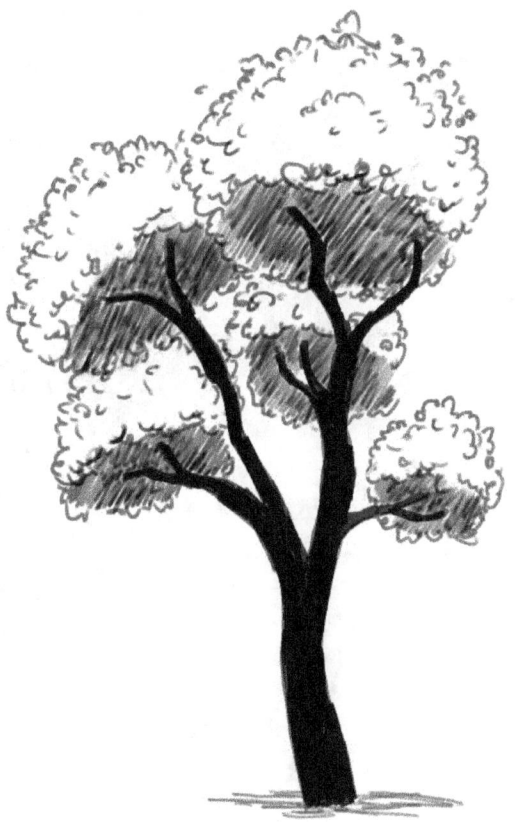

Recognizing and Reproducing Structures

Another method that helps us to represent trees better is the recognition and reproduction of structures. These structures can be found in the treetops of many trees. They allow the character of a certain tree species to emerge to its fullest.

The structures are created by the growth of branches, twigs and foliage, which bundle leaves and create a certain optical rhythm. These structures can be worked out, above all, by including shadows.

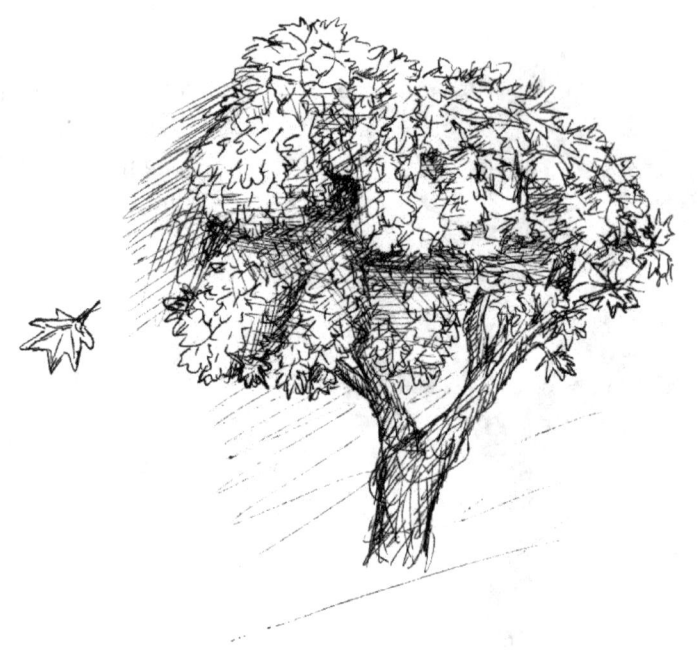

Indian ink sketch of a maple tree

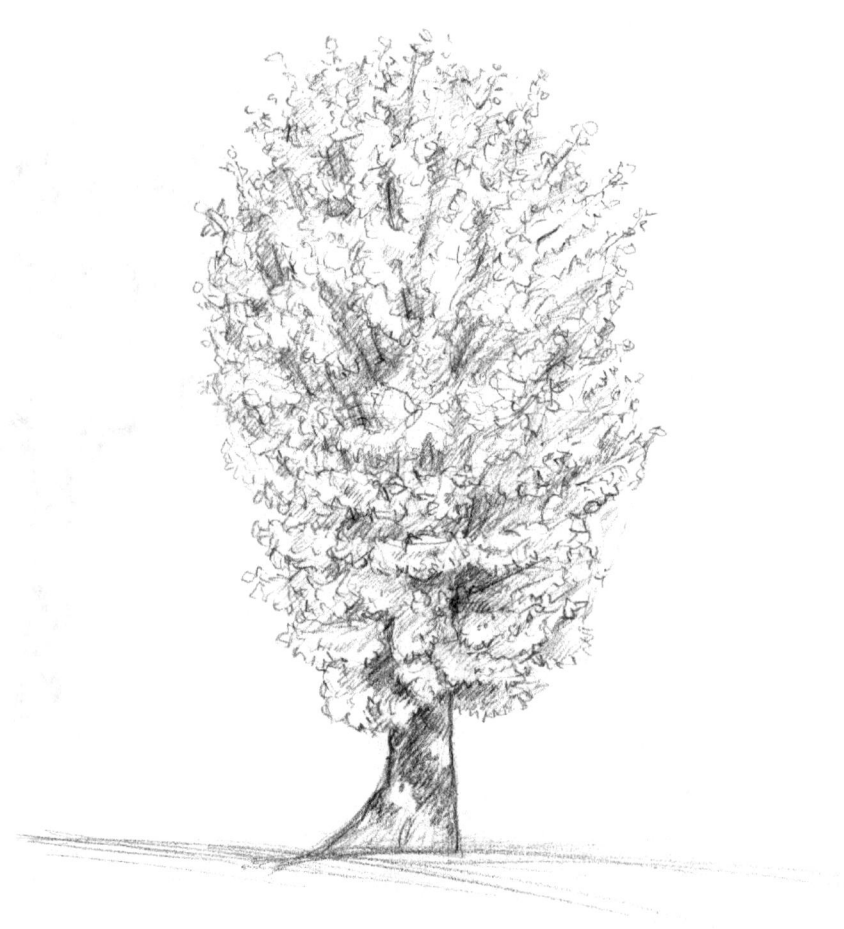

Drawing the Tree Trunk and Branches

For the drawing of the tree trunk and the branches there are two particularly important aspects to consider. On the one hand the **rejuvenation** (i.e. the gradual thinning) with progressive branching and on the other hand the natural **growth**.

In order for your drawing to look natural, you should make sure that the trunk becomes thinner and thinner towards the top. If the trunk divides into several individual trunks, these will become much thinner. You can assume that the cross-sectional area of the individual trunks corresponds in sum to the cross-sectional area of the individual trunk.

The same applies to branches. Branches become continuously thinner. If a branch splits, the rejuvenation is correspondingly stronger. Finally, the branches end in very fine branching.

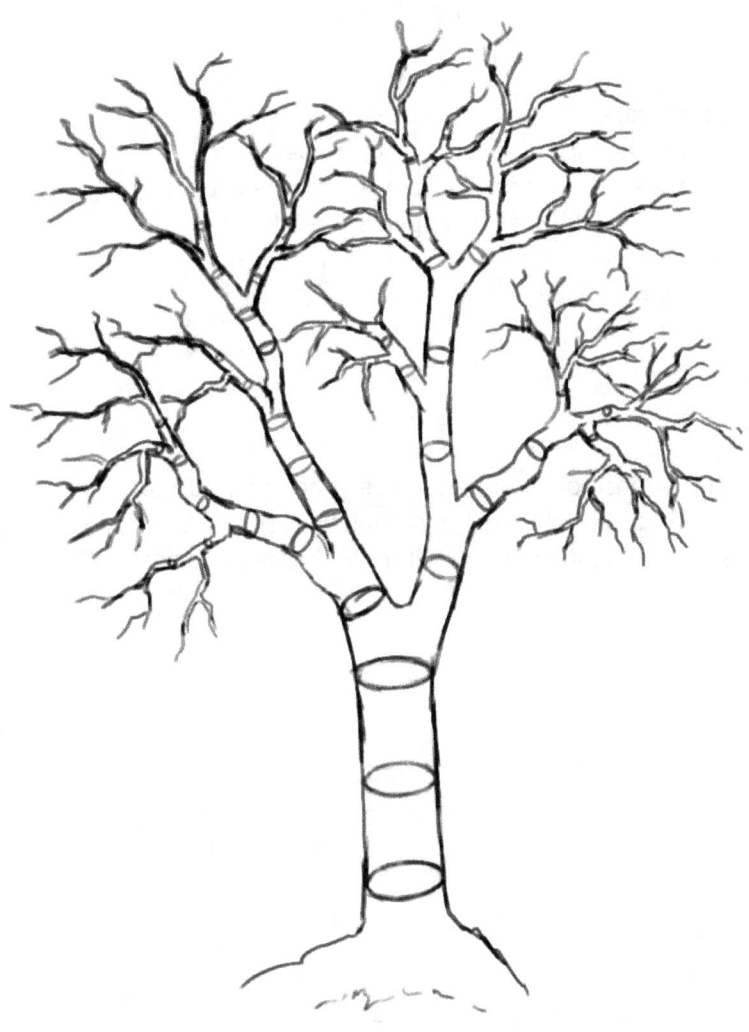

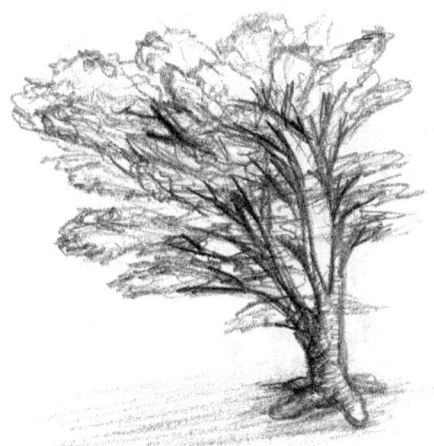

When observing the growth of branches, as well as trunks, always pay attention to the peculiarities of the tree species you want to draw. Each tree has its own form, which you have to reproduce. This is the only way to create a natural looking drawing.

Drawing Roots

Since the representation of roots causes difficulties for many beginners, in this subchapter precisely this topic is to be illuminated. The main focus is on the transition between tree and soil.

When drawing, it is worth studying the motif carefully, as the appearance of the roots can vary greatly from tree species to tree species. The most important thing here is whether the tree disappears directly into the ground or whether the roots spread out visibly on the earth's surface.

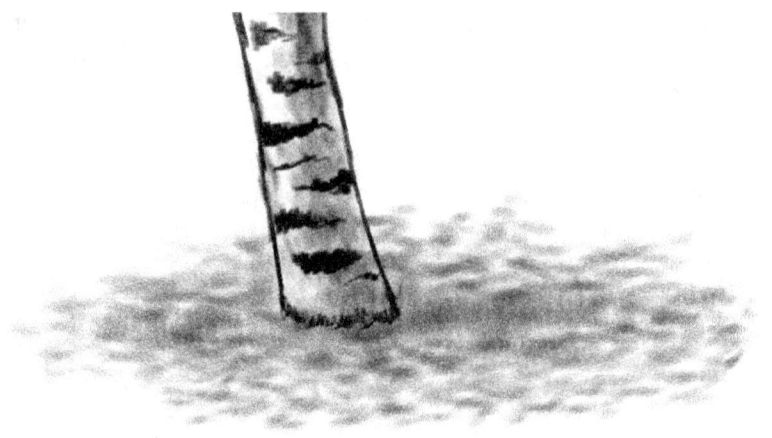

Tip:

The transition between tree and ground can be beautifully concealed by depicting some blades of grass, which makes the picture look especially natural.

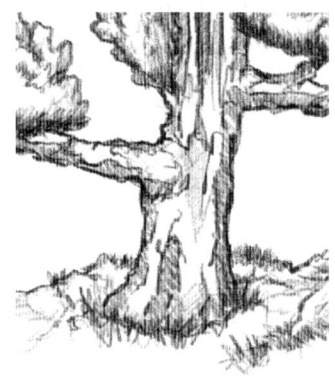

Tip:

Roots that are still visible on the surface can be imagined as branches buried halfway in the ground. The transition between tree and ground can be beautifully concealed by depicting a few blades of grass, making the picture appear more natural.

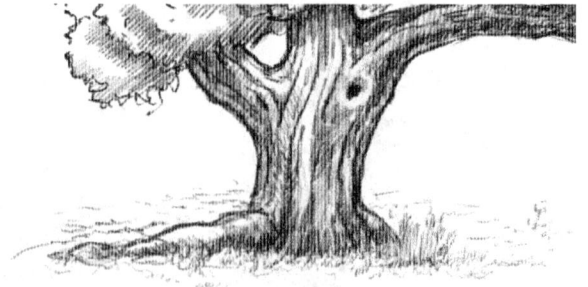

Elements of a Landscape Drawing

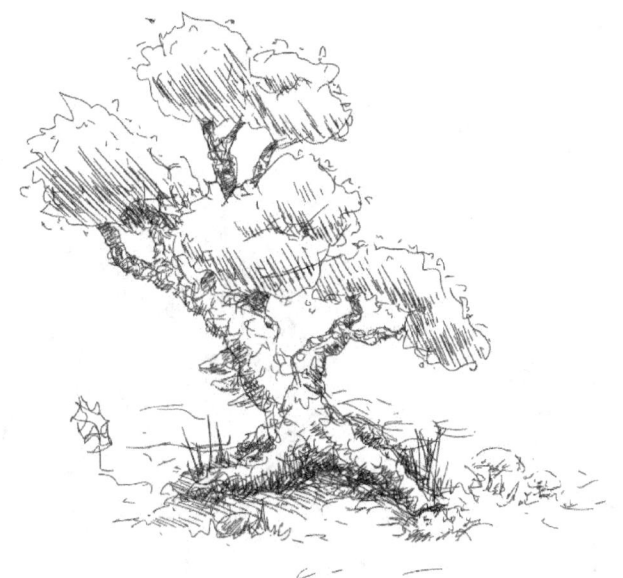

It is usually sufficient to depict three root outgrowths in order to achieve a credible visual effect.

Drawing a Tree Step by Step

When drawing a tree, it is best to start by sketching the approximate shape relatively roughly. Draw the trunk, the visible branches and the crown of the tree. Do not draw the lines too firmly – this way you can erase them later or keep them as inconspicuous as possible in the later drawing.

The next step is to work out the contours more precisely. The trunk and the branches are depicted more precisely and attention is paid to the rejuvenation of the branches with increasing branching. The crown is given a contour that gives a hint of individual leaves.

In order to make the drawing appear natural, the contour of the crown should be sketched as unevenly as possible and open shapes should be created.

Then you can already indicate the first shadows within the tree crown. Think about how the shape of the treetop looks in its spatial extension and where shadows should be created.

Template for practicing hatching:

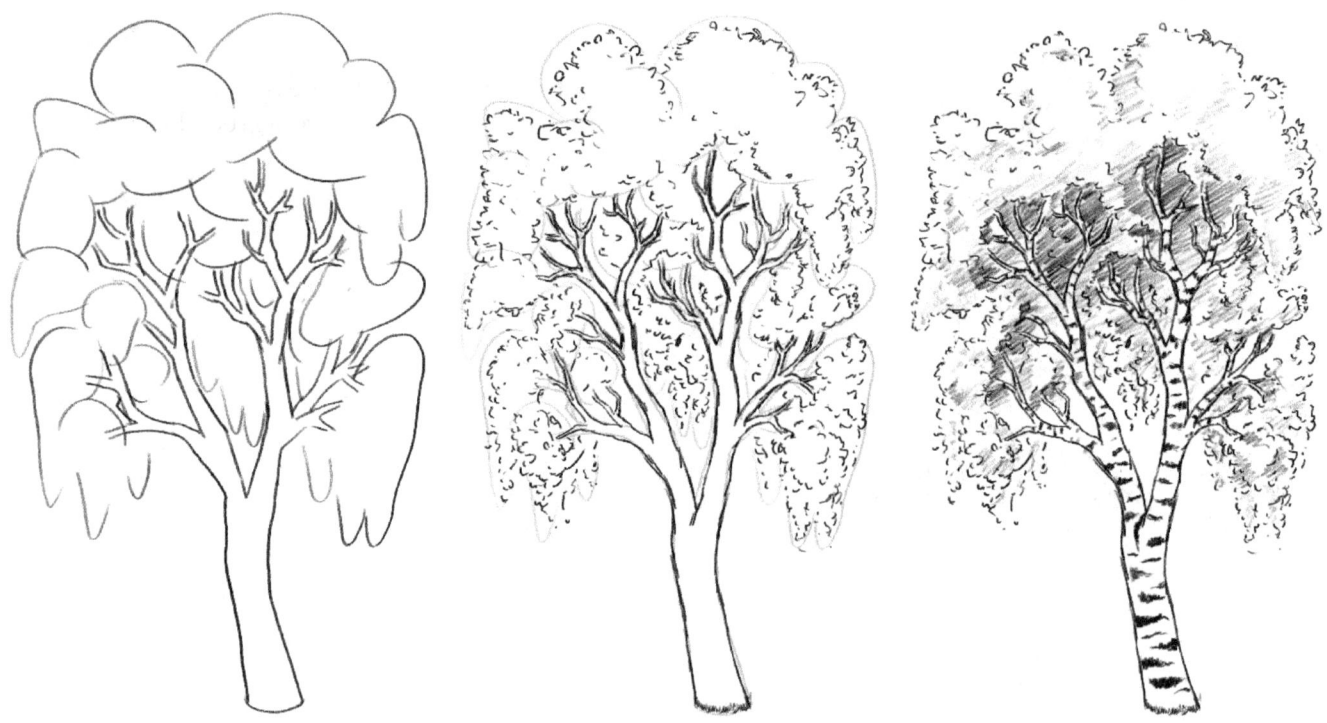

Since the rough shape of the tree is now defined, you can continue with the detailing and shading. When shading the treetop, it is best to use a hatching style that conveys a kind of leaf texture. A curly hatching style, for example, is a good choice.

In the last two steps the trunk is shaded and the cast shadow of the tree is drawn. Then the drawing is complete.

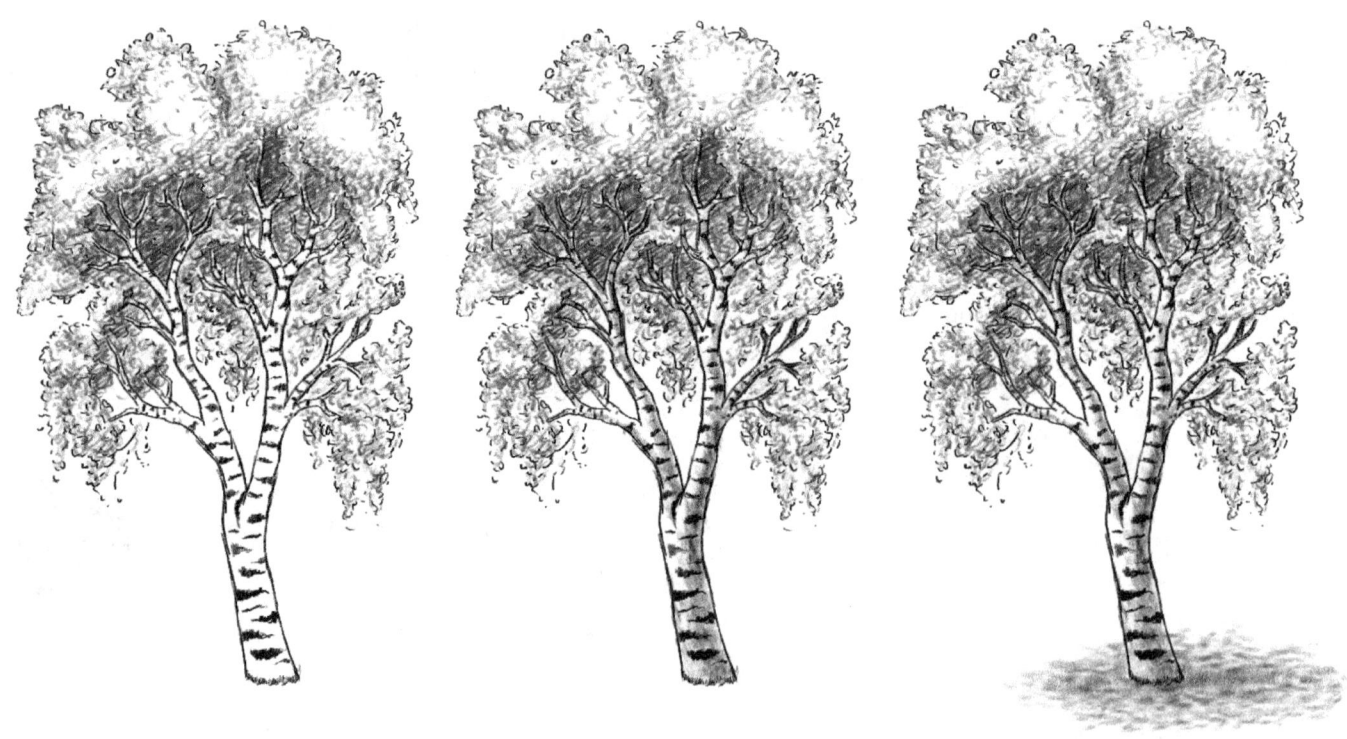

3.3 Different Species of Trees

If you want to draw trees, it is advantageous to know some species and their optical characteristics. If you have an awareness of the typical characteristics of a tree species, you can also accurately depict them.

Birch

Birches have small leaves and a white trunk with dark stripes, which makes the birch unmistakable. The thin branches hang partly down like grapes.

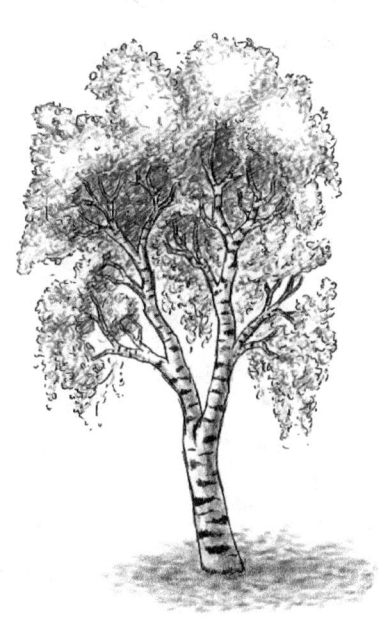

Cypress

The shape of cypresses is dense, slender and pillar-like. They often adorn roads and paths and impress with their noble and graceful appearance.

Oak

An old oak offers a wonderful motif. It has a massive, gnarled trunk, which can also have grown somewhat asymmetrically. It has large leaves that can form a broad crown. The crown of an oak tree usually spreads out at a small distance from the ground.

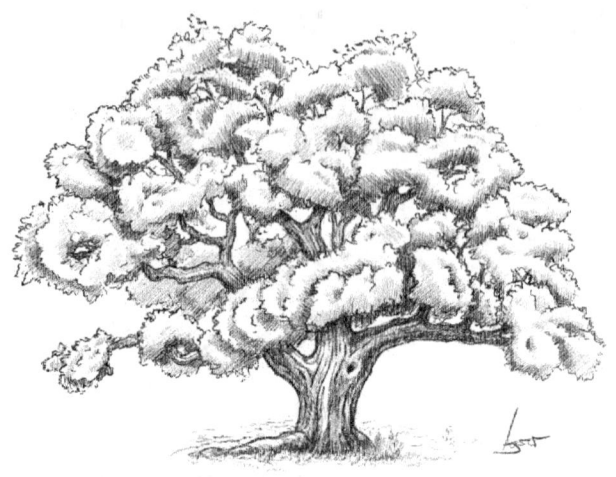

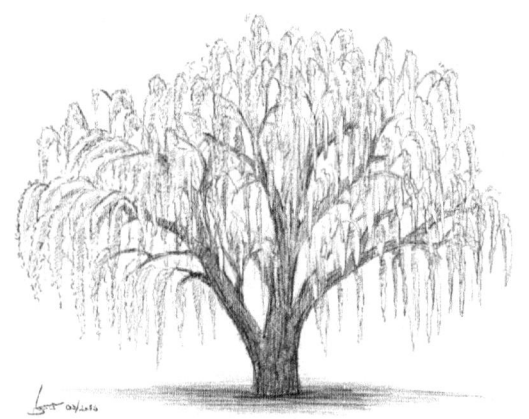

Weeping Willow

Weeping willows grow on humid and loose soils next to bodies of water. Their hanging branches with thin foliage are especially characteristic.

Pine Tree

The pine is a coniferous tree. It grows very tall, but does not become excessively broad. The branch growth starts a little further up and the branching is not particularly pronounced. Typical are also some bare branches here and there.

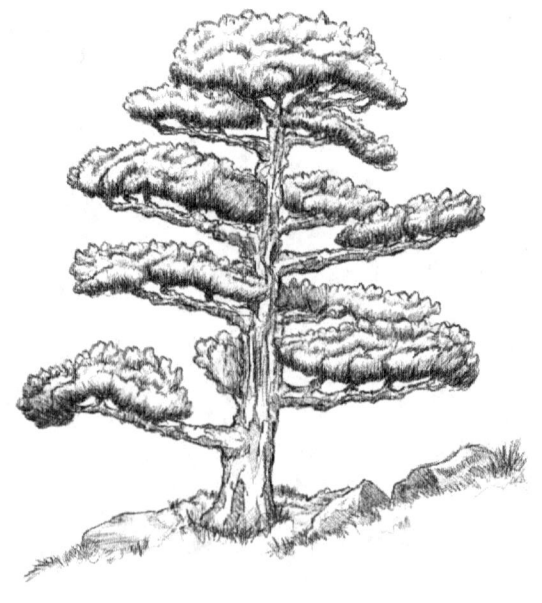

Elements of a Landscape Drawing

Spruce Tree

The spruce grows tall, but remains relatively narrow. The branches are very close to the ground. Their growth is usually denser than that of a pine.

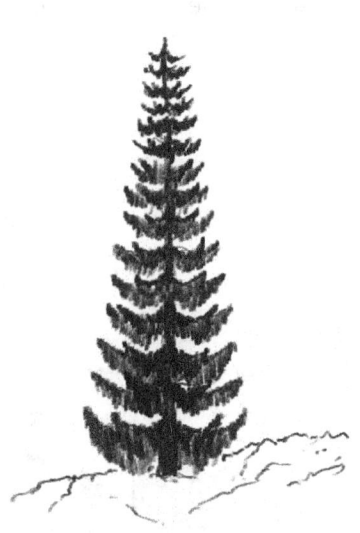

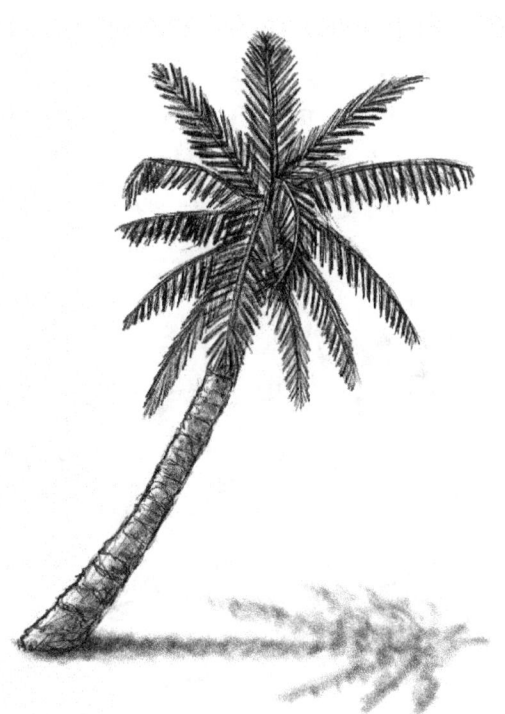

Palme

Palm trees have a long, rather thin trunk, no branches, and the long, pointed palm leaves are typical. Their roots are often not visible on the earth's surface.

3.4 Wooden Structures

Wood has a very characteristic and unmistakable structure. In this exercise you can try your hand at drawing a wooden surface. The motif is a wooden bench, as it can be found in many landscapes. Note that we can see three different types of wood structure. The seat is a cut tree trunk, where we look at the frontal view of the surface with the bark removed. In the side view one can see the annual rings, whose structures continue on the upper side. The lateral surface corresponds to the cut across the trunk, while the upper surface corresponds to the cut along the trunk. The backrest also shows the structure of the cut lengthwise through a tree trunk, with some additional structures of branches.

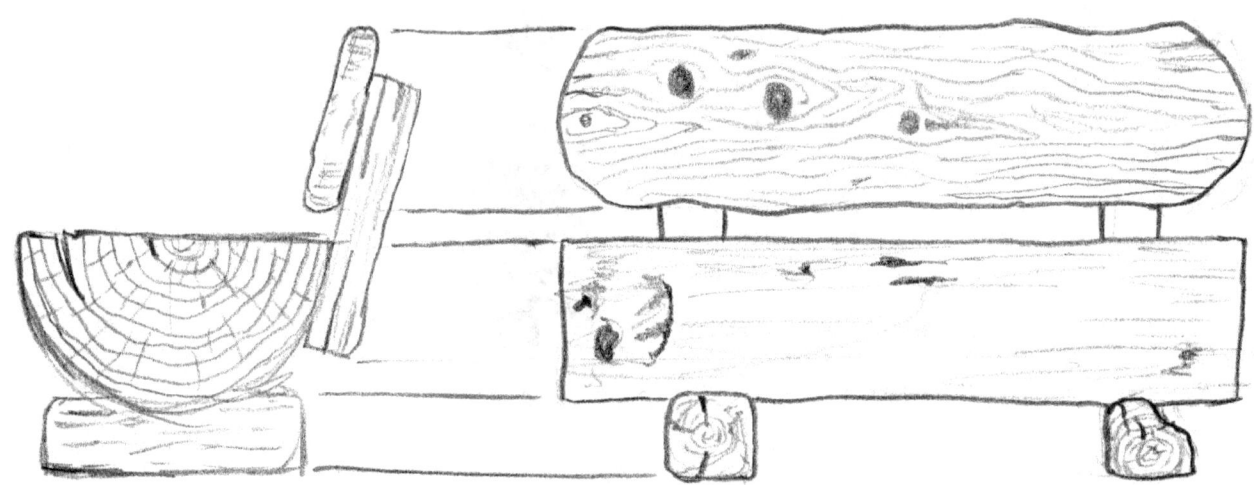

Drawn in perspective, not only the structures but also the forms have to be considered. Through representation of the wood structure the form of the motif is demonstrated even further.

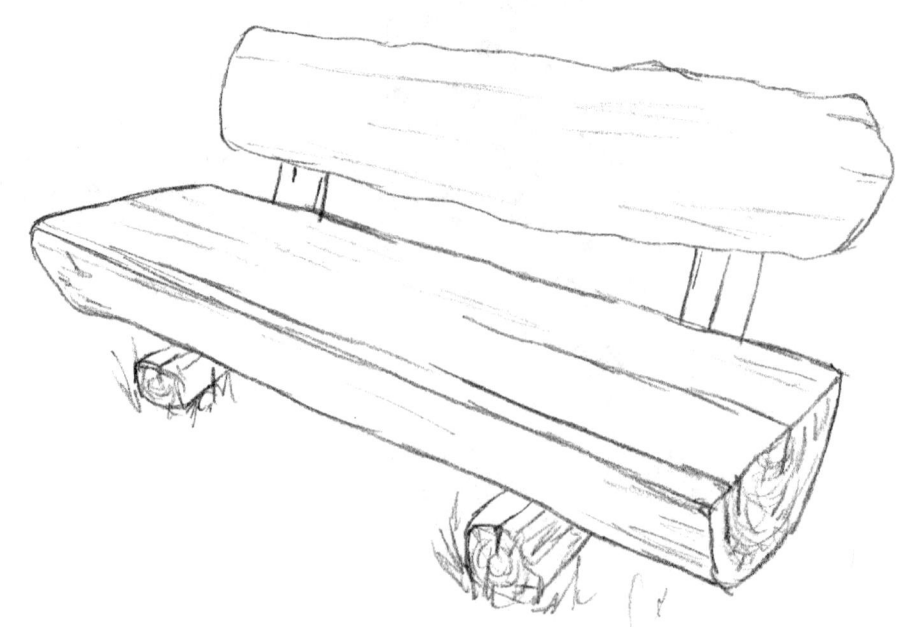

Elements of a Landscape Drawing

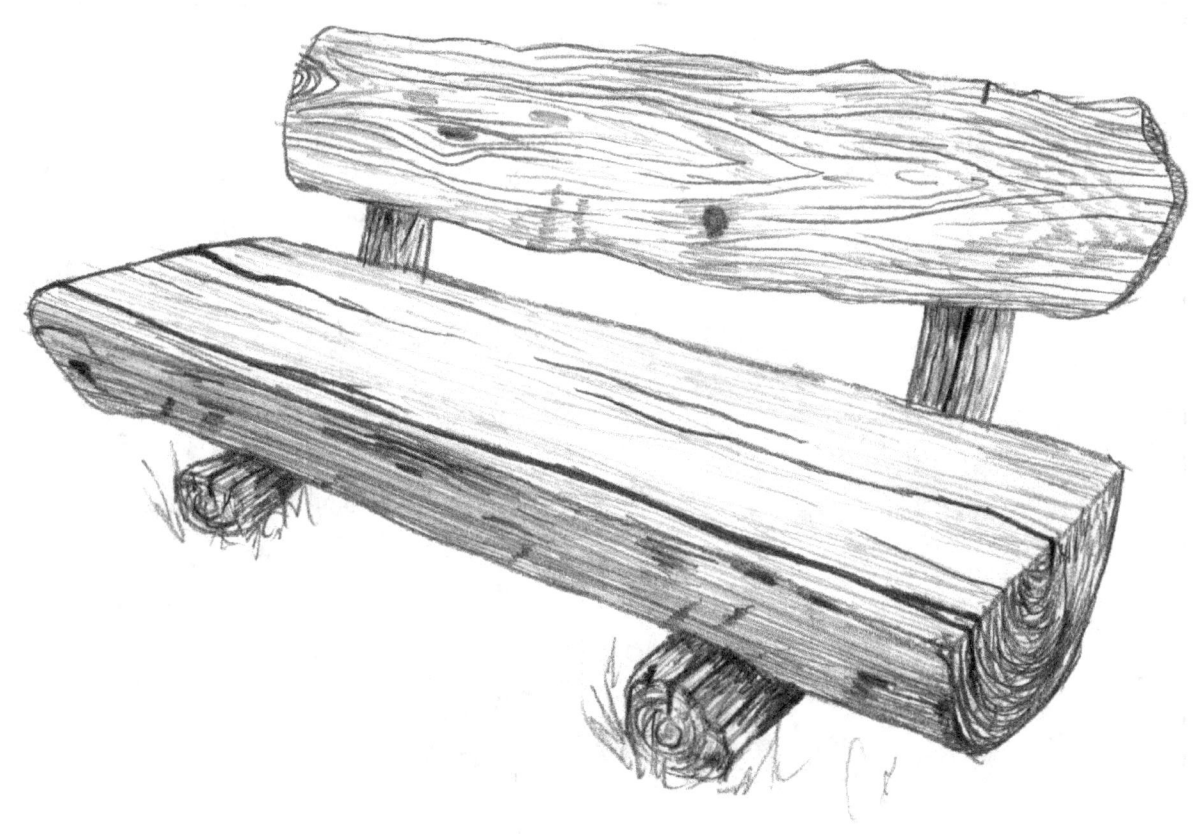

3.5 Stones, Boulders, Mountains

Stones, boulders and mountains are objects that occur again and again in landscapes. It is not easy to draw them because, like trees, they often consist of countless details. Especially with mountains, you have to be careful not to go into too much detail.

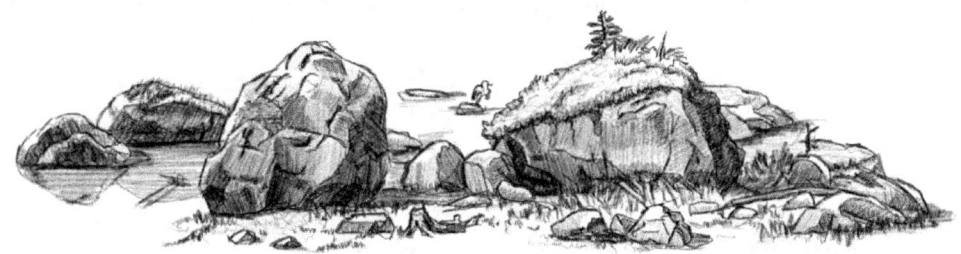

Stones and Boulders

Stones, boulders and mountains are objects that occur again and again in landscapes. It is not easy to draw them because, like trees, they often consist of countless details. Especially with mountains, you have to be careful not to go into too much detail.

Depicting shadows next to a stone

In this sketch a stone can be seen in the side view and from above. The lines represent the light that illuminates the stone. According to the direction of light, shadows form on the back of the stone. The front side, on which the light shines very directly, is particularly bright.

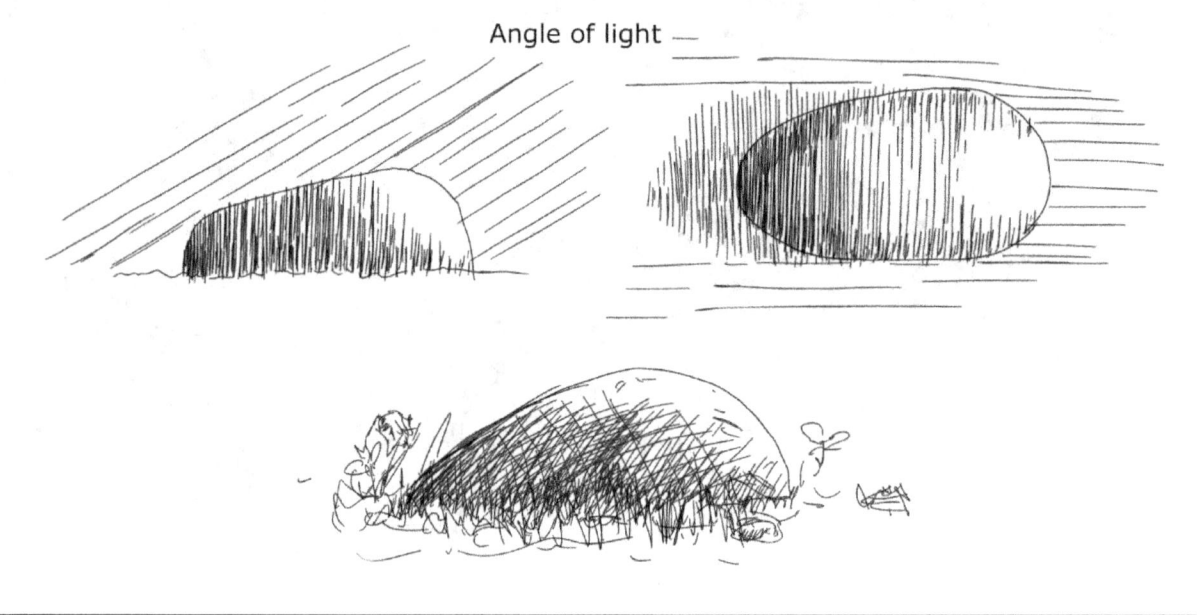

Drawing a Group of Stones Step by Step

The best way to learn how to represent stones is in a small exercise. We want to draw a small group of stones or small boulders as they often times appear in a landscape drawing. For this we start with the sketching of the contours.

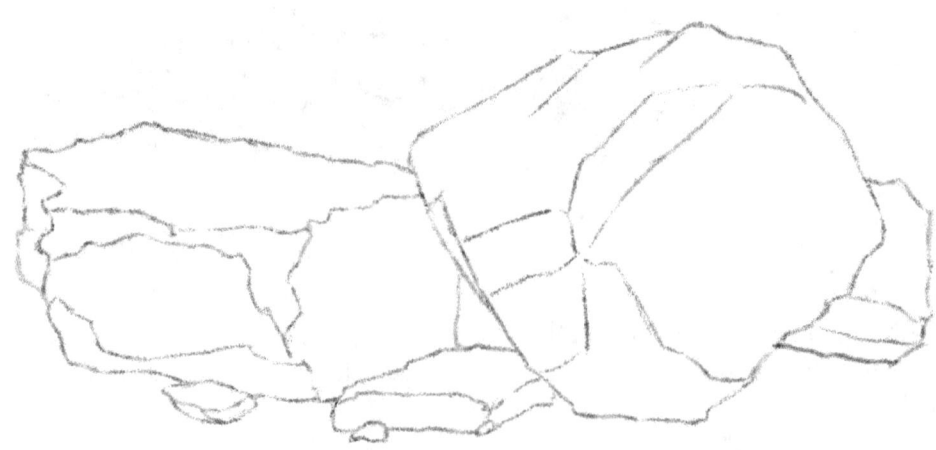

Elements of a Landscape Drawing

The next step is to hatch the first shadows. You can start with the lighter tonal values, because darkening afterwards is easier than lightening again. In this case, a simple parallel hatching was sufficient. You can also use any other hatching technique, as well as any drawing technique.

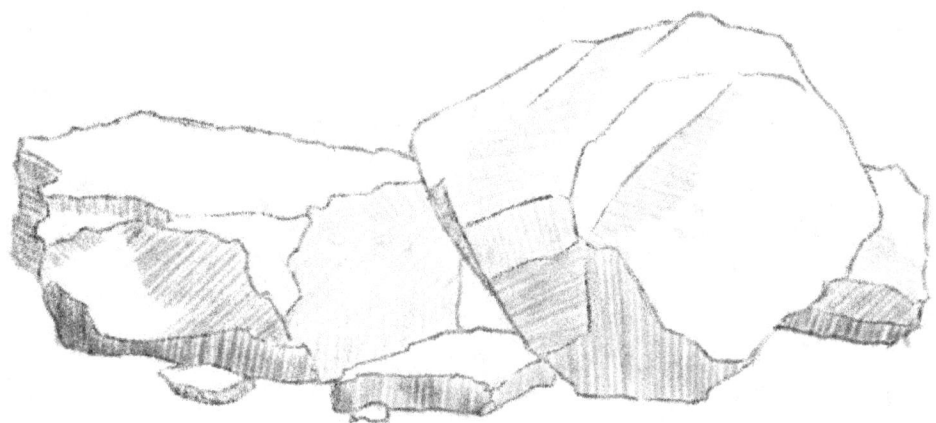

Then you can display the drop shadows. Pay attention to the shadows that one stone casts on another. In this example, the large stone casts a shadow on two other stones at the front.

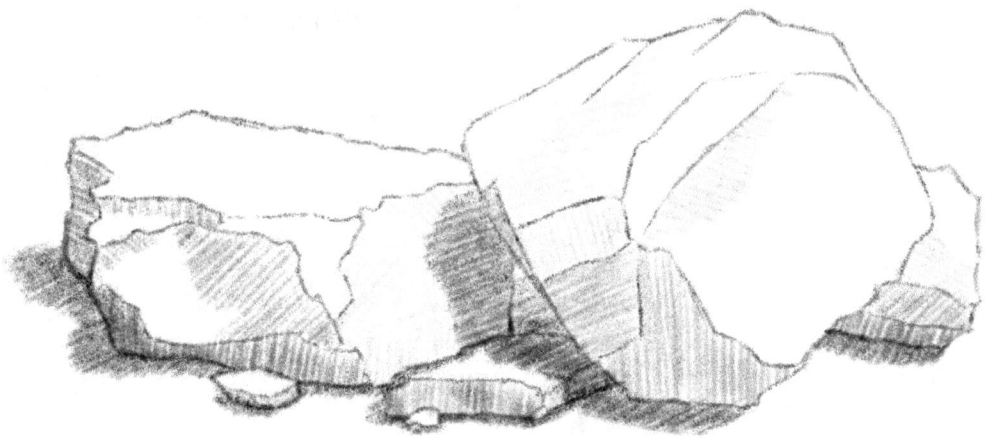

In the last step, important details are drawn so that the shape of the stones becomes even more visible. In addition, you should now work out the darkest areas again, as they increase the contrast and consequently the tension in the picture. In addition, the three-dimensional effect of the motifs is also enhanced. In this context, the phrase "work out" means that the darkest areas are deliberately designed to be very dark.

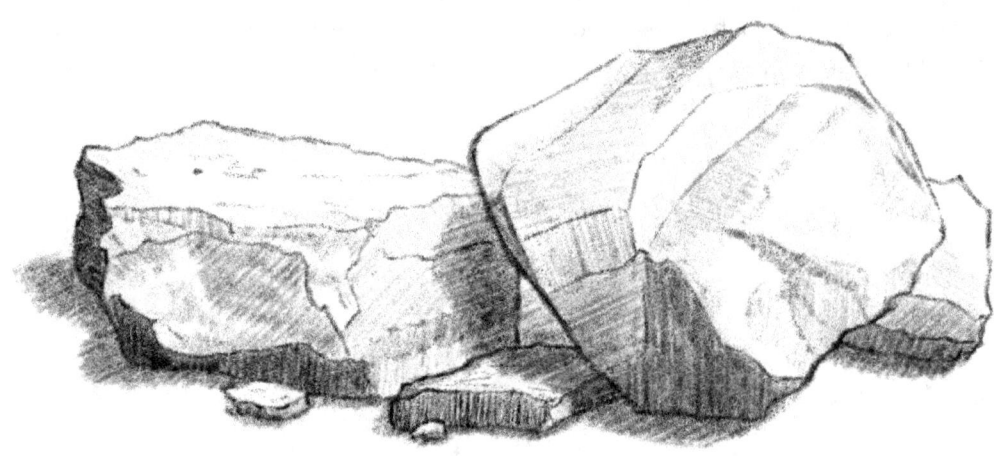

Template for quick practice:

Mountains

The representation of mountains is often a challenge for beginners. It is not easy to reproduce the interlocked structure while capturing the typical look of the mountain. In simple terms you can imagine a single mountain as a pyramid. In reality, however, you often stand in front of an entire mountain range, which corresponds to a series of pyramids that are interlocked with one another.

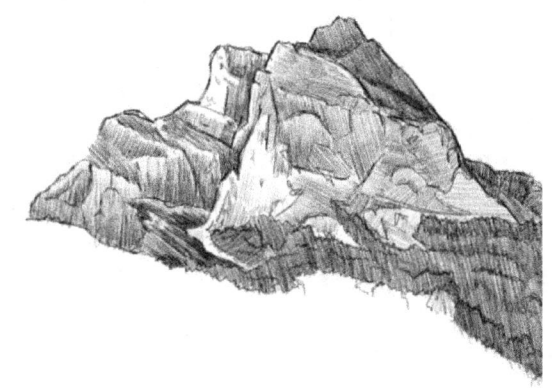

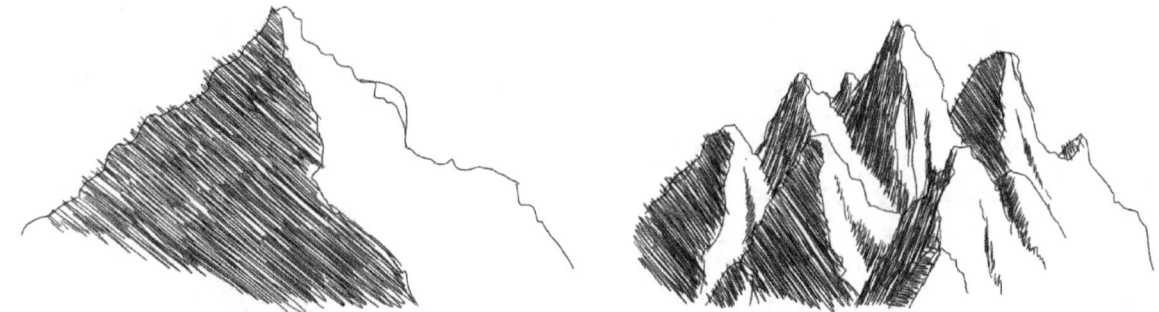

Individual mountain in its basic pyramid form (left) and mountain range (right)

In addition to this, there are irregularities, cracks and edges that give rise to typical rock structures. Try to represent these rock structures as realistically as possible without getting distracted by too many details.

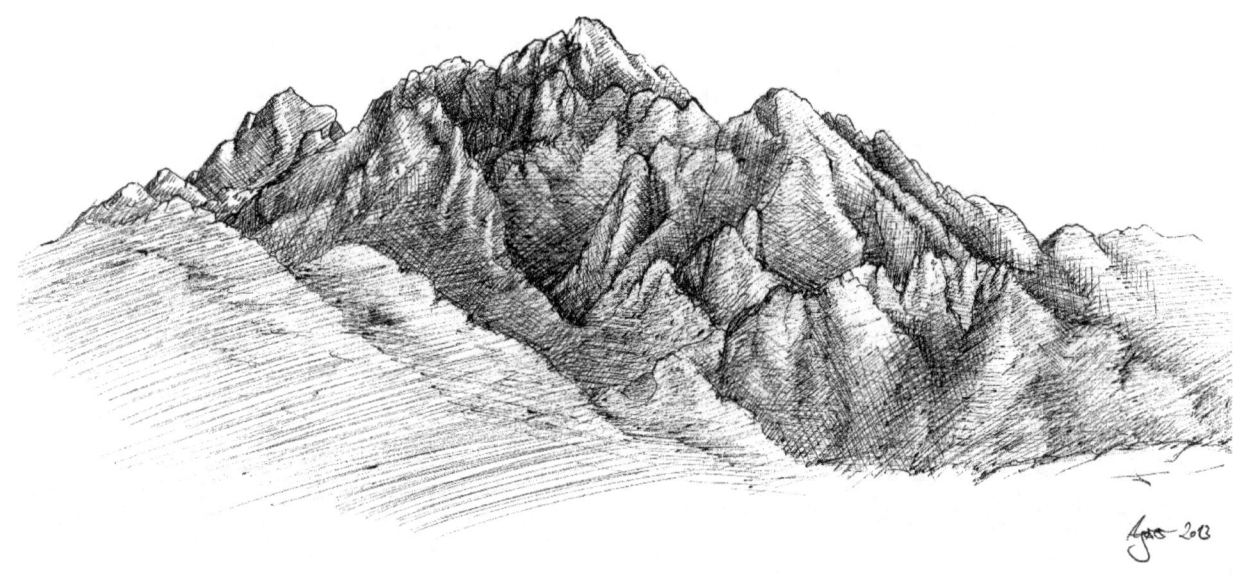

What many beginners also overlook when drawing mountains is the shading. This is because even if mountains are huge bodies, shadows appear on their surface just like any other body. Observe exactly which surfaces are in the shadow and which ones are in the light before you start drawing. Try to understand how the shape of the mountain is described by light and shadow.

Drawing a mountain step by step

First, you should sketch the contour of the mountain and the most prominent edges.

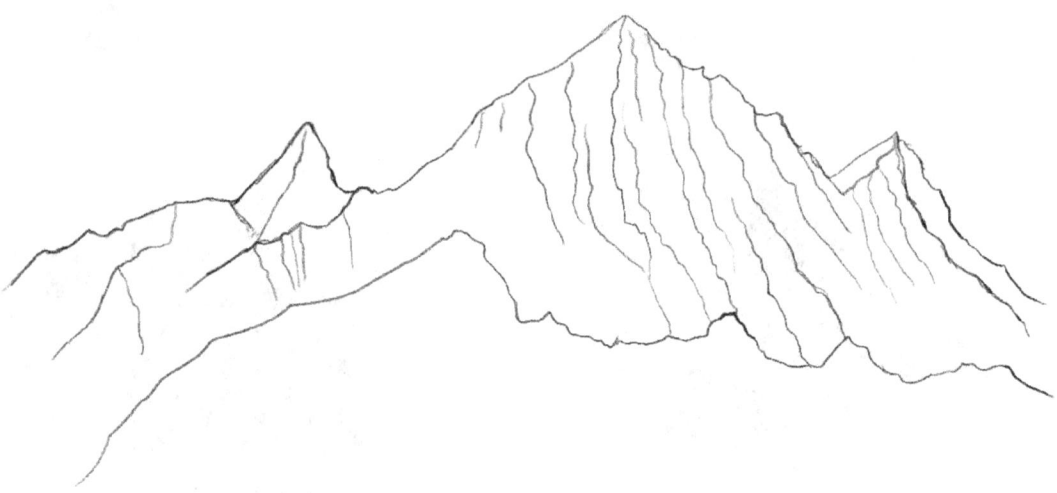

Observe where the light is coming from. In this example the sun shines from the back left onto the mountain range. Accordingly, the areas to the left are brightly lit, while the right flanks are shaded. Shadows also appear in the furrows, while sunlight falls on projections.

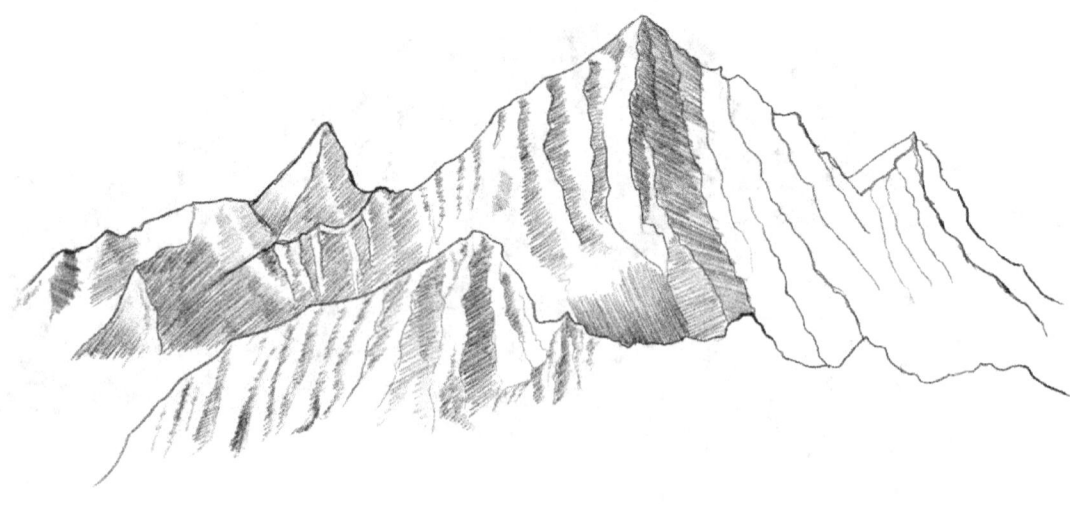

In this manner you can now gradually shade the mountain range. It is sufficient if you work with a few different tonal values. This keeps the complexity of this exercise low. A quickly sketched sky rounds out the drawing.

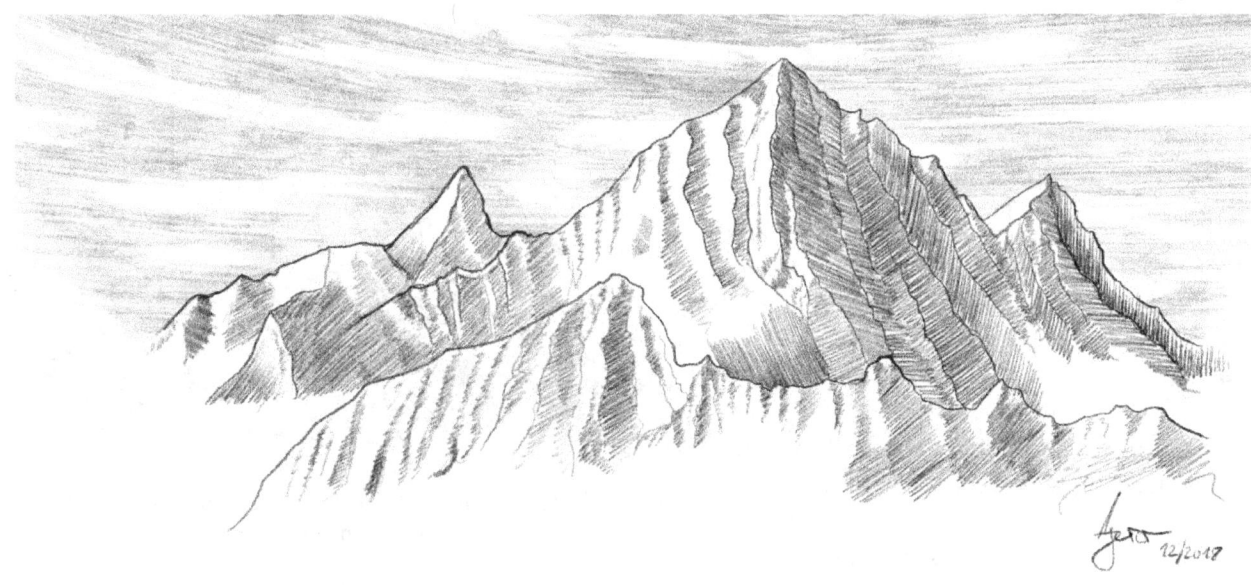

Template for quick practice:

3.6 Clouds

Clouds always become a topic when it comes to the representation of the sky. This aspect is often neglected when drawing - whether it is because you think that the sky is less important, or because the representation of clouds causes difficulties. However, it is precisely the sky that gives the final touch to many landscapes.

Particularly during the heyday of landscape painting in the 17th century, artists devoted two thirds of the picture surface to the sky, making the sky the dominant and most expressive aspect of the work. By depicting clouds, the artists conveyed movement, atmosphere, drama as well as the depth of spatial area.

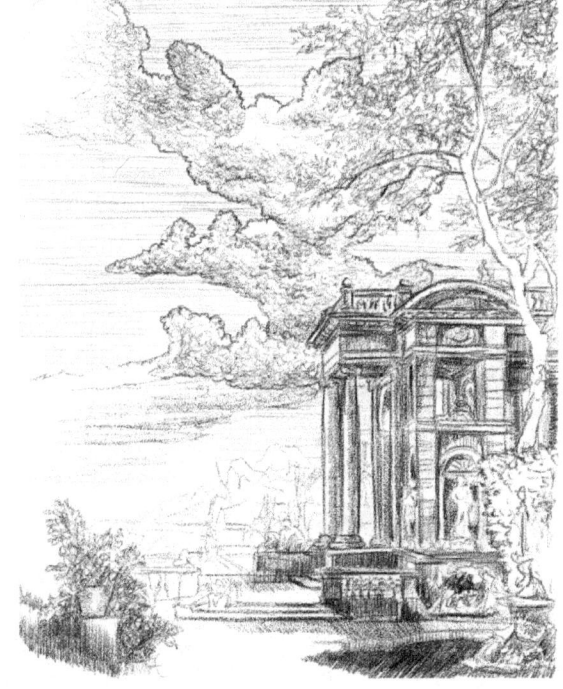

Drawing Clouds

Drawing clouds is actually not very difficult. You can also emphasize their contours in a drawing. This does not correspond to reality, but underlines the graphic character of the picture.

Shadows, for example, can be reproduced with shape-describing hatching or chaotic curled hatching. What is easily overlooked is the fact that clouds have a shadow on their underside.

The shape of a typical cloud can be imagined as a recumbent egg flattened on its lower side. When detailing the form further, mountain-like shapes and structures similar to the foliage of a tree emerge.

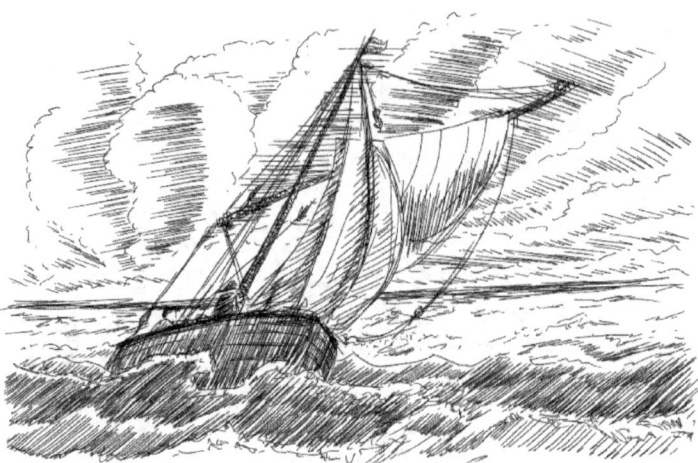

Indian ink drawing after the painting "Stormy Sea with Sailboat" by von Jacob van Ruisdael

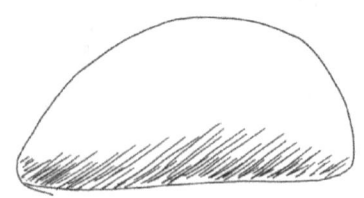 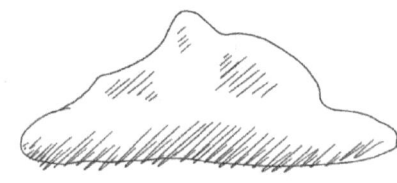 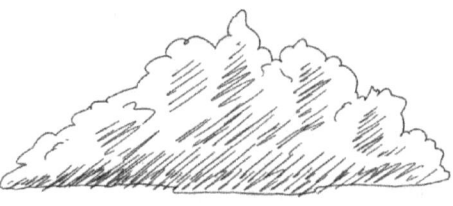

The transition from basic geometric form to cloud

Drawing a Cloud Step-By-Step

The Contour

With the contour you can proceed almost in the same manner as with a tree. Always draw the small curvatures of the lines unevenly so that the shape looks natural.

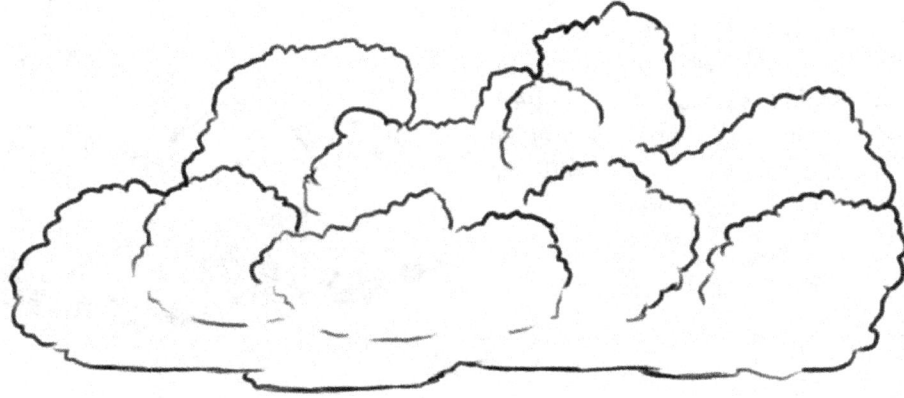

Shadows

The shadows on the underside of the cloud are important - they are often left out by beginners. You can work with small, arched lines.

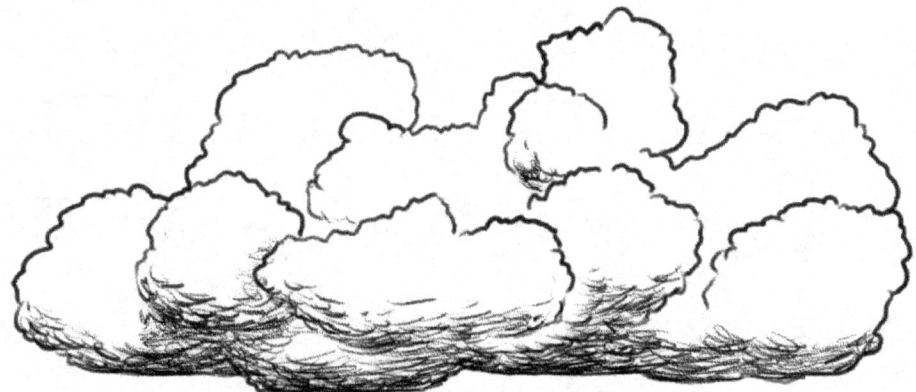

Further Shadows

Further shadows follow. Shading can be used to describe the three-dimensional shape of the cloud.

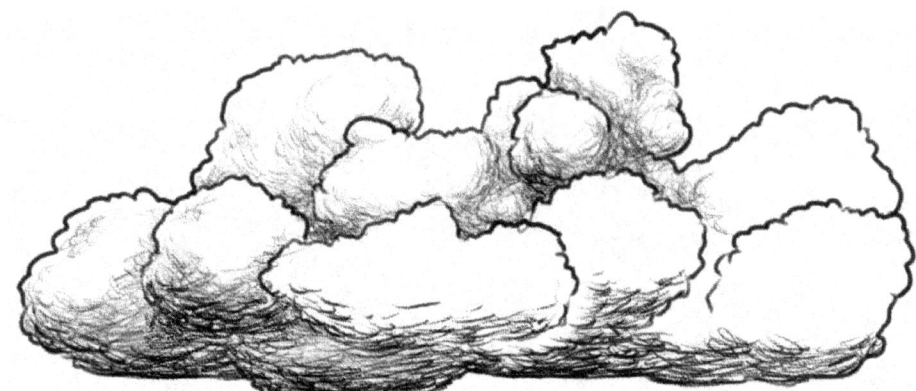

Completion

Then you can complete the sketch by working on the remaining surfaces and, where necessary, darkening them again or lightening them with a kneaded (art) eraser.

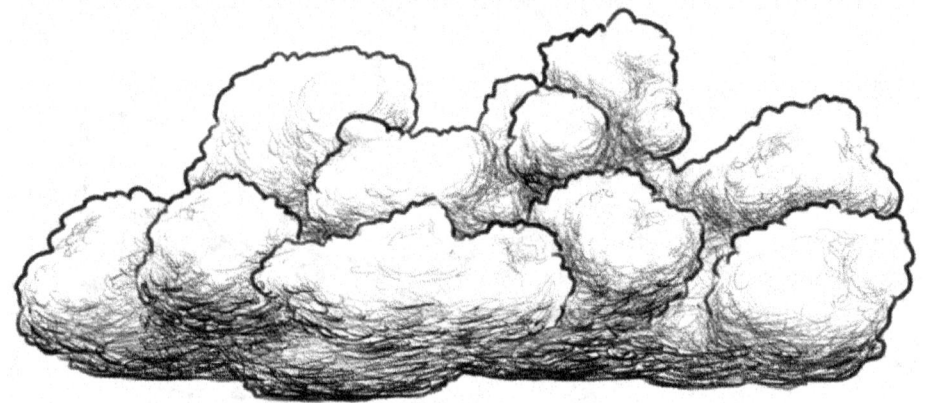

| Template for quick practice: |  |

Another way to draw clouds is negative drawing. With this technique the contour is not drawn directly. Instead you draw the sky and leave the area of the cloud free - a negative shape is created. Then the shadows of the cloud can be displayed.

Two Common Errors when Drawing Clouds:

1. The contour of the cloud is drawn too evenly (left). An uneven line, on the other hand, appears more natural and interesting (right).

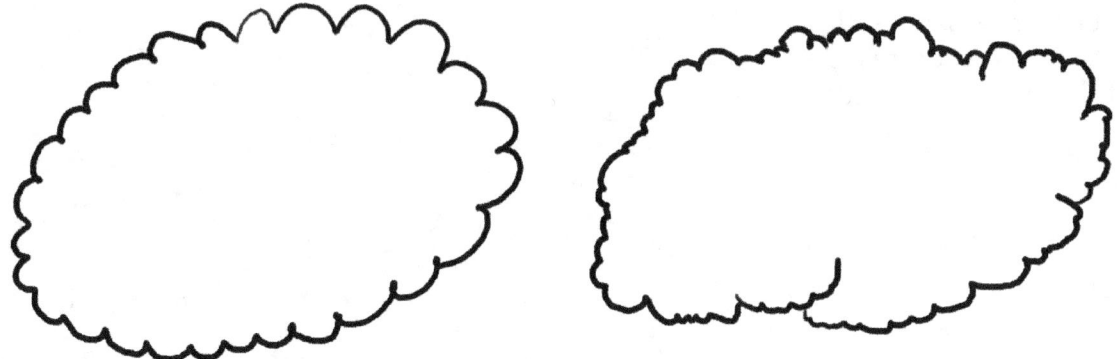

2. Clouds are simply displayed in white. In reality, however, shadows also appear on their surface.

Kinds of Clouds

In order to be able to implement clouds precisely in drawings, one should also know a few of the most important cloud types. Basic knowledge about clouds is useful, because certain clouds are associated with a corresponding weather system. Rain clouds in bright sunshine are a contradiction. These are things that one should consider when drawing a landscape.

Cumulus

The cumulus cloud is also called heap cloud or sheep cloud and represents the classic "picture book cloud". It has a sharply defined shape and a flat underside. Cumulus clouds mostly occur in sunny weather. The parts illuminated by the sun shine in bright white.

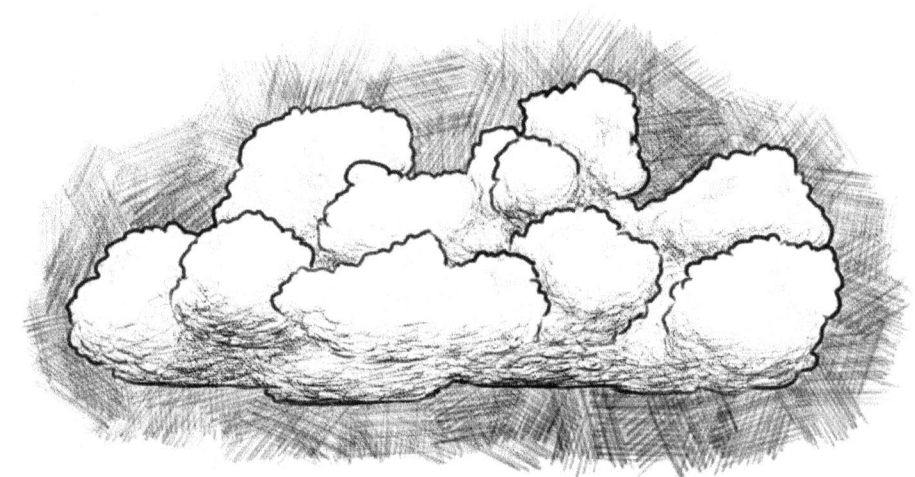

Cirrus

The word cirrus comes from Latin and means "lock of hair" or "fringe". The cirrus cloud is an ice cloud at a great height. They appear as bright white, delicate threads or narrow bands with a silky shimmer. Their edges are usually frayed by the high winds.

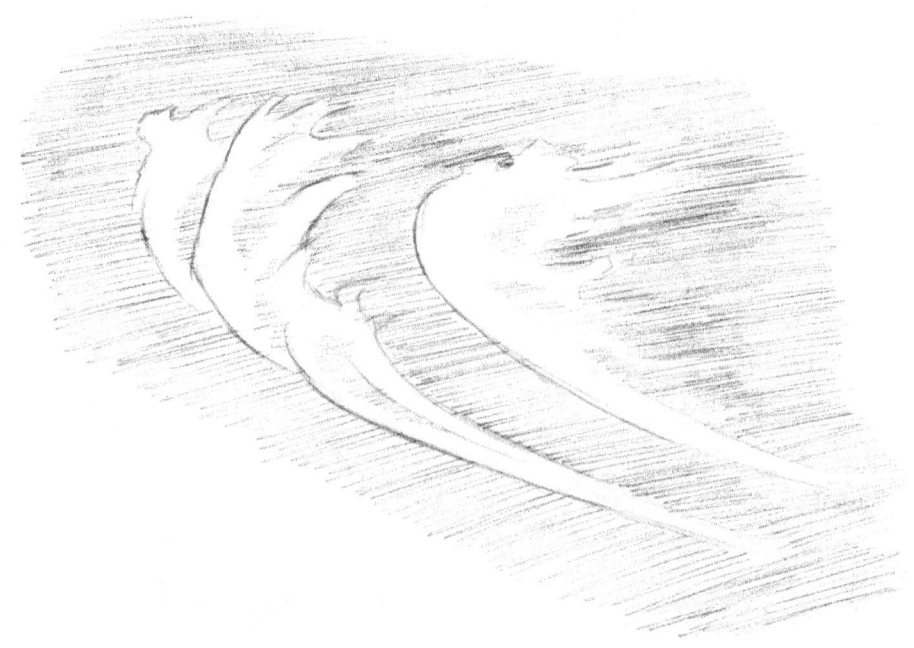

Elements of a Landscape Drawing

Cumulonimbus

Cumulonimbus is a rain cloud that stretches vertically like a tower. The upper part of the cloud extends like an anvil, giving it a particularly impressive and characteristic appearance.

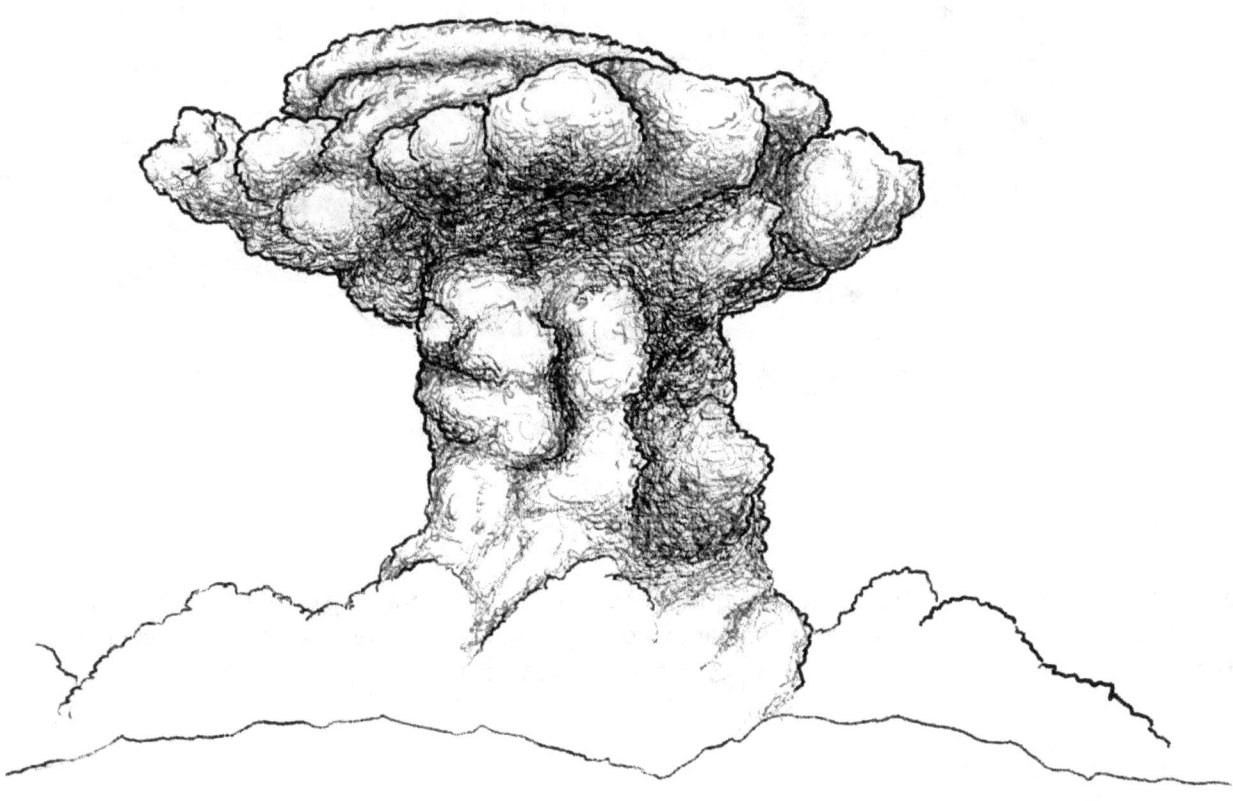

Nimbostratus

Nimbostratus is a more or less contourless, blue-gray cloud cover. It usually begins at medium altitudes and often causes prolonged precipitation.

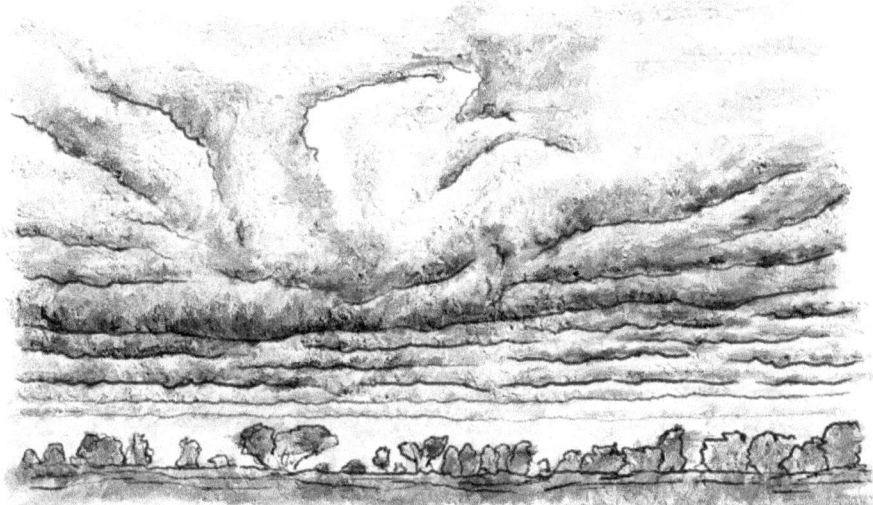

3.7 Water

Water can occur in different variations in landscapes. It can appear as a river, lake, sea or even as a waterfall. Here you will learn techniques for depicting these different forms so that you are prepared for any eventuality.

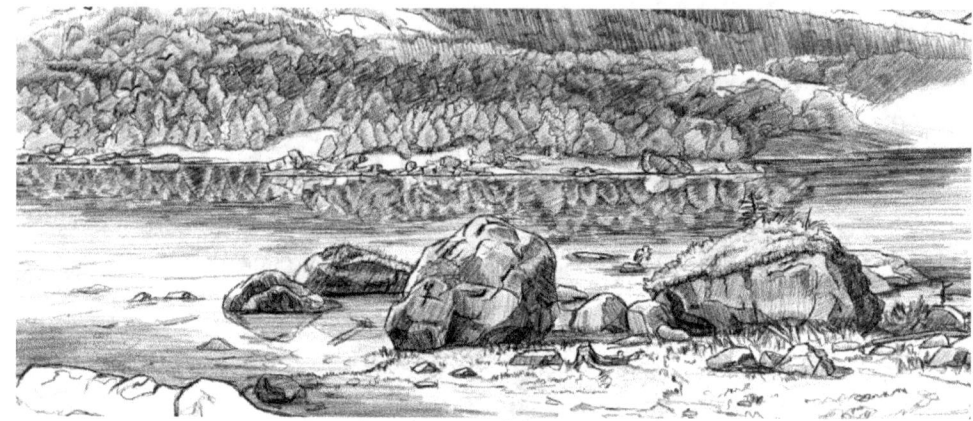

Standing water: reflections in a lake

Rivers

The challenge in depicting a river is the movement of the water. As a draughtsman, in a still picture you have to convey to the observer that the water is constantly flowing. Additionally, the objects are reflected in the water at the edge of the river - at least as long as the current is not too wild.

Start your drawing by sketching the river and its surroundings. Draw some higher objects like the trees in this example.

In the following chapter you will also learn tricks to make this sketch even better. This refers to the vanishing point perspective.

For now it is enough for us to draw without this method.

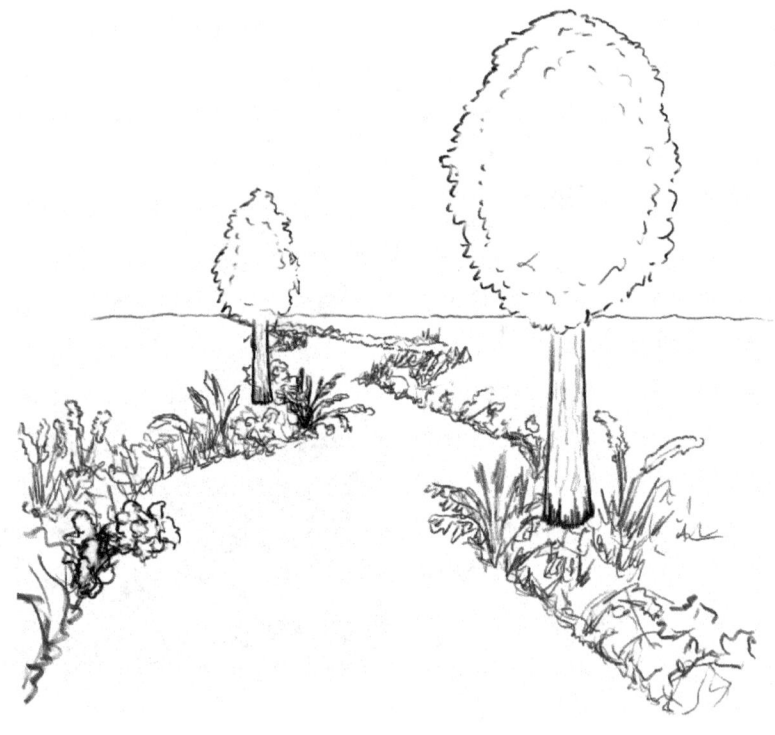

Elements of a Landscape Drawing

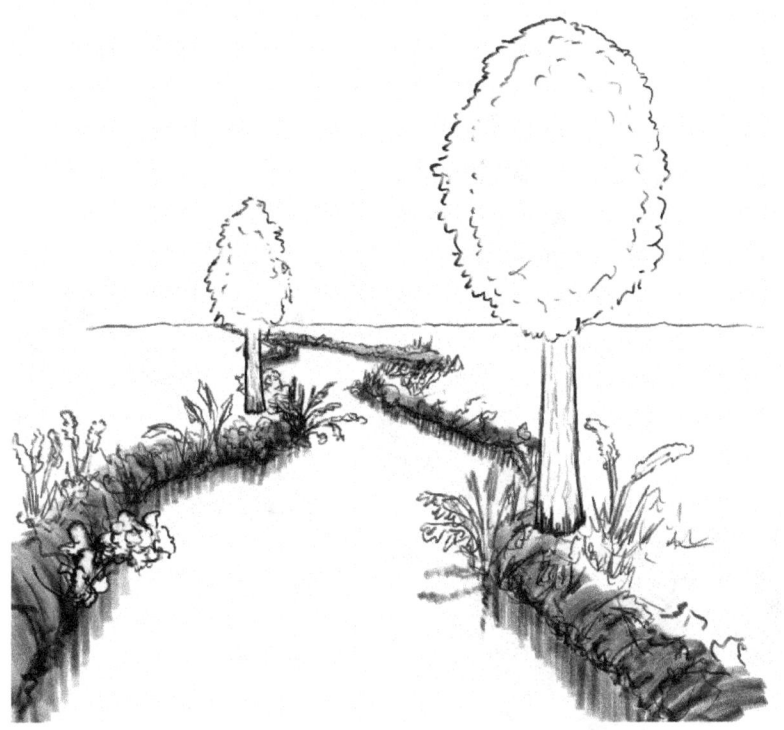

Now the riverbank follows. You don't have to go into detail here. It is enough to darken the shore. Then you can draw with vertical lines the reflection of the bank in the river. As in the example shown here, you can also draw the reflection of a few longer blades of grass. This increases the effect.

In the next step you can also mirror the trees and other higher objects. Now it looks like the river is standing still like a lake. There is no movement in the water to recognize.

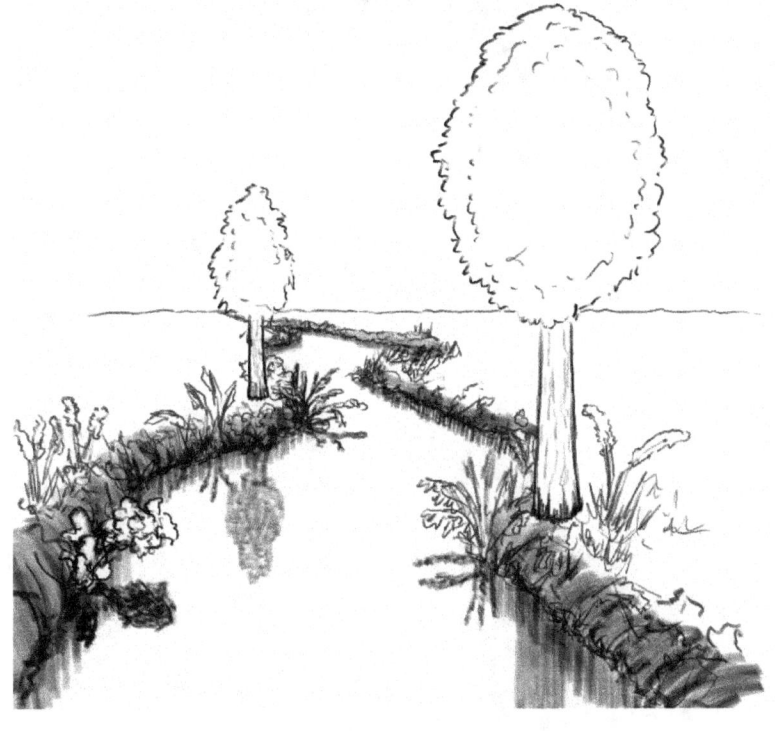

You can indicate the movement of the water with a few wavy lines. Towards the back you have to draw the lines smaller to get a perspective effect. Then the small drawing is ready.

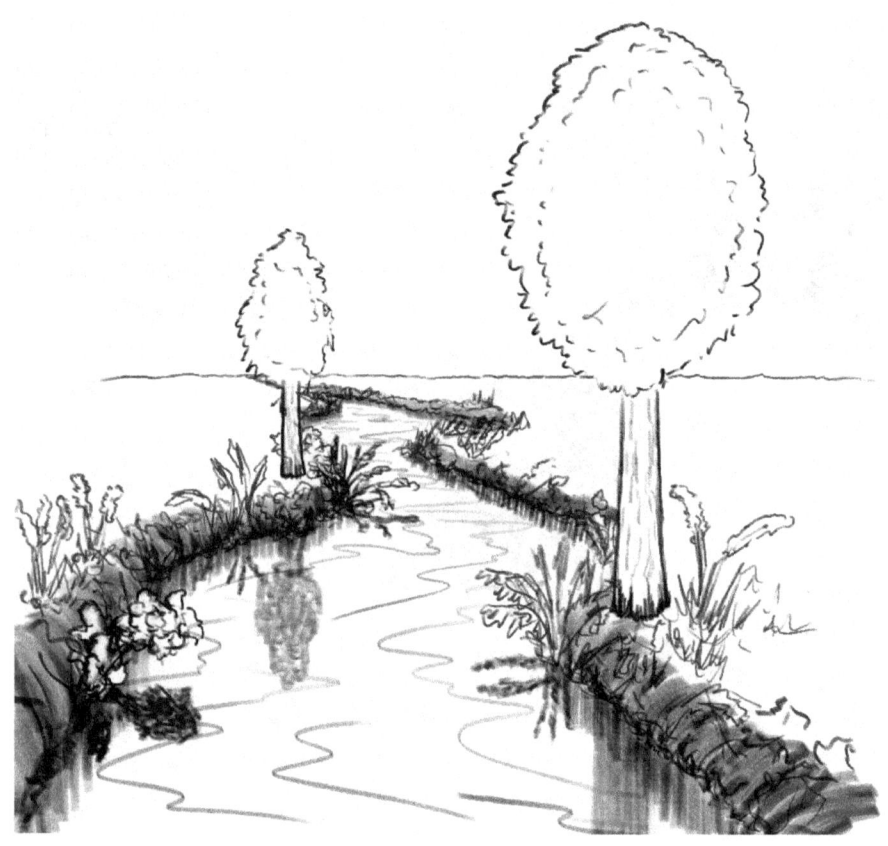

Shoreline and Sea

As with the river, the sea is also moving water. In addition, there are clearly visible waves in the sea. Depending on the weather, these waves are very small or extremely large. This increases the degree of difficulty a bit.

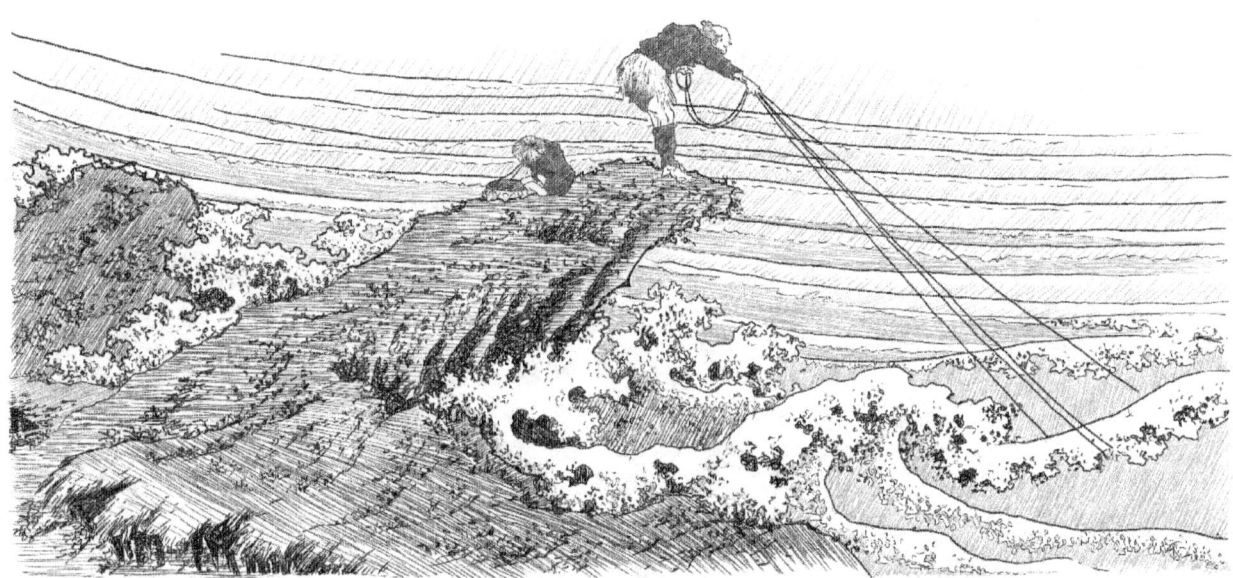

Representation of surging waves that are crashing against the rocks
Taken from a Japanese colored woodcut by the artist Hokusai

We now draw a small exercise sketch for which we begin with a simple line drawing. Small waves should be first suggested here, which look a bit like mountain ranges. At the transition between water and beach, foam can also be suggested.

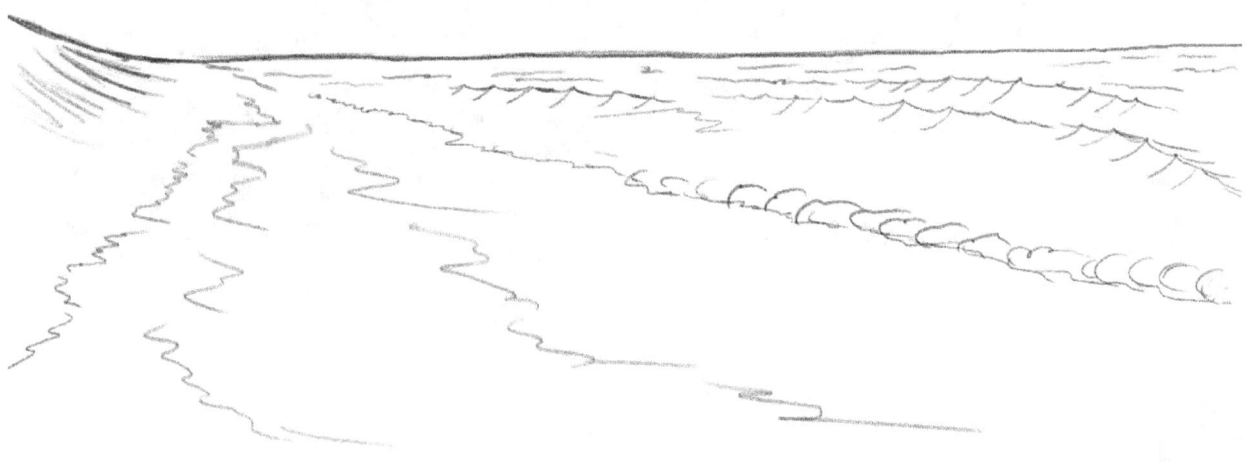

The next step is to structure the water more strongly. The shapes between the beach and the big wave are foam that floats on the surface of the water. The shape of the waves can be illustrated by further lines, which at the same time shade the waves. In the background, hills have also been indicated.

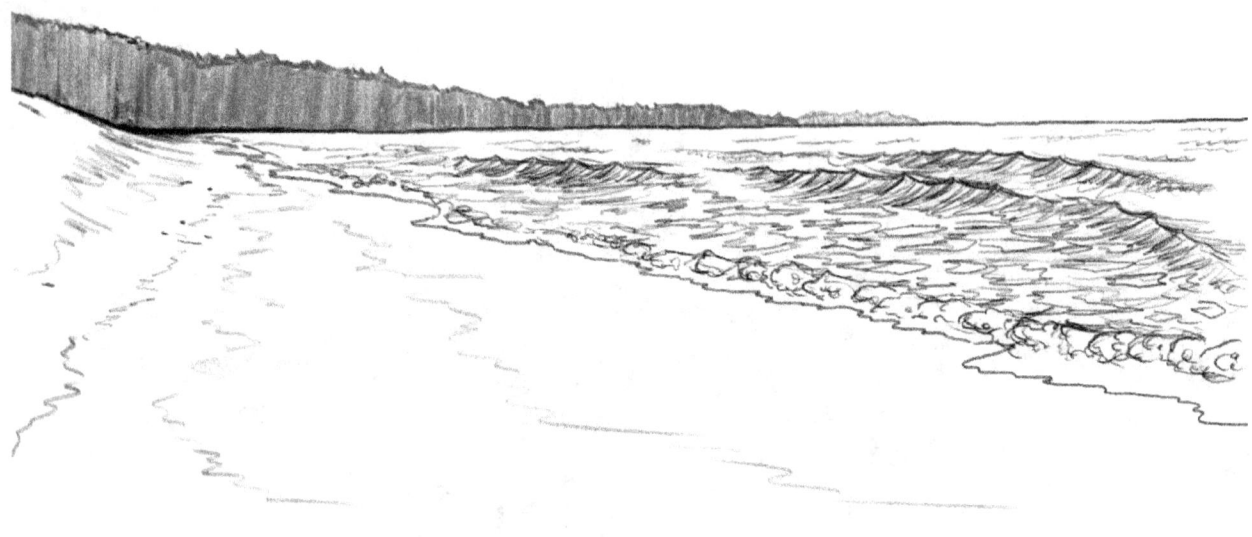

Now you can darken the rest of the water. This will make the foam and the waves even more visible. It is important that the waves always have bright areas so that they stand out from the rest of the sea. On the other hand, the backside of the waves can be shown darker.

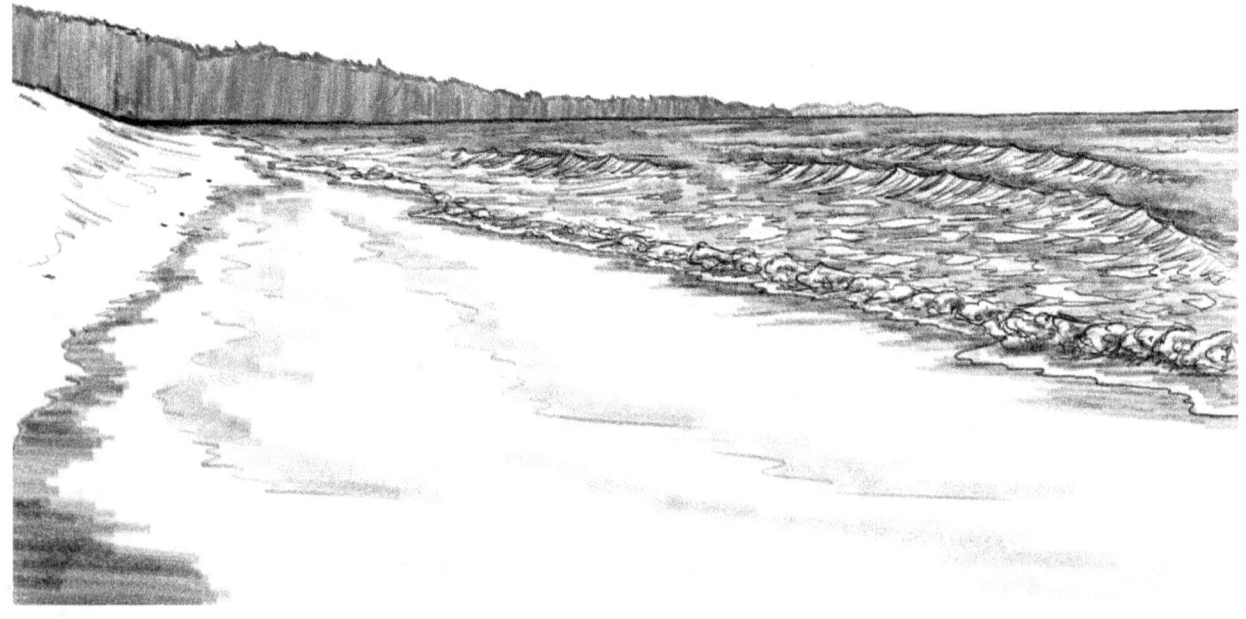

Waterfalls

Even stronger movement has to be depicted with a waterfall. Here water flows down at high speed. A lot of water and haze is whirled into the air.

For the following exercise you simply imagine a cliff face. The water of a river falls down this cliff face and over the centuries has cut out wide swaths through the stone. Start your drawing with this cliff wall and leave enough space for one or two waterfalls. The suggestion of a treetop borders the left side of the picture.

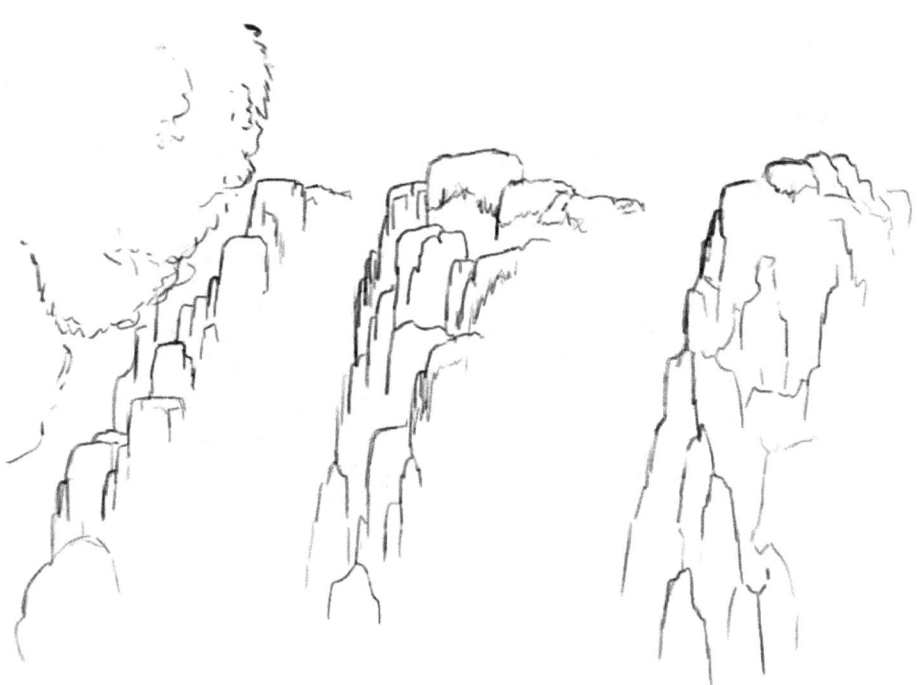

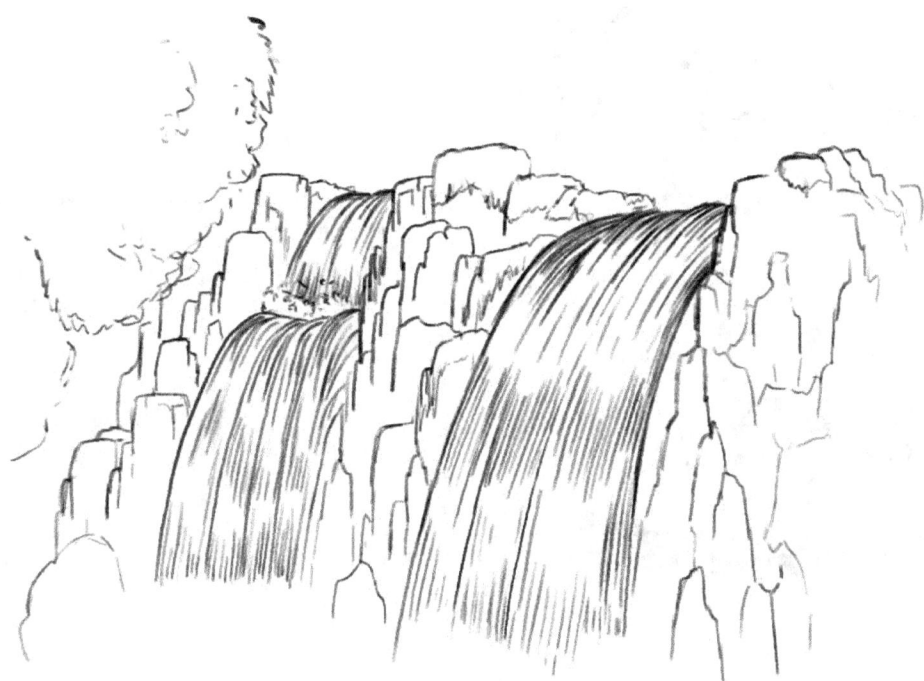

Now you can draw the waterfall. Draw the outlines of the water streams and other lines in the direction of the flow. You can depict the reflection of the sunlight by leaving certain areas white.

Where the waterfall hits the ground, a lot of water is whirled up. You can do this in a similar way with treetops or clouds. The calmer water below can be drawn with horizontal lines.

I have also sketched a tree in the rock face to make the picture even more vivid.

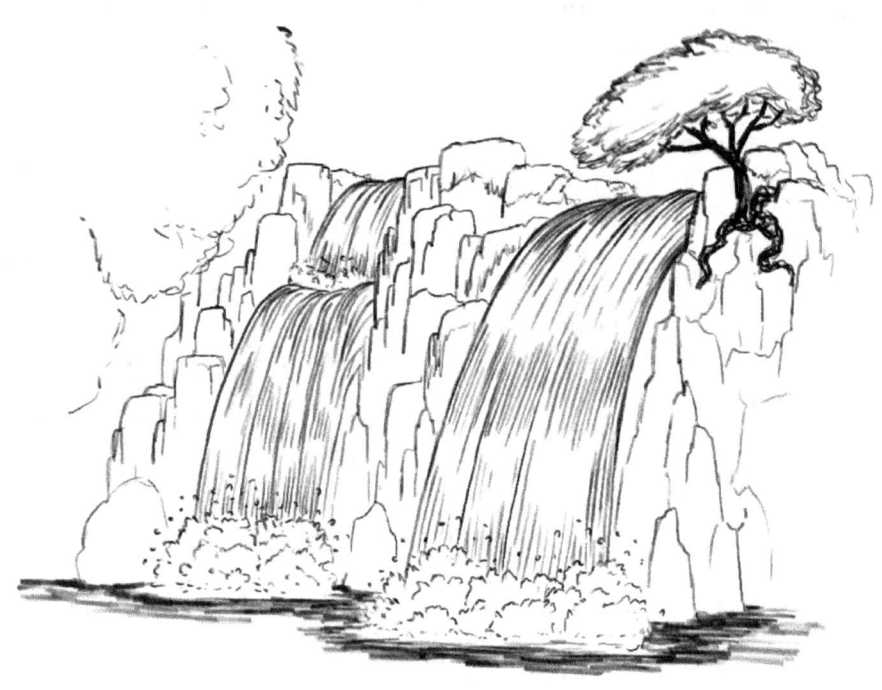

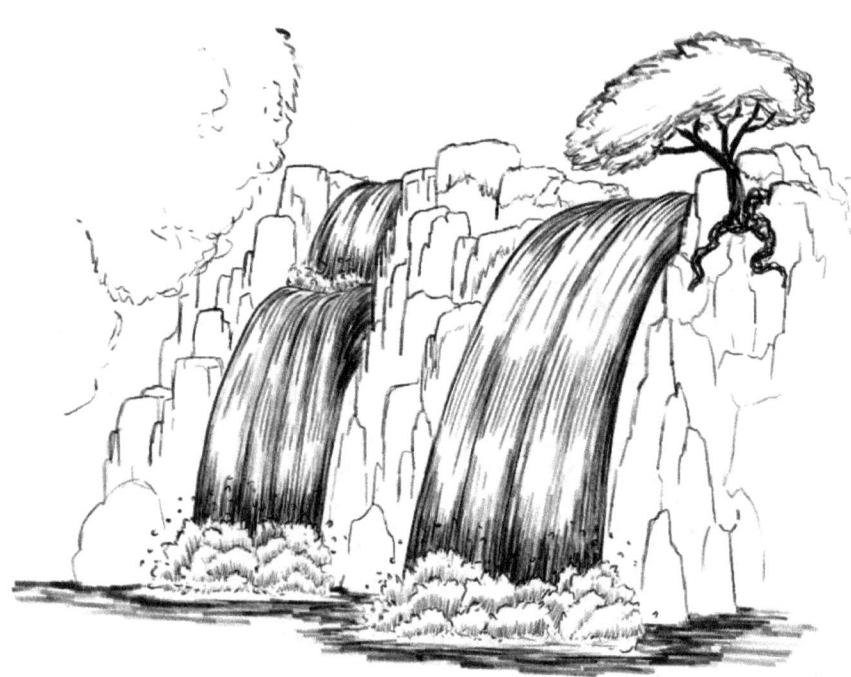

And now you can shade the waterfall. Especially in the lower part you can make the waterfall very dark, which makes the cloud of water even more visible.

Elements of a Landscape Drawing

Additionally, further soft shadows accentuate the form of the waterfall even more. Once the cliff wall has also been shadowed, the drawing is complete.

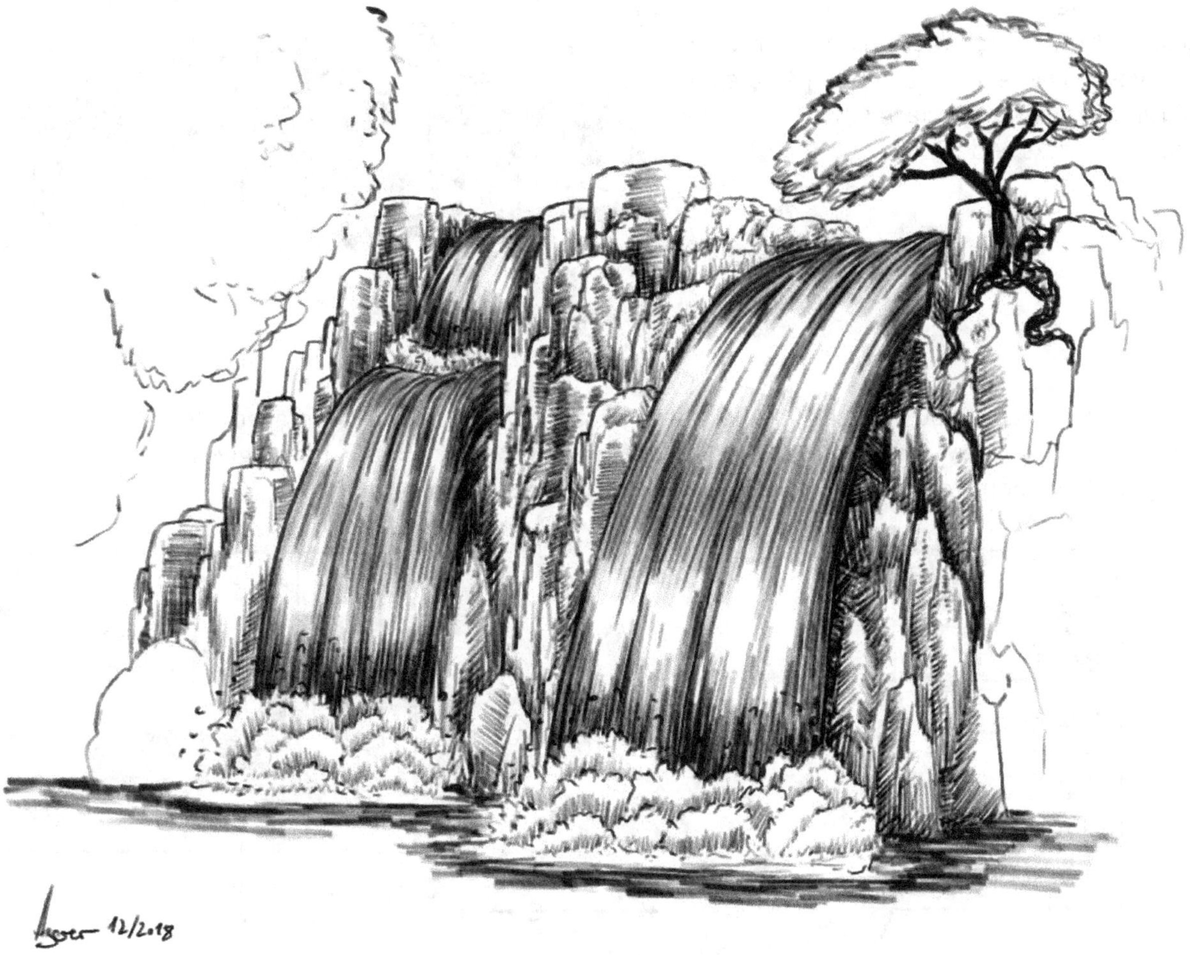

Template for quick practice:

Buildings

Buildings also occur relatively frequently in landscapes, especially since cities also fall under the category of landscape. An important task in the representation of architecture is to reduce the level of detail. It is often enough to suggest details and structures that repeat themselves only a few times in order to create the illusion of a certain surface structure - such as roof tiles, bricks and the like.

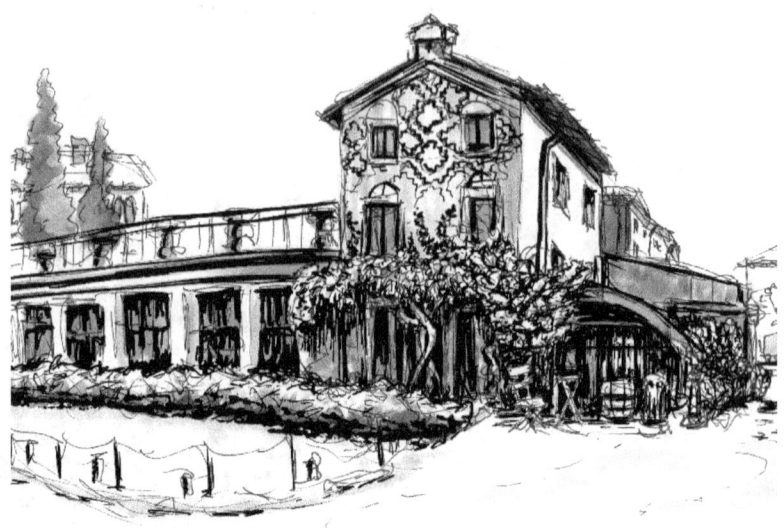

In the drawing below you can see in the detail sections how complex, detailed elements can appear very authentic by using a few intuitive strokes. The overall view, on the other hand, gives the impression that the building has been depicted with all its details.

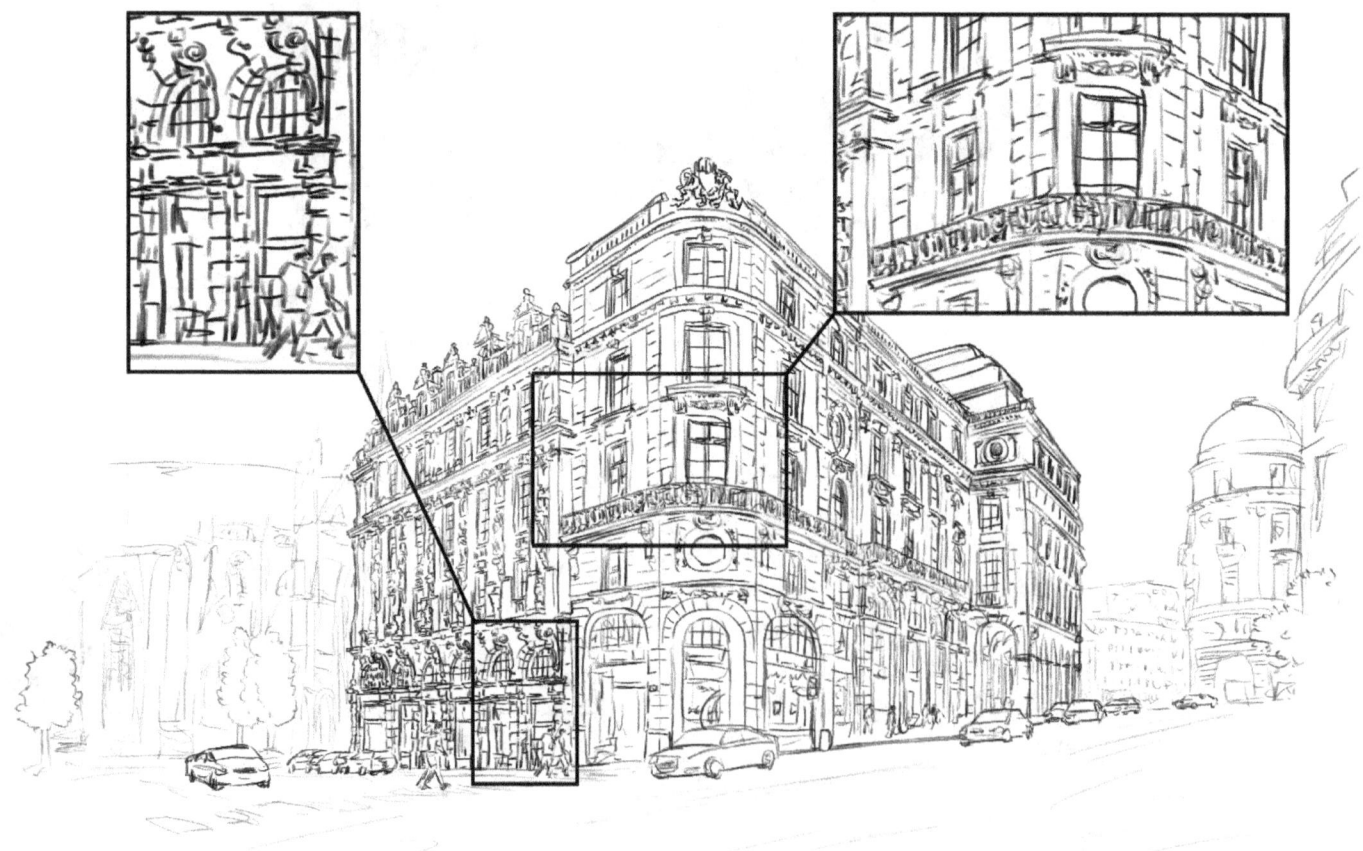

Drawing of a building with details

Elements of a Landscape Drawing

Another aspect that is very often associated with architecture in landscape paintings is perspective representation. This is perspective representation with the help of vanishing points, which is often ignored in pure landscape drawing, because more work is done according to feeling while other methods are used to convey space and depth.

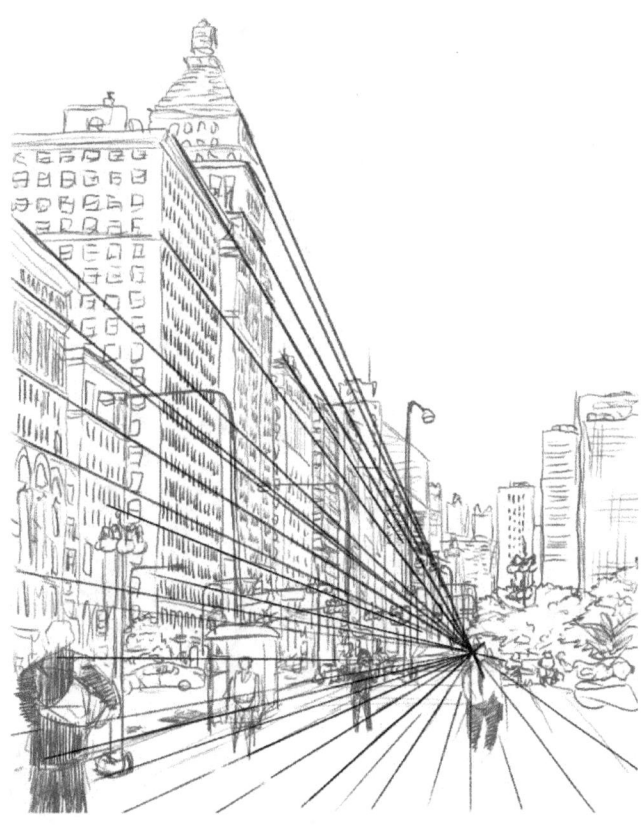

The subject of perspective drawing conveniently represents the perfect transition to the next chapter, which deals with precisely that subject.

Representation of Space and Perspective

» He who changes his perspective, sees things in an entirely different light. «

- Engelbert Schinkel -

4 Representation of Space and Perspective

4.1 Introduction

This book is dedicated to the topic "Drawing in Perspective". Primarily, it involves so-called vanishing-point perspective. By making use of vanishing-point perspective, it is possible to realistically display objects, landscapes and architecture. A persuasive illusion of reality is thus created on paper.

The depth of space becomes visible the clearest from a larger distance. Therefore, the depiction of depth plays especially with landscape pictures a major role. In order to allow this sense of space to emerge upon a two-dimensional drawing surface, diverse graphic aids are frequently deployed. In the following pages you will become acquainted with the most important methods.

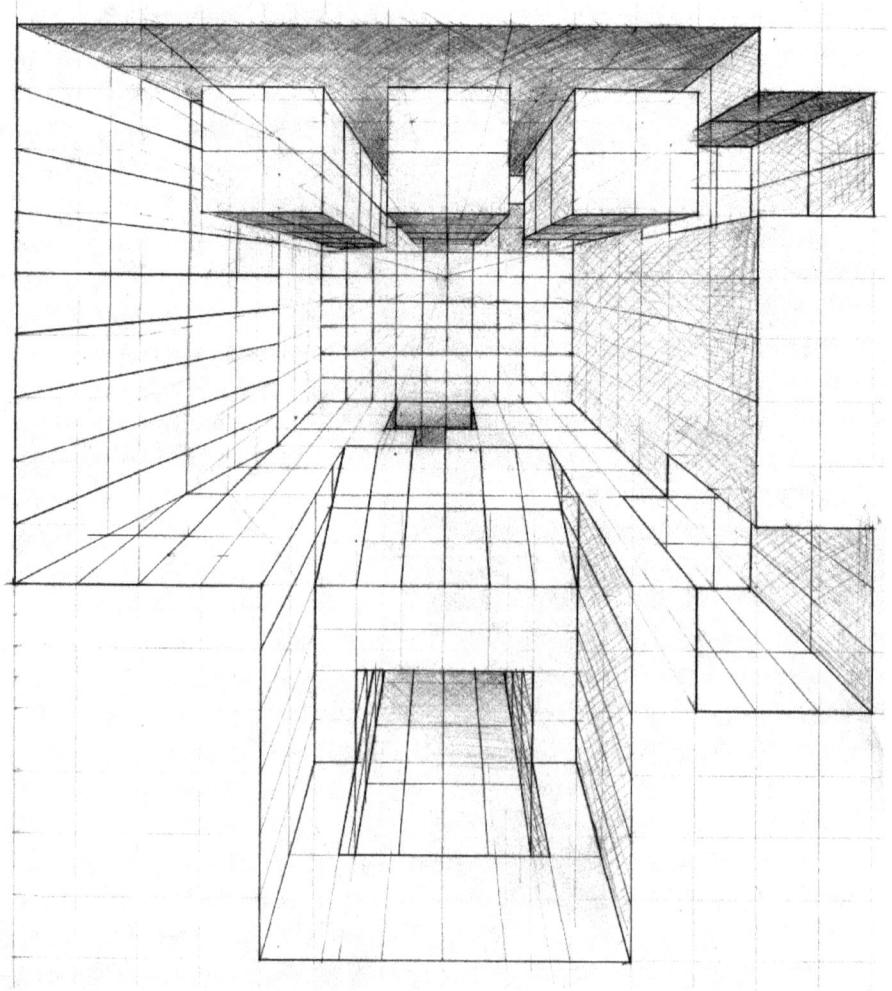

Geometric construction using the vanishing point perspective

Representation of Space and Perspective

Proper Composition of an Image

A simple principle for achievement of the effect of space and depth is to fulfill the expectations of the observer. This means that we represent the space in the manner that he is accustomed to and anticipates according to his own experience. Specifically: those objects that lie on the ground, i.e. in the lower area of the drawing, are located in the foreground, and those objects that are in the upper section are more likely located in the background. Thus we make it easier for the observer of the drawing to get his bearings within the image, and the impression of a three-dimensional landscape is more readily conveyed in this manner.

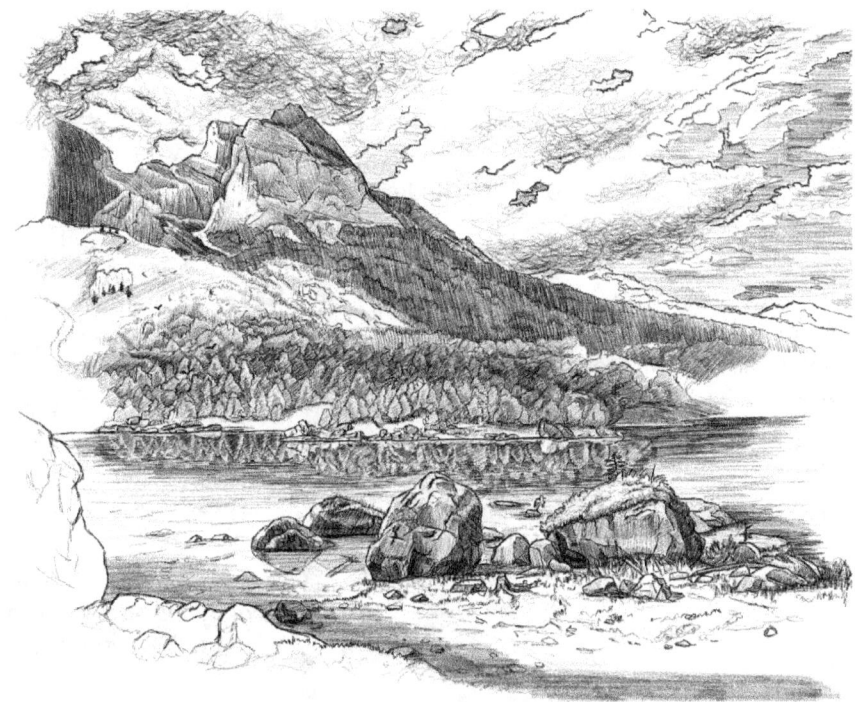

*Landscape with a classic composition
(Drawing based on a painting by Carl Rottmann)*

Overlapping

The effect of spatial representation is optically reinforced when the image is constructed in several upright planes. These planes can contain trees, a house, a car etc. The planes are laid out at varying distances and overlap one another. Due to the fact that the planes overlay one another, it is immediately obvious to the observer that the various objects in the image are located at different distances.

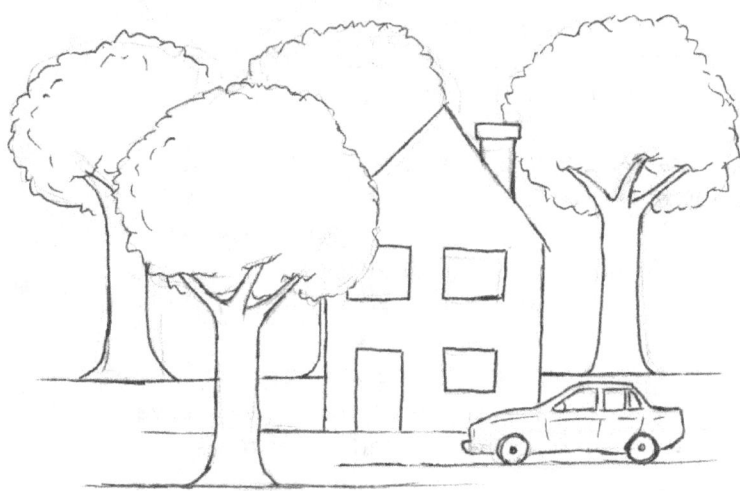

Levels

The effect of the spatial representation is visually enhanced by building up the image in several levels. These levels could include trees, a house, a car, etc.

In many cases, the overlap method is combined with the level method. The levels are at different distances and overlap each other. As the levels overlap, it is immediately obvious to the viewer that the different image objects are at different distances.

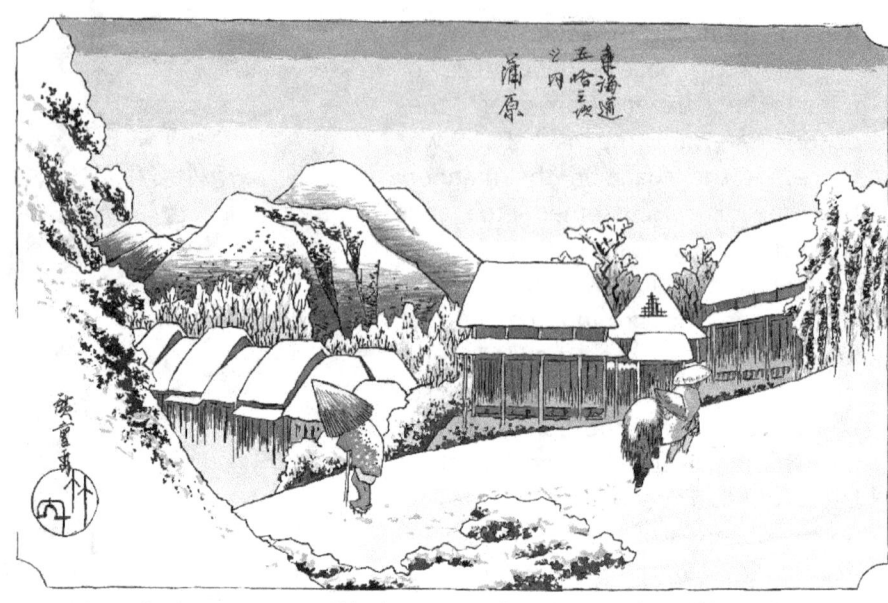

Replica of a Japanese woodblock printing: "Station Kambara" from the series "The 53 Stations of Tōkaidō"; Original: Utagawa Hiroshige

Perspective Foreshortening

Perspective foreshortening is an effect that becomes particularly distinct when we view, from straight ahead, an object that stretches out into the distance. For example, we look at an outstretched arm or a branch directly from the front.

The graphic problem arises as a lot of "information" is compressed into very little space in this foreshortening of perspective. Such views are not only difficult, but also unusual to draw. They often contradict the experience stored in our brain.

Unbiased seeing and observing are important approaches here. The vanishing point perspective is also a particularly effective method for representing such views.

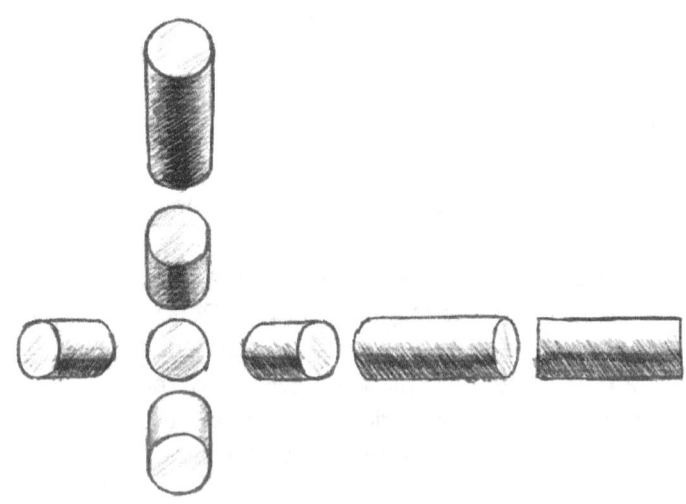

Perspective shortening of a cylinder

Representation of Space and Perspective

Vanishing Point Perspective

The last method of spatial representation to be introduced here is vanishing point perspective. The procedure here is much less characterized by feeling and intuition than the previous methods. Vanishing point perspective is first and foremost a technical method. But more about that in the remainder of the book!

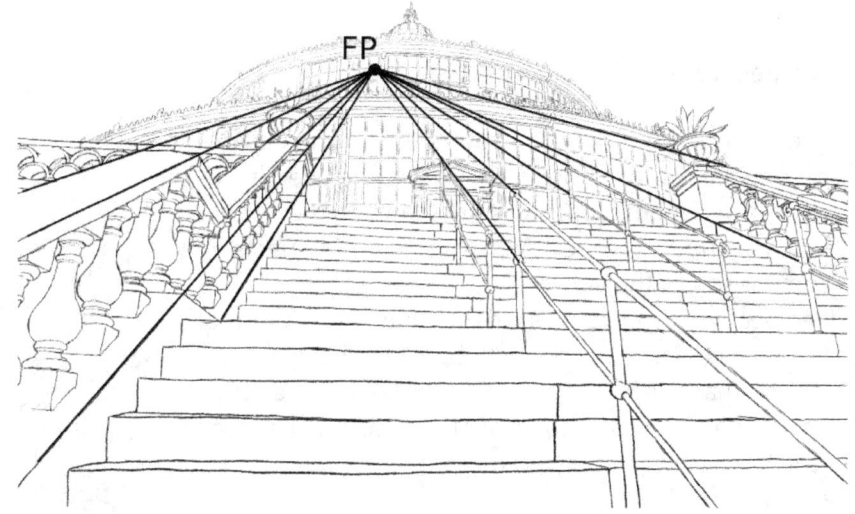

Example of the perspective representation of a staircase

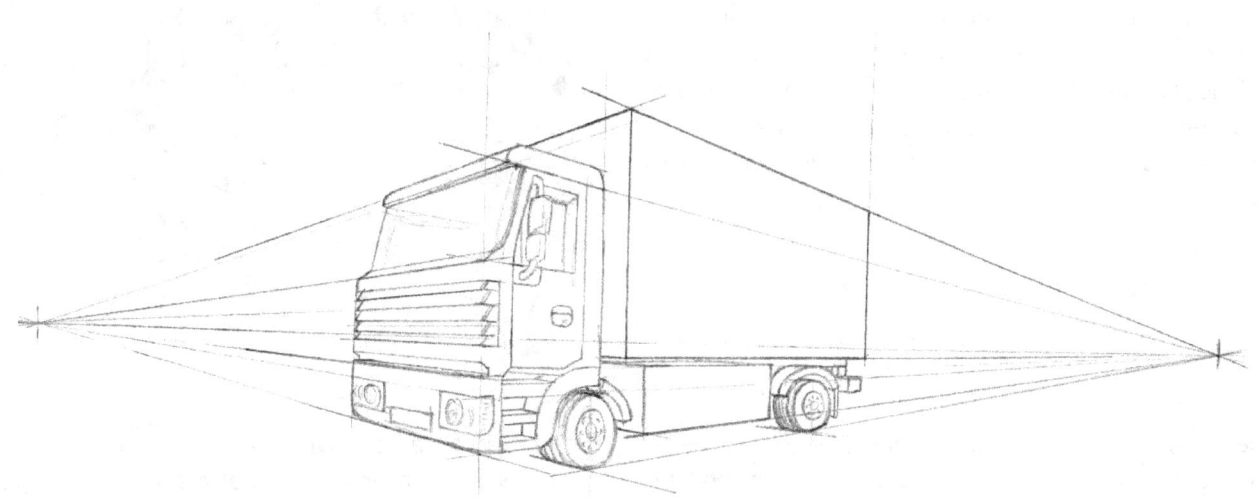

Perspective drawing of a truck

4.2 Vanishing Point Perspective – the Basics

General Information about Vanishing Point Perspective

Perspective

The term perspective refers to the spatial circumstances of objects in space. Perspective is always dependent on the standpoint of the viewer and describes the relative distances of objects in comparison to the viewer.
Perspective only changes when either the location of the objects or that of the observer changes. This means that the perspective does NOT change when only the observed section of the picture is changed (e.g. in a zoom-in using a camera).

Vanishing Point Perspective

Vanishing point perspective presents a graphic method with which we can represent three-dimensional objects on a two-dimensional surface with the use of perspective. This involves a construction procedure that is both technical and artistic. The objective here is to create the illusion of a three-dimensional space, even though the drawing, i.e. the surface of the canvas, is only two-dimensional.

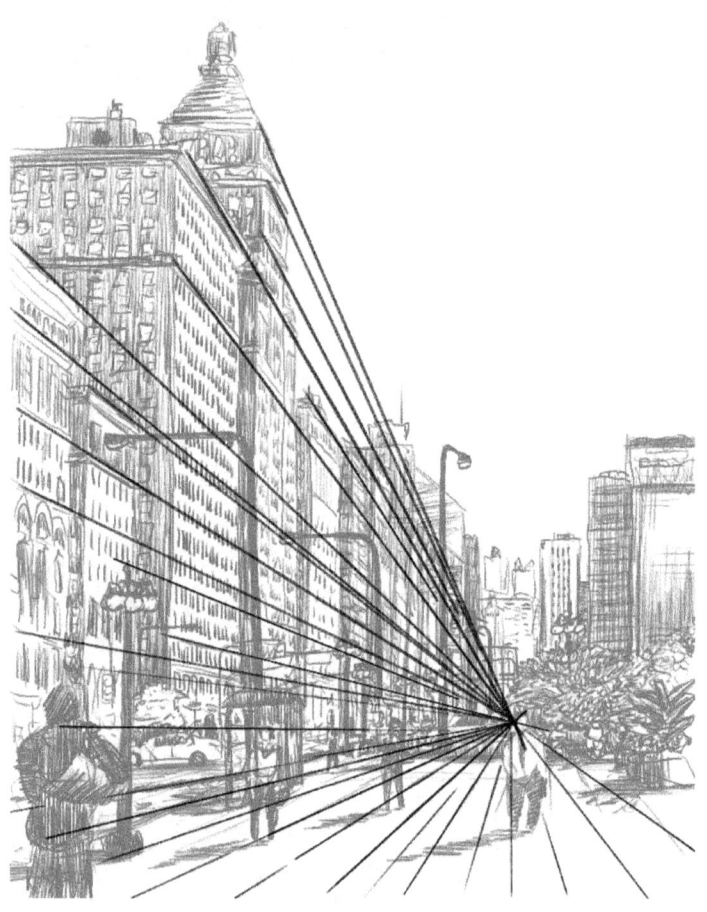

The perspective perception is characterized above all by the fact that we perceive objects the smaller the further away they are from us. This reduction occurs because the rays of light enter our eyes at a shallower angle when an object is further away.
Another effect of perspective is that we see more objects in the distance than in our vicinity. In principle, this phenomenon has the same origin as the previously described effect of objects getting smaller in further distance.

Construction of Vanishing Point Perspective

At the beginning of this chapter we will have a look at the individual elements of vanishing point perspective. The simplest form of perspective representation requires a horizon, a vanishing point, vanishing lines and, of course, an object that we would like to draw spatially.

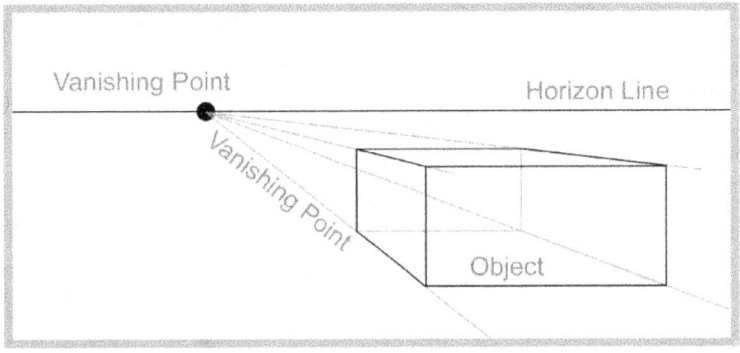

The most important terms

The Horizon

The horizon is the separation line between the ground and the sky. The technically correct description, however, would be "the line at which the view from below and the top view are separated". This means that one looks down (top view) at everything that is located below the horizon line – one is thus looking at the upper face of the object. Conversely, everything that is located above the horizon line is viewed upwards (view from below) – it is thus seen from below.

Even though the Earth is a sphere, the horizon is always perceived as a horizontal line. Obviously, mountains, hills, canyons and such interrupt the horizon line – in order to execute a drawing in perspective, we are forced to just imagine the horizon here.

It is furthermore important that the horizon is always placed at eye level with the observer! The horizon is the most important element in a drawing with vanishing point perspective, and is therefore drawn first.

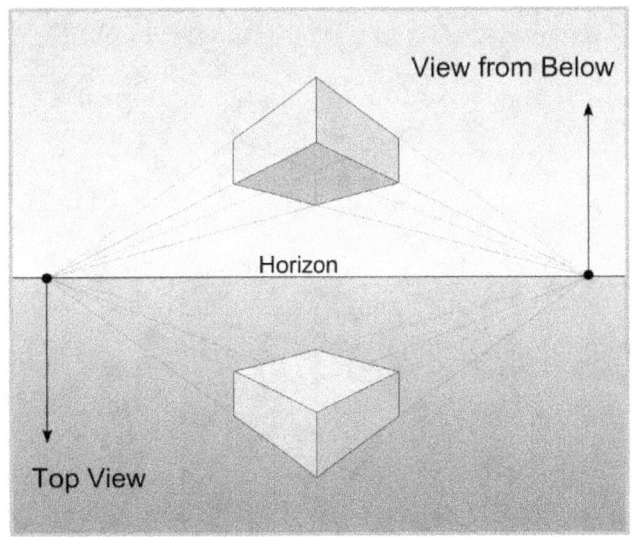

Vanishing Point and Vanishing Line

After the horizon line, the vanishing point is the second most important element in a drawing in perspective. With vanishing point perspective, all lines vanish into (i.e. are aligned in) one or several points. These points are called vanishing points. The aligned lines are also called vanishing lines and are frequently extended out to the vanishing point to aid construction of the drawing.

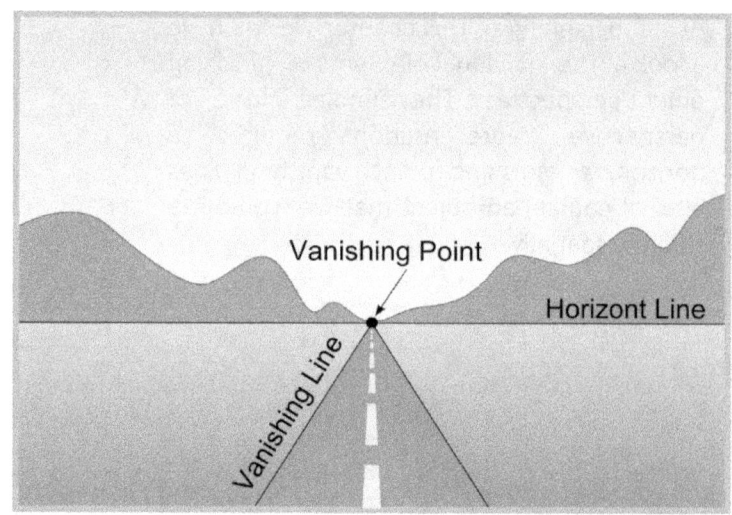

A few important rules for vanishing points and vanishing lines:

- Depending on the spatial position and the form of an object, an individual vanishing point can suffice for representation, or several vanishing points are required.
- Vanishing points that are referenced underground are always located on the horizon line.
- Lines that run parallel to one another vanish into a common vanishing point.

4.3 Central Perspective with one Vanishing Point

For central perspective with a (main-)vanishing point, the objects to be displayed are situated with their front surface parallel to the picture plane. We as observers are thus looking straight at the frontal face of the objects.

It can be said that the vanishing point is the point at which the observer's visual axis meets the horizon.

This type of perspective is certainly the simplest form. Only lines that lead back into the depth of space disappear into a vanishing point. Vertical lines are always vertical. Horizontal lines that run parallel to the horizon remain horizontal and do not align/disappear. The entire frontal face is thus not distorted through perspective.

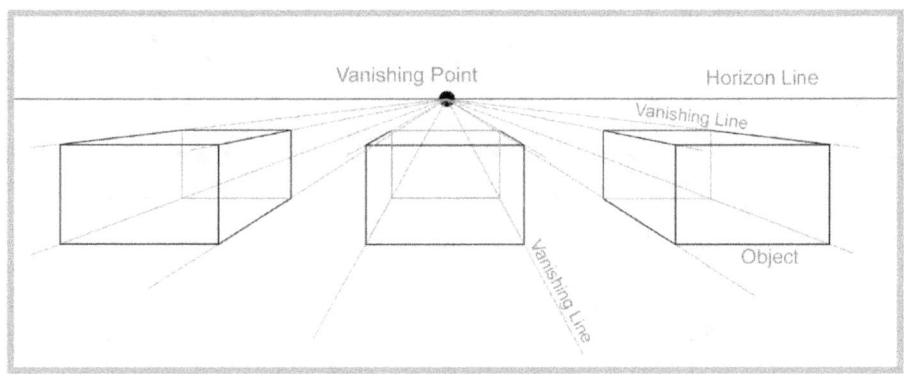

Three cubes in central perspective with one vanishing point

Central perspective with one vanishing point, however, can only be used when the represented objects stand vertically on the base plane and stand with one surface head-on to the observer, i.e. the front is parallel to the picture plane.

Exercise – Central Perspective with one Vanishing Point

And now we would like to translate, with a small exercise, the theoretical principles from the previous chapter into practice. A box with one vanishing point should be drawn in central perspective. As you proceed, you can view the picture series step by step. A clarification of the individual steps will follow the drawings.

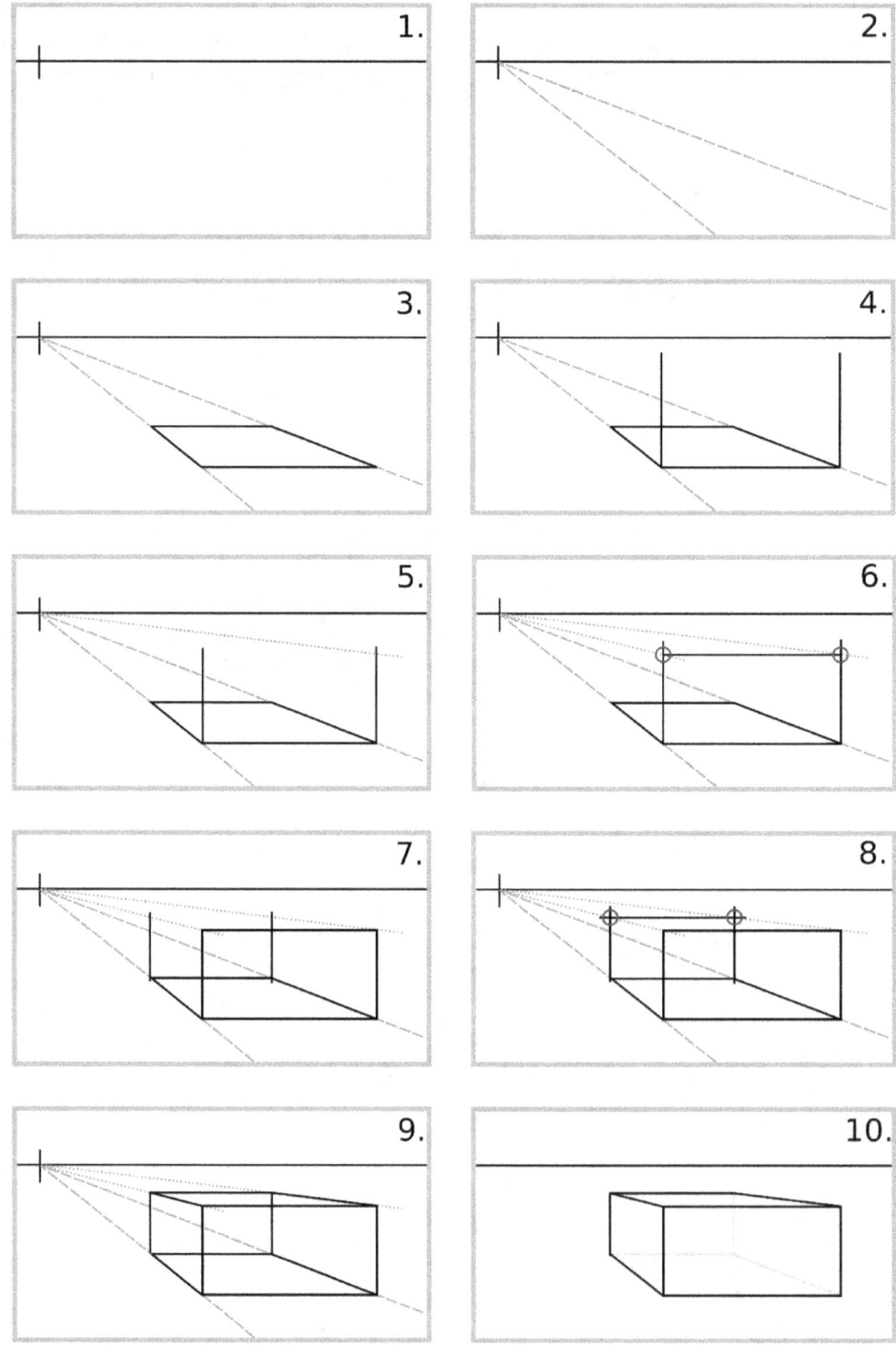

1. As you can see in the first image (upper left), we begin with the horizon line. It is drawn at any desired position. In this step we can also determine the vanishing point at the same time.

2. Now you can draw two vanishing lines that will determine the width of the box. These vanishing lines emerge out of the vanishing point and run in a direction towards the observer.

3. The base of the box is defined by two horizontal lines that intersect with the two vanishing lines.

4. At the corner points of this square, two vertical lines are drawn upwards. These lines represent the edges of the frontal face of the box.

5. Two more vanishing lines are then drawn which intersect with the two vertical lines. The height of the box is determined in this step. The two vertical edges of the box must be intersected at the same height. Step 5 can be executed together with step 6, so that it is a bit easier.

6. In this step, a horizontal line is extended out from one of the two points of intersection – this refers to the two points of intersection between the vertical lines and the new vanishing lines. This line represents the front upper-edge of the box.

Moreover, the point of intersection for the second vanishing line, which we have already drawn in Step 5, would appear due to the horizontal line. Thus one could also proceed in such a manner that one draws only one vanishing line at first, then the horizontal upper edge of the box and, finally, the second vanishing line.

7. In the seventh step, two further vertical lines are drawn on the two back corner points of the floor area.

8. The new points of intersection can once again be connected to each other by a horizontal line.

9. And now you only have to represent the upper face of the box by drawing in the upper vanishing lines.

10. If you now remove the extraneous construction elements (vanishing point and vanishing lines), you'll get the completed box drawing in perspective. The hidden edges are represented in light grey in the drawing.

Using the Vanishing Point Method

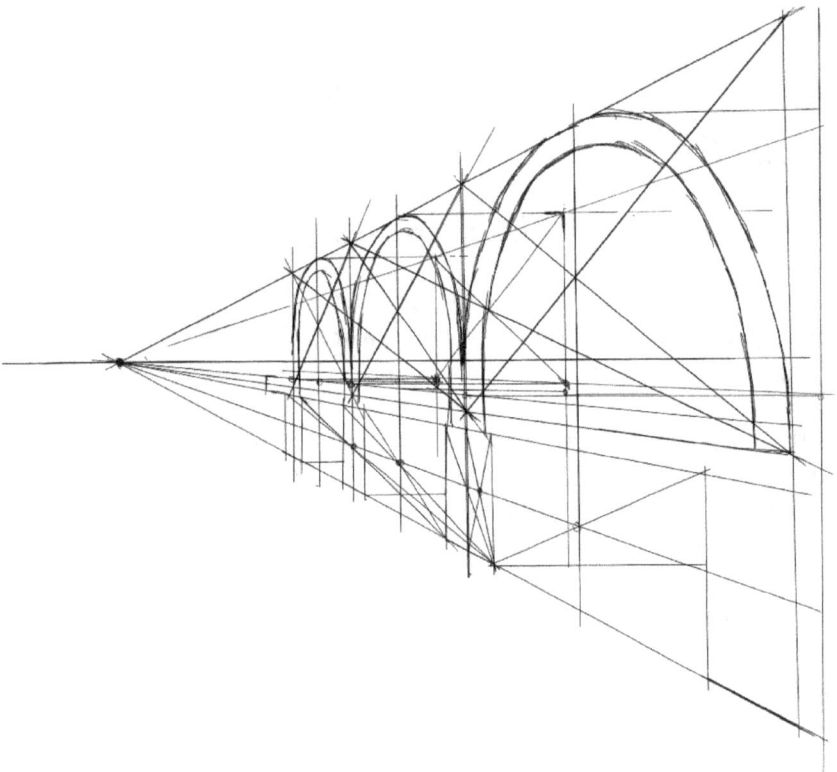

With the aid of vanishing point perspective, relatively complex motifs can be constructed with a single vanishing point. This example shows a bridge with steel structures.

Using perspective methods, objects with the same proportions can be repeatedly depicted at different distances. Also arcs can be sketched with perspective distortion.

Often it makes sense to first carry out the rough proportioning and structuring with the methods of vanishing point perspective and then to start working purely as a draughtsman.

In this way, pictures are created that appear very realistic and at the same time retain their artistic spontaneity and lightness.

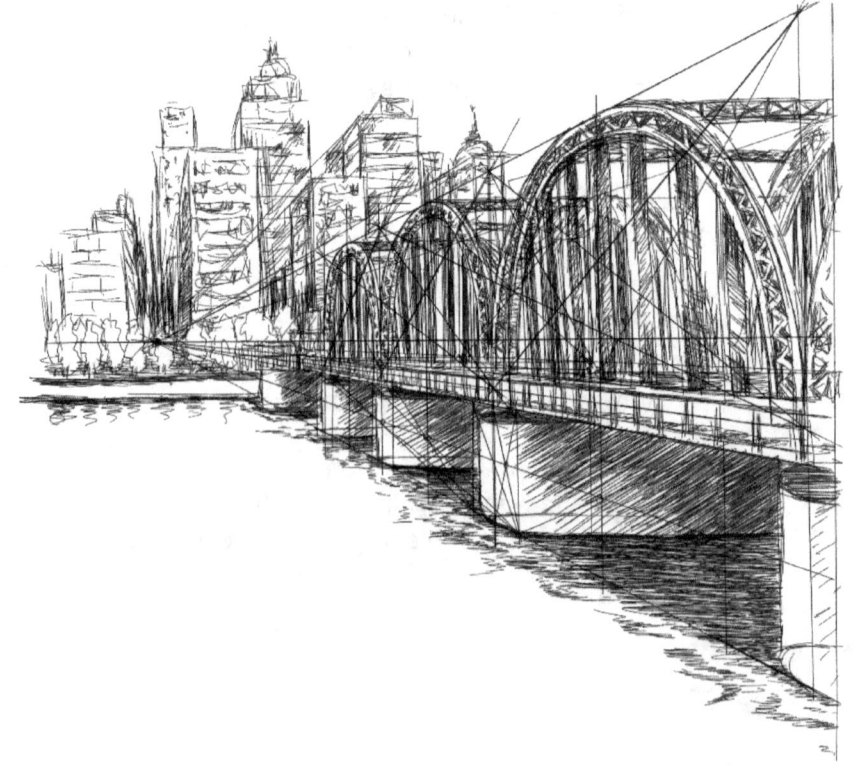

Representation of Space and Perspective

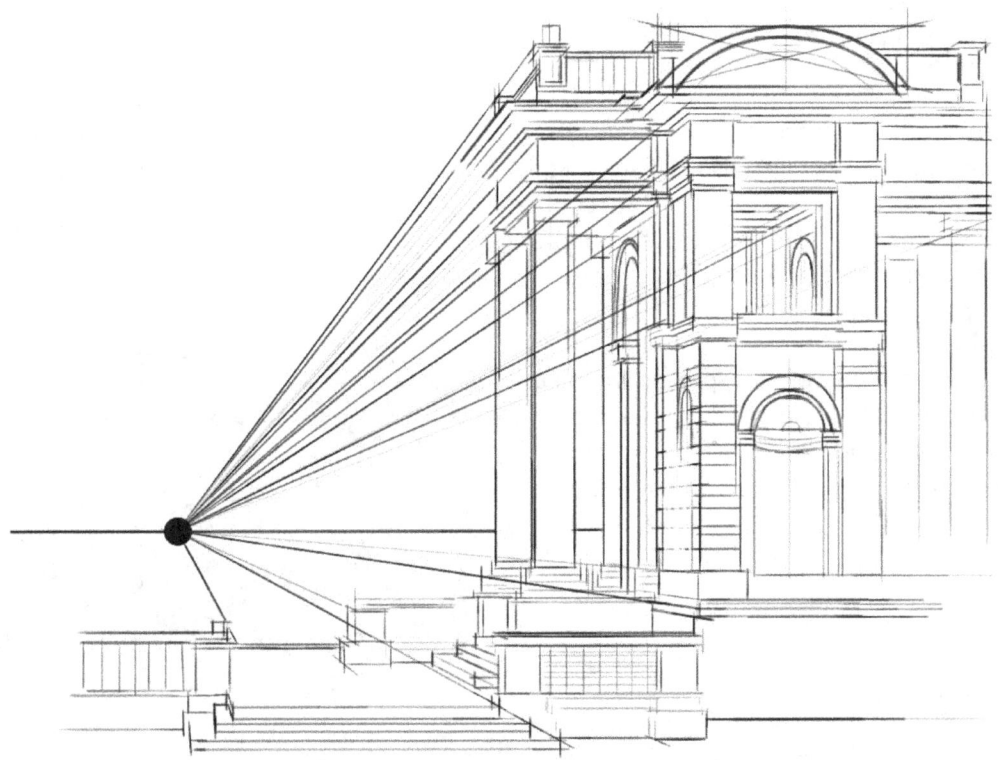

Construction of a complex structure drawn in central perspective, taken from a painting by Claude Lorrain

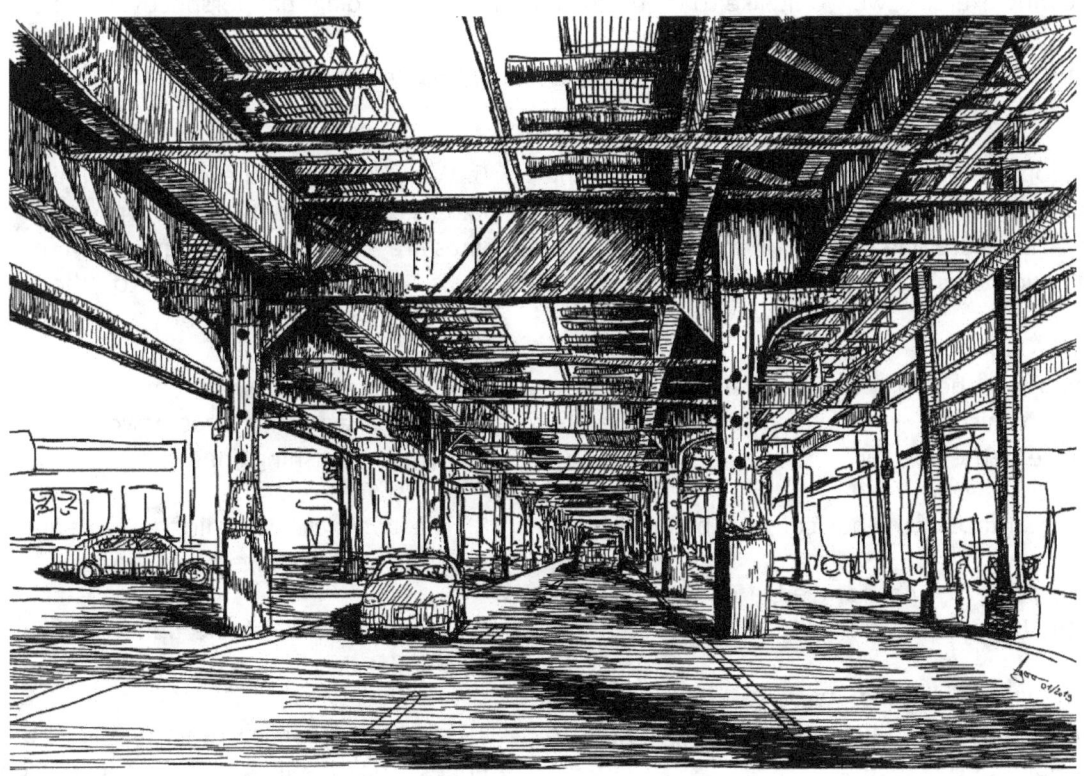

Drawing in central perspective with a vanishing point

4.4 Diagonal Perspective

In this chapter you will learn how you can draw objects in diagonal perspective (also called oblique perspective or two-point perspective). The central perspective covered in the previous chapter, included the limitation that one could only represent objects in perspective from the front.

Diagonal perspective, conversely, presents objects that are positioned at an angle (oblique) to the observer – as portrayed in the picture below. You will learn how to deploy this technique in the following exercise.

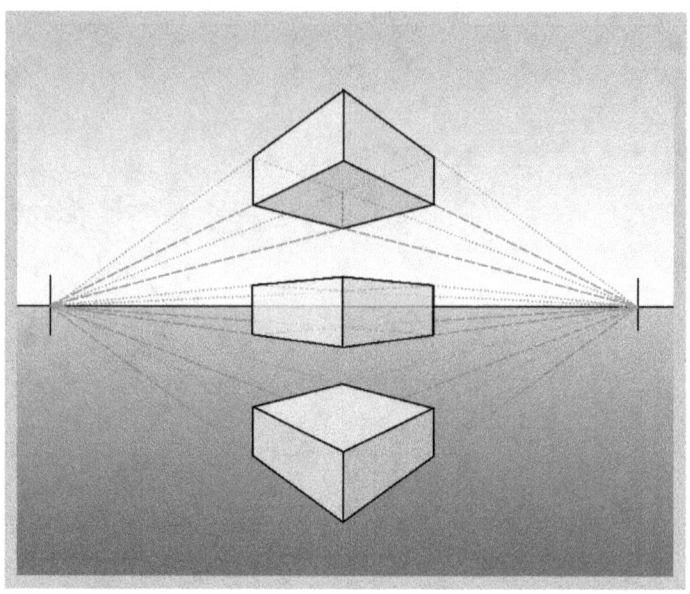

Drawing a Box in Diagonal Perspective

In the following exercise, we would like to try to draw a simple box in diagonal perspective. This object represents one of the simplest motifs for this technique.
You can find the step-by-step development of the box on the following page.

1. For diagonal perspective we need two vanishing points (similar to the two vanishing points of the diagonals). Therefore, we first of all draw the horizon and mark two vanishing points – one left and one right.

2. Starting from the two vanishing points, we now extend two vanishing lines each which define the lower surface of the box.

3. The lower surface of the box can now be drawn in.

4. Next we come to the front edge of the box. The height of the box is then defined by this edge.

5. And now we extend two vanishing lines - respectively from the left and right vanishing point - to the upper point of the edge.

6. With the aid of these vanishing lines, we can now extend the two side edges up vertically. These two lines are automatically shorter than the front edge, as it is required according to the guidelines for perspective representation.

7. We can now draw two more vanishing lines up to the points at which these two side edges intersect the upper vanishing lines.

8. The two new vanishing lines define the height of the back vertical edge of the box.

9. Thus the form of the upper surface of the box is also defined.

10. If we remove all reference lines and the hidden edges, the drawing of a box in perspective is now complete.

Representation of Space and Perspective

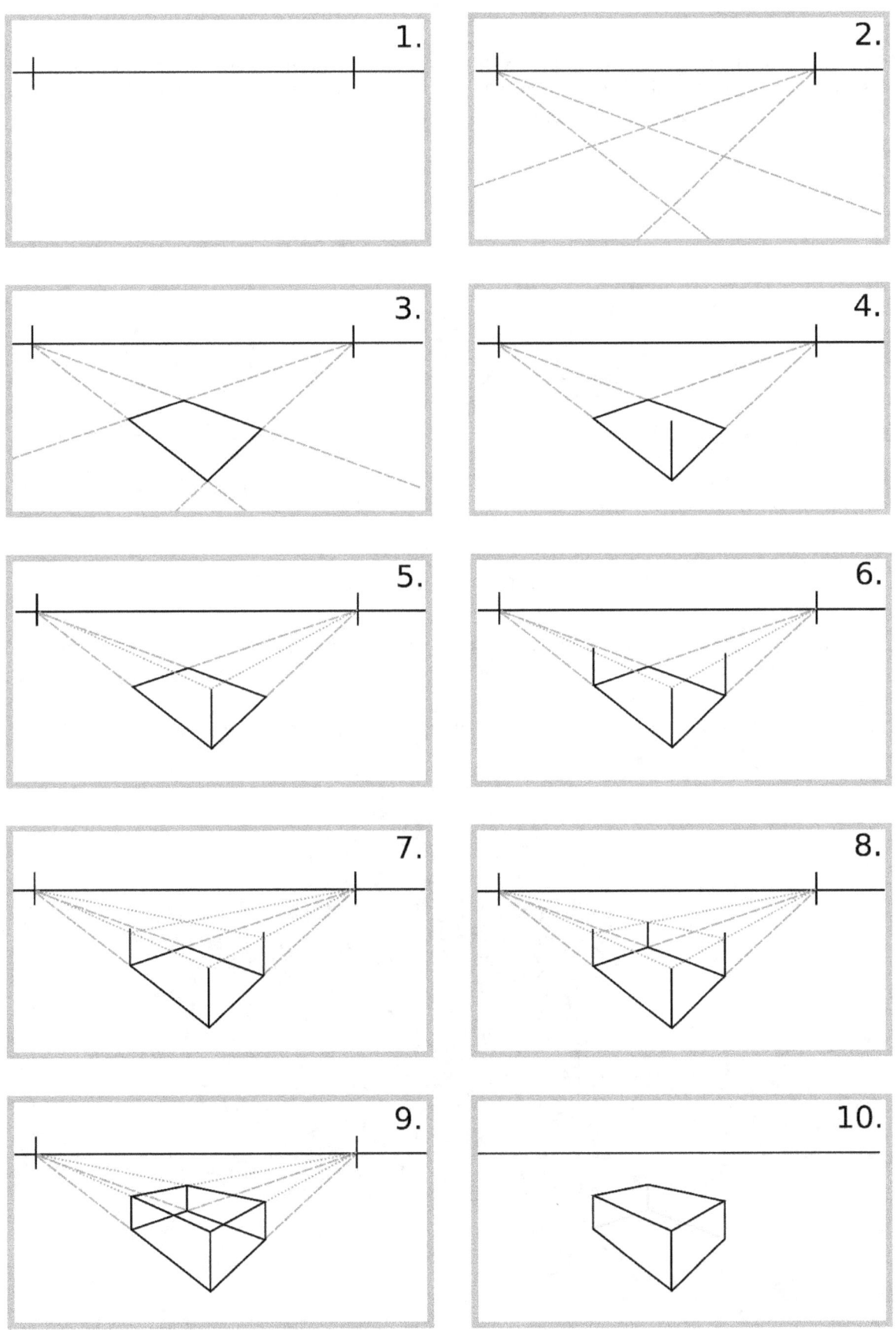

An Example of Two-Point Perspective

Two-point perspective is a very powerful instrument with which you can create impressive drawings. The following example shows a typical application where a building has been depicted. First you can draw the most important vanishing lines from the two vanishing points.

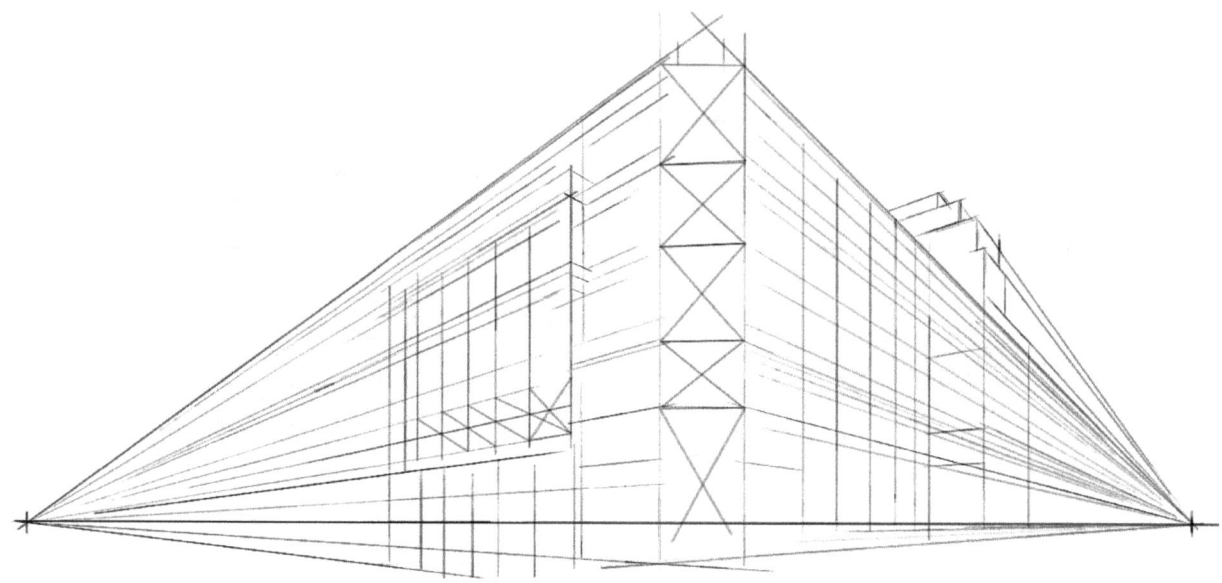

When drawing a building, you can then orient yourself along the vanishing lines. It is not necessary to construct every detail with the help of vanishing lines. Many things can also be drawn intuitively - orientation lines are sufficient in most cases.
In the city scene of this example, it is important to note that the road has a gradient.

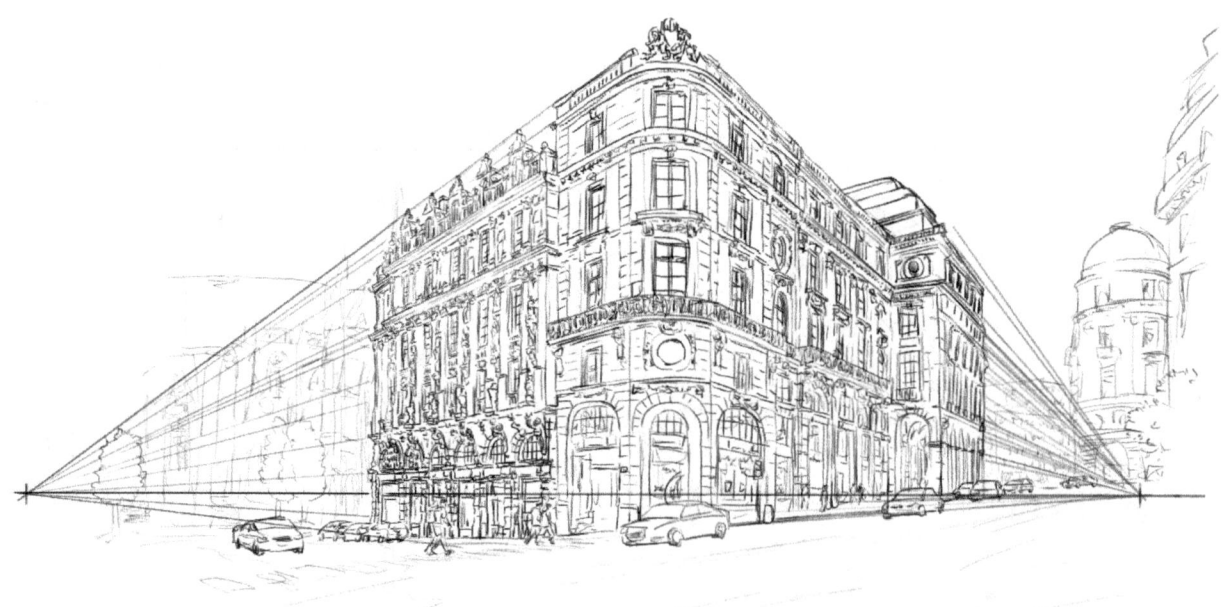

4.5 How to draw an oblique Plane

You will quite often encounter oblique planes in perspective drawings. In the example shown here, we represent a body that resembles a house. That means we have two symmetrical inclined planes.

The basic object is a box:

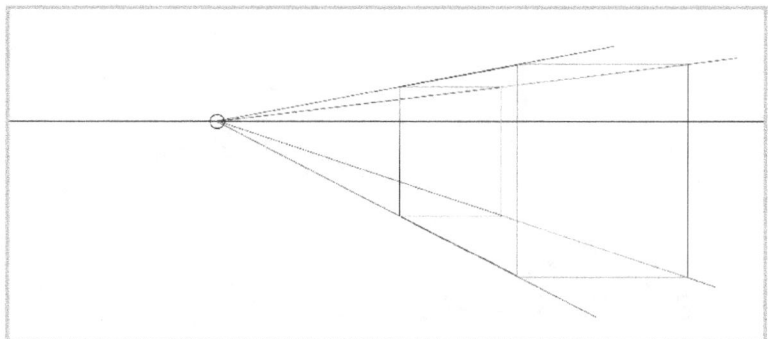

The thing that is however new here is the roof. A roof is an oblique plane that is, with a vanishing point in central perspective, still quite easy to depict.

Draw the diagonal lines of the end faces of the house, in order to determine the center point of these faces. Then a vertical line is drawn through each of the two center points.

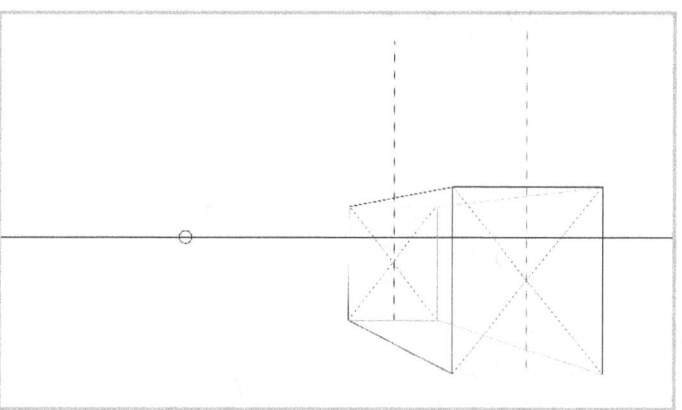

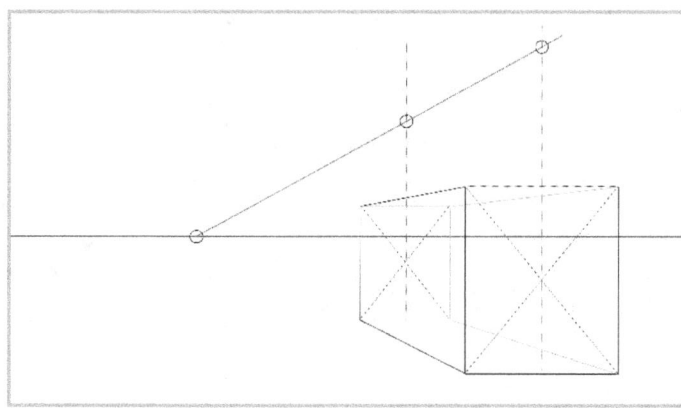

A vanishing line that intersects the two vertical lines forms the roof ridge (upper ridge of the roof).

And now you can draw the roof gable with the aid of the two intersection points. And now the house is finished.

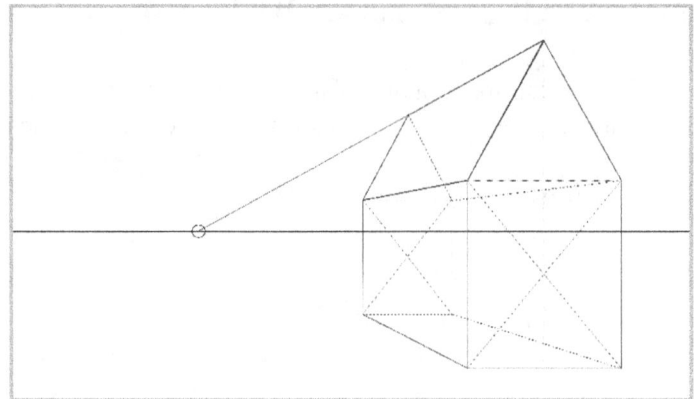

4.6 Exercise – a House with Side View

Now try to draw, on your own, a house with a side view. You can see in the drawing below what the final result will look like.

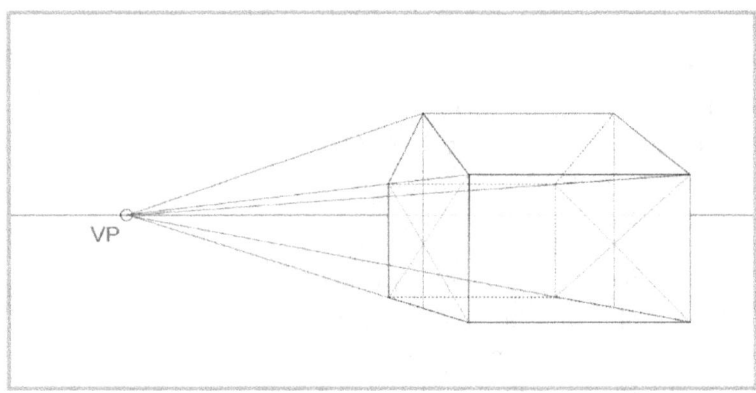

4.7 Drawing Diagonal Upright Planes

Up to this point, everything that we have drawn in diagonal (oblique) perspective was flat. This means that all of the surfaces were vertical or parallel to the floor. But what do we do if we want to draw a surface that lies diagonal to the base plane?
We want to take a closer look at this situation on the basis of the following example.

The new learning objective here is representation of diagonal planes. In the previous example with the house, the diagonal plane is of course the roof; but otherwise everything here functions as usual. You can, of course, translate the presentation technique for diagonal surfaces in a 2-vanishing-point perspective to any other possible situation – not only when you draw a house.

The initial situation here is a box, as you can see in the illustration below. You have already learned in previous exercises how to draw the box in perspective.

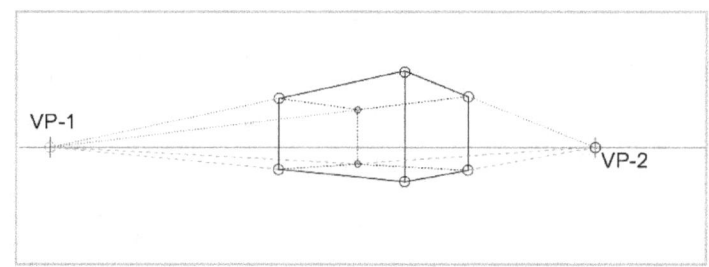

In order to draw the roof, the center point of the upper horizontal edge of the box has to be ascertained first. This must be carried out for both the front and back end-faces of the house.

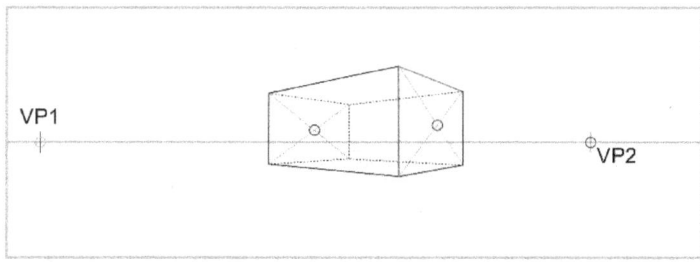

In order to determine the center point, we draw the surface diagonals of the two end-faces. Just take a look at the following image.

What you have achieved through this step is the respective center point within the two end-faces.

We then draw one line each, vertical to the horizon line, up through the two surface center points. The point, at which the lines intersect with the two upper edges of the box, is where the center point of the respective edge is located.

You should also extend these vertical lines a bit further up – we will need them for the following step.

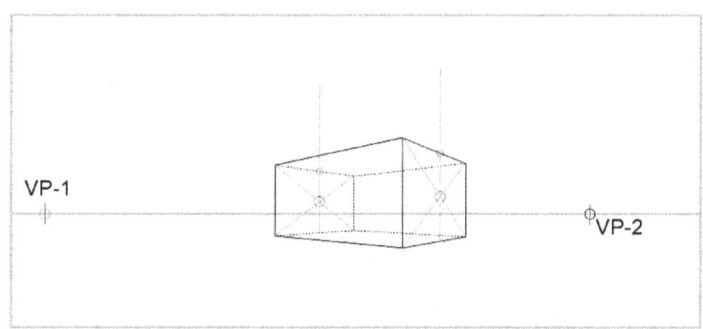

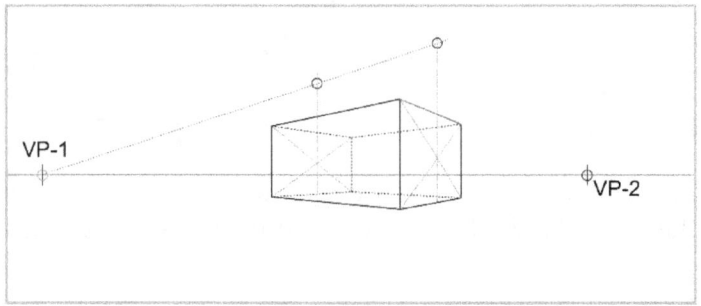

Now you need to draw the roof ridge, i.e. the uppermost edge of the roof. For this purpose, you first of all draw a point on the front vertical centerline. This point defines the height of the roof. And now you extend a vanishing line from vanishing point 1 out to this point. You will thus achieve the roof ridge and a further intersection point on the back vertical line.

With the aid of the vanishing line just drawn, as well as the two points of intersection, the roof of the house can now be easily drawn.

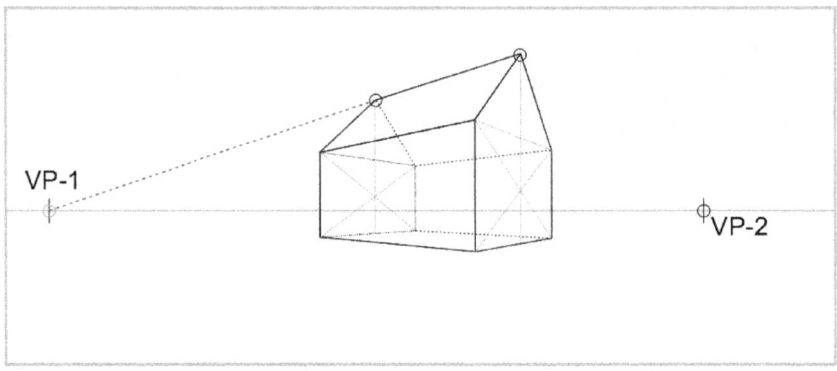

4.8 Drawing a Curved Pathway

The preferable version from a design point of view is a pathway that curves back and forth. The observer is motivated to follow the course of the path with his eyes. The image also appears much more natural and not so static.

In a drawing with perspective, one can create a curved road design by using several vanishing points. In order to achieve the points of intersection for the opposing road section, we draw a horizontal line at the desired location, as represented in the diagram below.
In order to optically improve the drawing, we need to round out the corners. It is necessary here to work with a bit of artistic intuition.

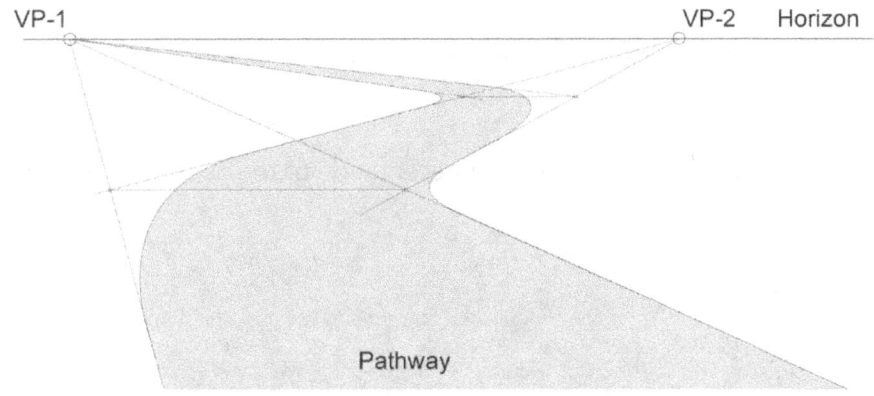

Curved pathway with two vanishing points

And now we have a construction that looks more complicated than it actually is. We proceed in the same manner as in the previous examples.
Simply draw a second horizon that lies above the normal horizon. Transfer the vanishing points (VP1 and VP2) to the second horizon (VP3 and VP4). And now begin with the front section of the pathway that you represent as a path with incline. The points of intersection of the curves (of the pathway without incline) can be transferred with the aid of vertical lines to the new vanishing lines. The respective vanishing lines of the corresponding vanishing points now run to these points of intersection.

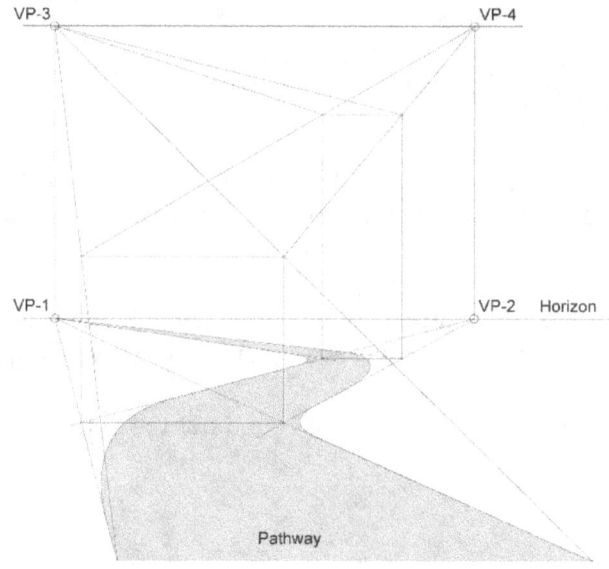

Auxiliary construction lines for the pathway with incline

And now we can draw the pathway with incline. Representation of the curves is ideally carried out freehand and by feel.

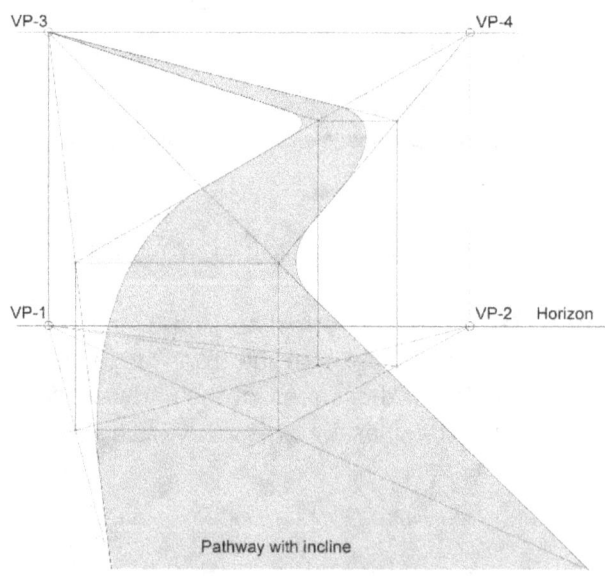

Curved pathway with incline

4.9 Exercise – Houses in the Mountains

And now you can try a more complicated exercise – a small landscape picture.

Simply draw several houses with various perspectives and at various altitudes. A road progresses between the houses and then extends upwards into the mountainous landscape. A few cliffs complete the picture.
The knowledge required to execute this exercise has been presented in the previous example and exercises. Thus, it is not so difficult.

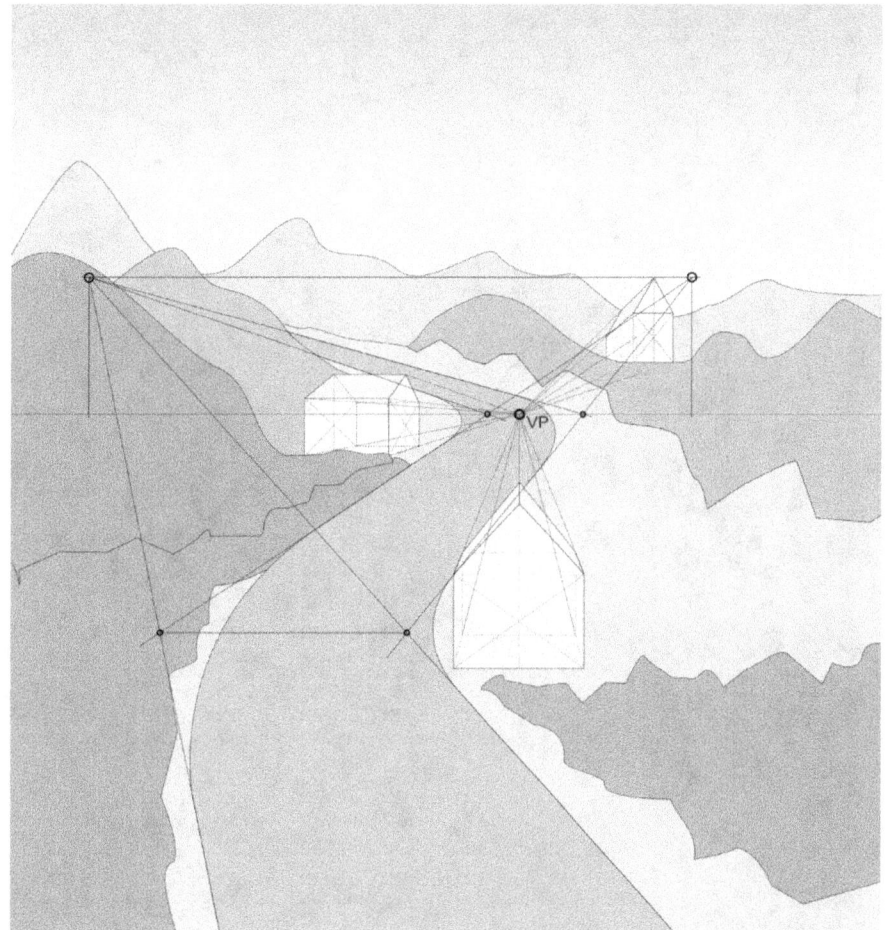

Cliff landscape with houses in various perspectives

You can now create a real drawing based on the perspective construction. You can transfer the previously made sketch on your drawing paper - for example with the help of a light table. With the knowledge from the previous chapter, you are now able to draw clouds, rocks and buildings.

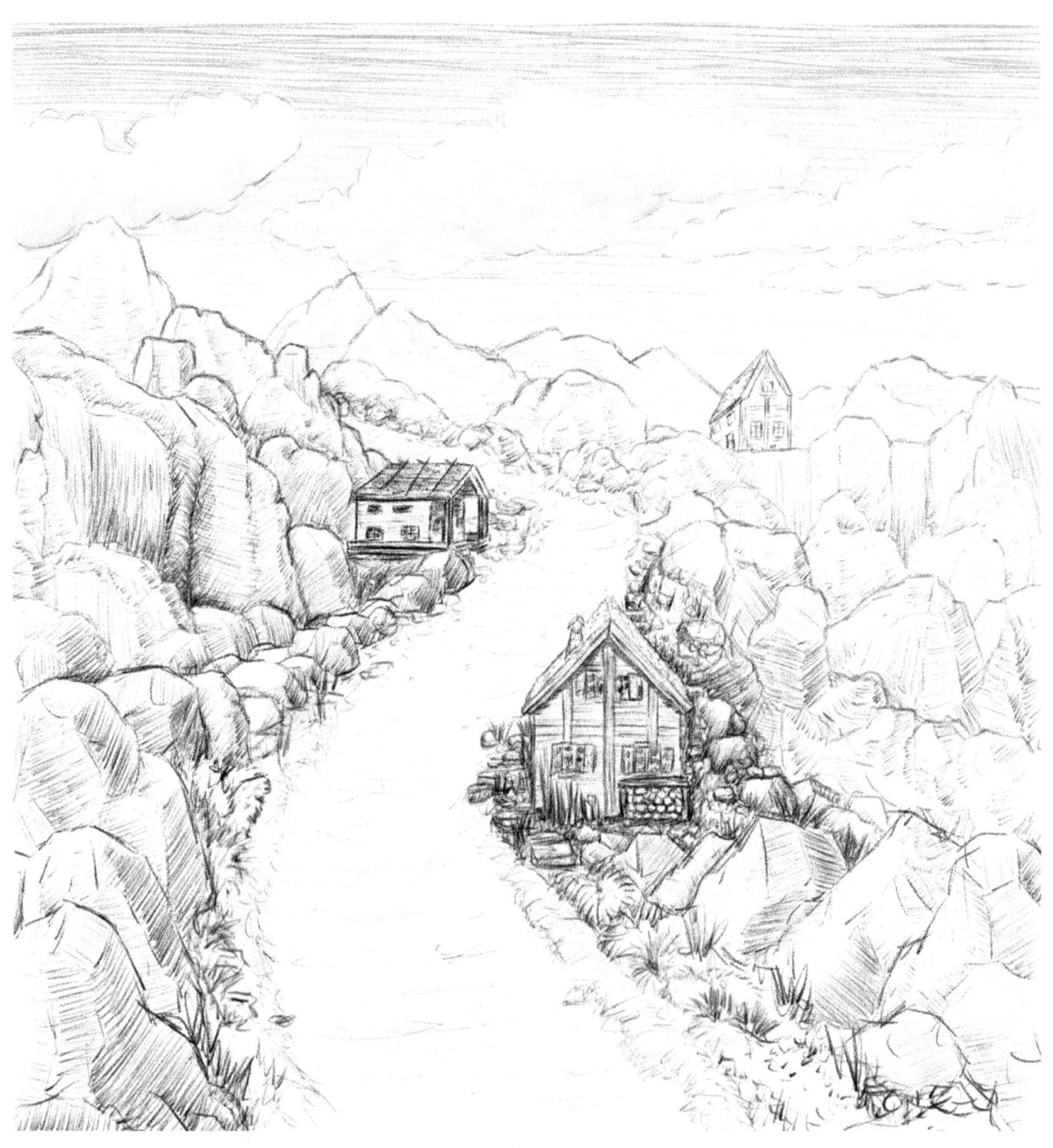

Finished drawing based on the perspective construction

4.10 Shifting a Defined height in Space

Shifting objects with a defined height in space is an easy task, but is frequently drawn incorrectly. This won't happen to you using the tricks from this chapter.
The motif for the following exercises is a tree. However, the method is also suitable for many other motifs, such as people, vehicles, buildings and much more.

Shifting along a Common Line

The simplest case involves all objects lying on a single, common line. All that is necessary then is a single vanishing point and two vanishing lines, which define the height of the objects in each depth of the depicted space.

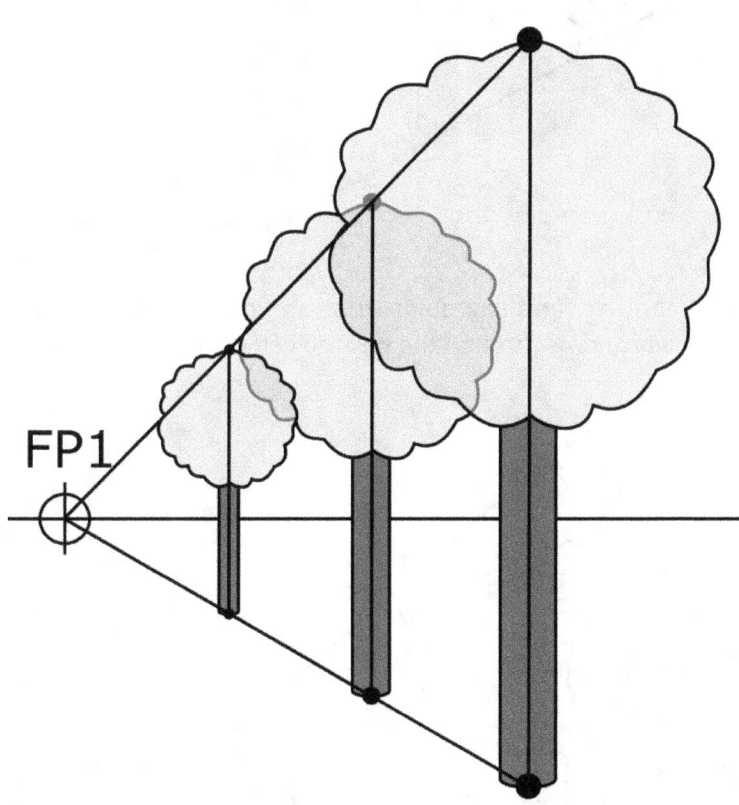

Shifting to a Chosen Position in Space

Shifting becomes more difficult when the objects are randomly distributed in space. In other words, how can one shift the tree from our example to the marked position while, at the same time, assuring that its height is properly represented in perspective?

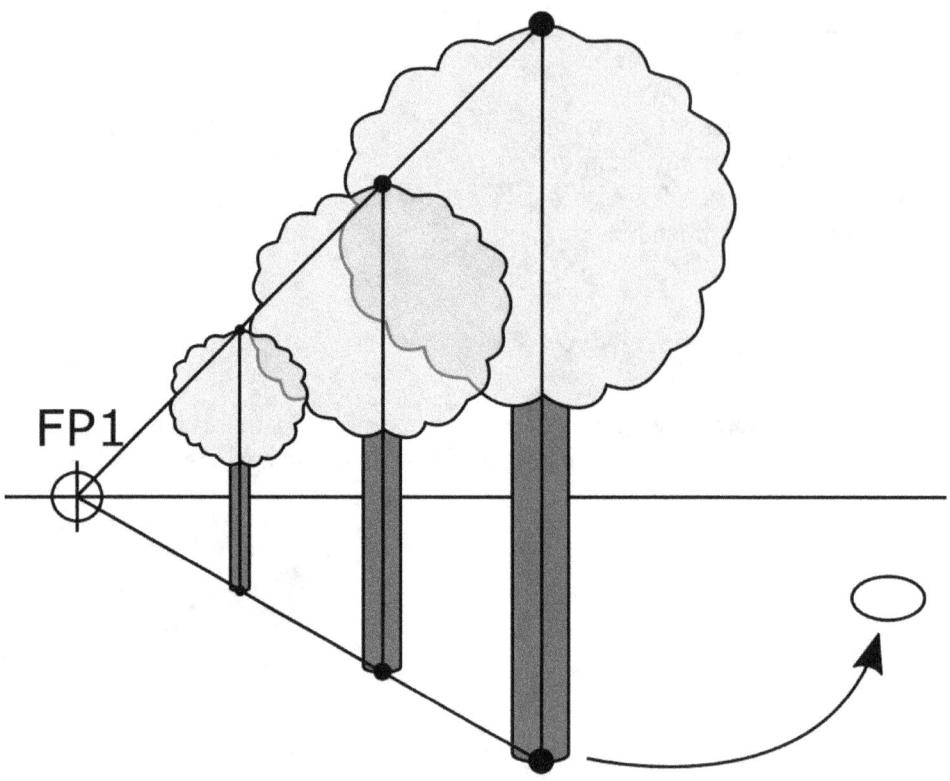

To solve the task, you need another vanishing point. You can find it by drawing another vanishing line from the existing lower vanishing line, which runs through the new object's point of view. With an upper alignment line you get the height of the object.

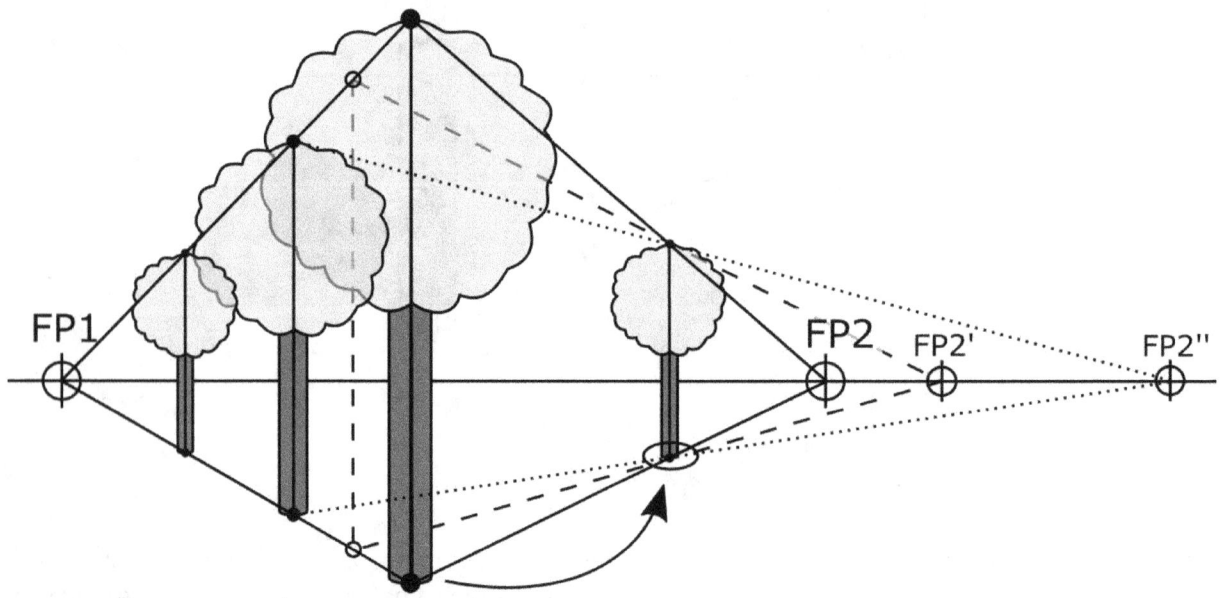

In addition: The alignment lines can start from any point on the alignment lines of the reference object, as can be seen by the dotted and dashed lines in the drawing. However, this results in different vanishing points (FP2' or FP2"). It is also important to measure the height using a vertical line.

Shifting to a Recess or an Elevation

It is a bit more difficult if you want to move an object with the same height to a lower or higher plane. In the drawing of the example two approaches are shown.

In the recess, the alignment lines (from FP1) of the reference object were drawn to the edge of the recess. Then the height (a) was moved down and from there a lower alignment line was drawn through the position of the new object. The result is FP2. With the help of the marked height (a) you can define the height of the shifted object with a second upper alignment line.

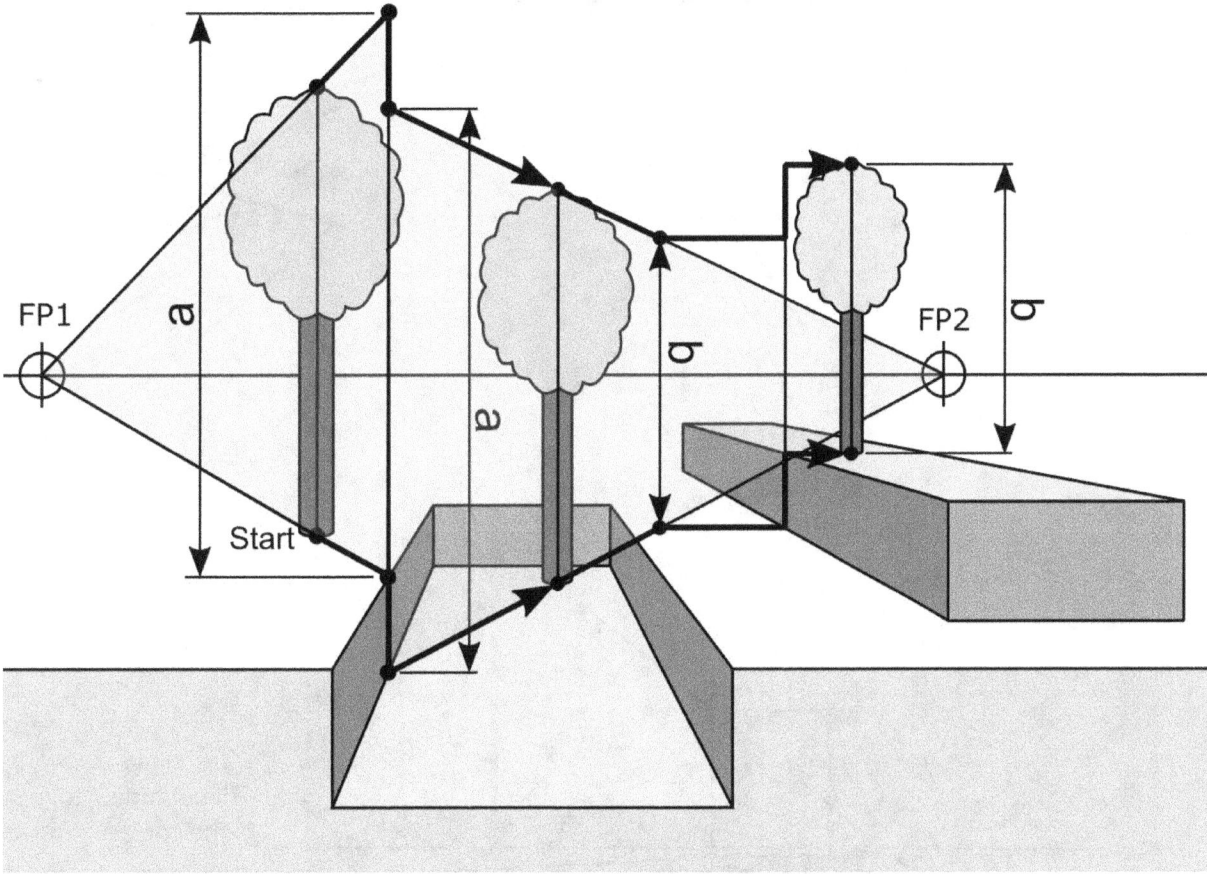

In the other case - used here for the tree on the elevation - one walks on a pair of related alignment lines (starting from FP2) in the depth of the room until one has reached the appropriate depth. Then draw two horizontal lines to the edge of the elevation, move the height scale (b) to the new plane, and then move back on horizontal lines to the position of the new object.

Example

In the following pictures you can see an example for the use of the described method. The picture shows a river with a winding course and two trees on its banks. In the representation of the trees you can use the technique of shifting equal heights. You don't have to limit yourself only to the total height of the trees; you can also transfer the dimensions of the treetops.

In the following sketch you can see the construction on which the drawing should be based.

The next picture shows the freehand drawing of the landscape together with the construction lines.

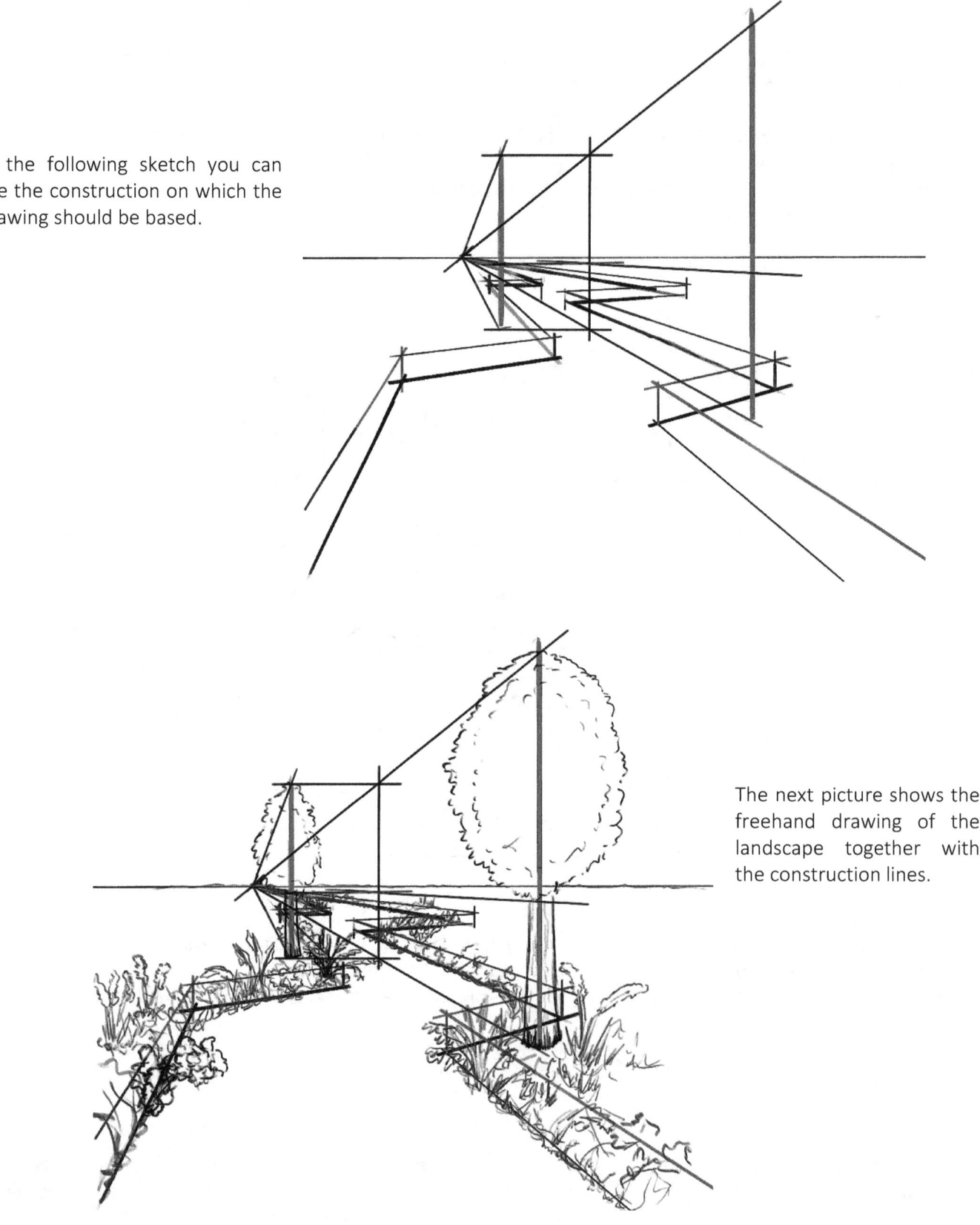

Picture Design and Composition

» Talent is revealed in the design and art in the execution. «

- Marie Freifrau von Ebner-Eschenbach -

5 Picture Design and Composition

The success of a painting does not only depend on artistic and craft skills. From the very beginning, a lot of attention should be paid to the harmonious design of the picture. The more thought the artist invests prior to the first stroke on the paper or canvas, the more beautiful the picture can become. The depiction of a natural scene on flat paper is subject to its own laws of drawing and painting. Therefore, after the selection of the motif, it is worthwhile to think carefully about how it will be implemented on the canvas or drawing surface.

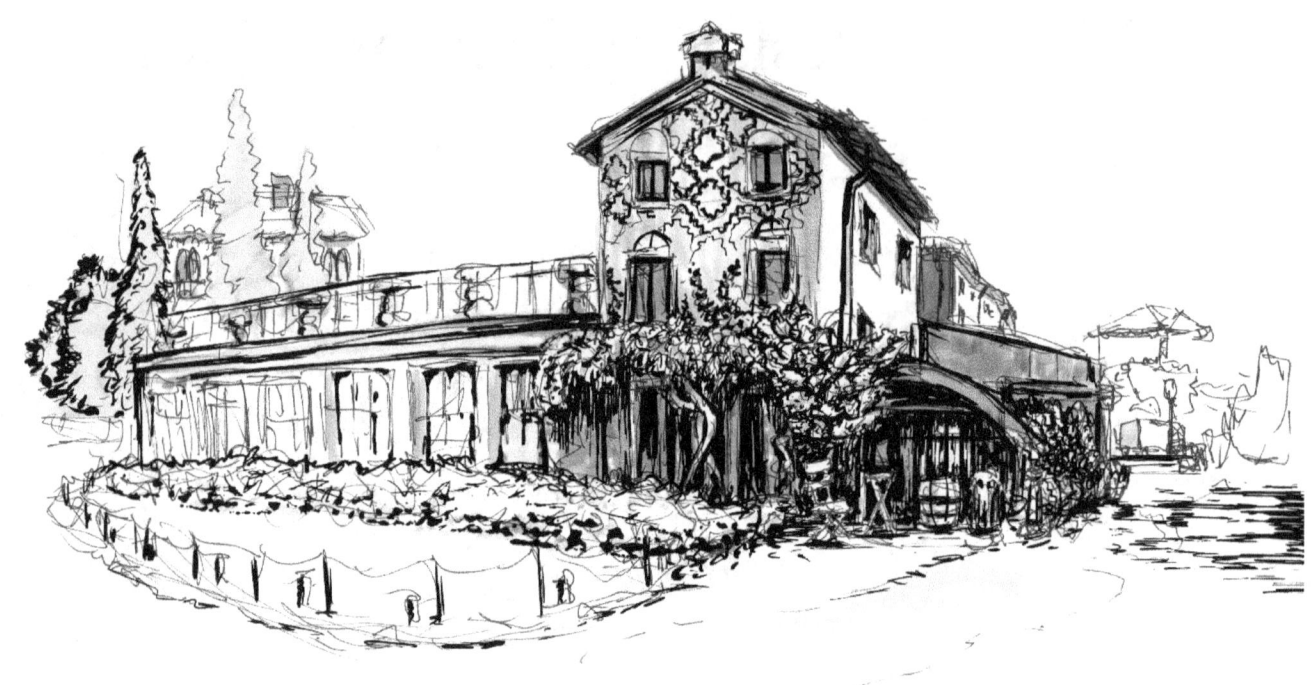

Sketch with Indian ink

From my own experience I can confirm that one can improve a picture considerably with a certain amount of planning. From a relatively static and unexciting presentation you can develop your own picture into an interesting and dynamic work of art. In retrospect, I was always glad that I didn't spontaneously start the final picture with the first idea, but rather gave the composition the opportunity to really develop itself. By means of small tricks and improvements the picture effect can already be increased quite a bit. Sketches always help me a lot.

Picture Design and Composition

5.1 Methods for Subdividing an Image

In this chapter we deal with methods of image subdivision. This is one of the most important composition techniques, because subdividing a picture is an enormous help for us in the creative process. With the subdivision of the basis for the image, one determines in principle the basic structure of the work. The methods presented here help the artist to create a successful composition that can appear balanced or even exciting. However, one should always be aware that the described techniques are only orientation aids. It is neither a panacea nor a guarantee that a good picture will be created in the end.

Symmetry – Center Lines and Diagonals

In image composition using central axes, the image is divided into two halves of equal size. The center axes can be used individually or together. The diagonals extend from one corner of the image to the other. This method can be used again and again with landscape pictures.

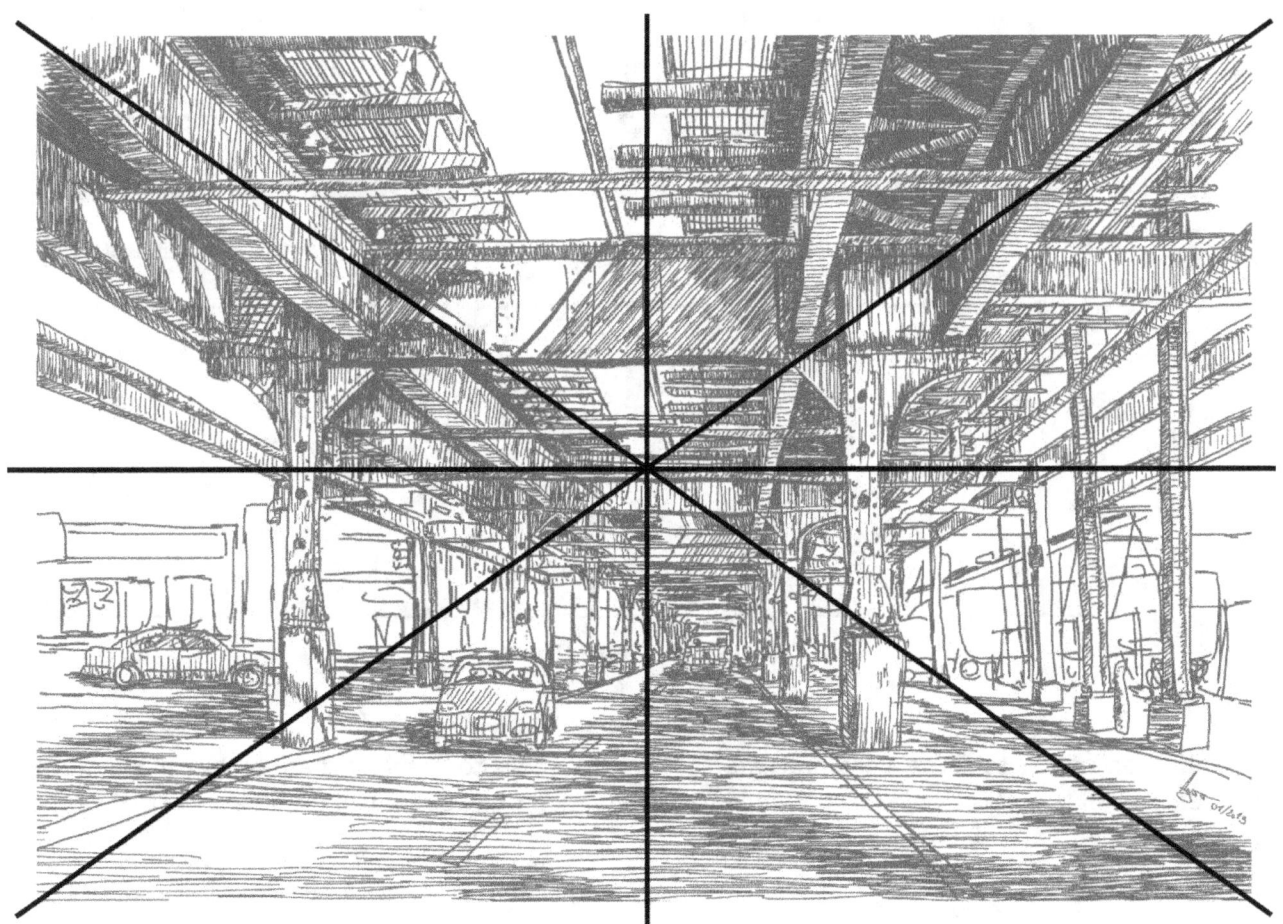

Roadway with steel construction - designed with an approximately symmetrical structure

Composition of pictures by means of central axes and diagonals was often used in the Renaissance, since paintings in this period were often constructed symmetrically. Nowadays, this method is rarely used, as the opinion that the main motif should not be placed in the middle has prevailed.

The Golden Ratio

The golden ratio is an aid for subdividing images according to a defined ratio. The resulting lines can be used to align image objects. The subdivision can be used both vertically and horizontally. In addition, the subdivision can be made in such a way that the entire image is subdivided into nine rectangles. The intersection points that result can also be used to align image objects. The golden ratio is one of the best known design techniques and is very often used for landscape motifs.

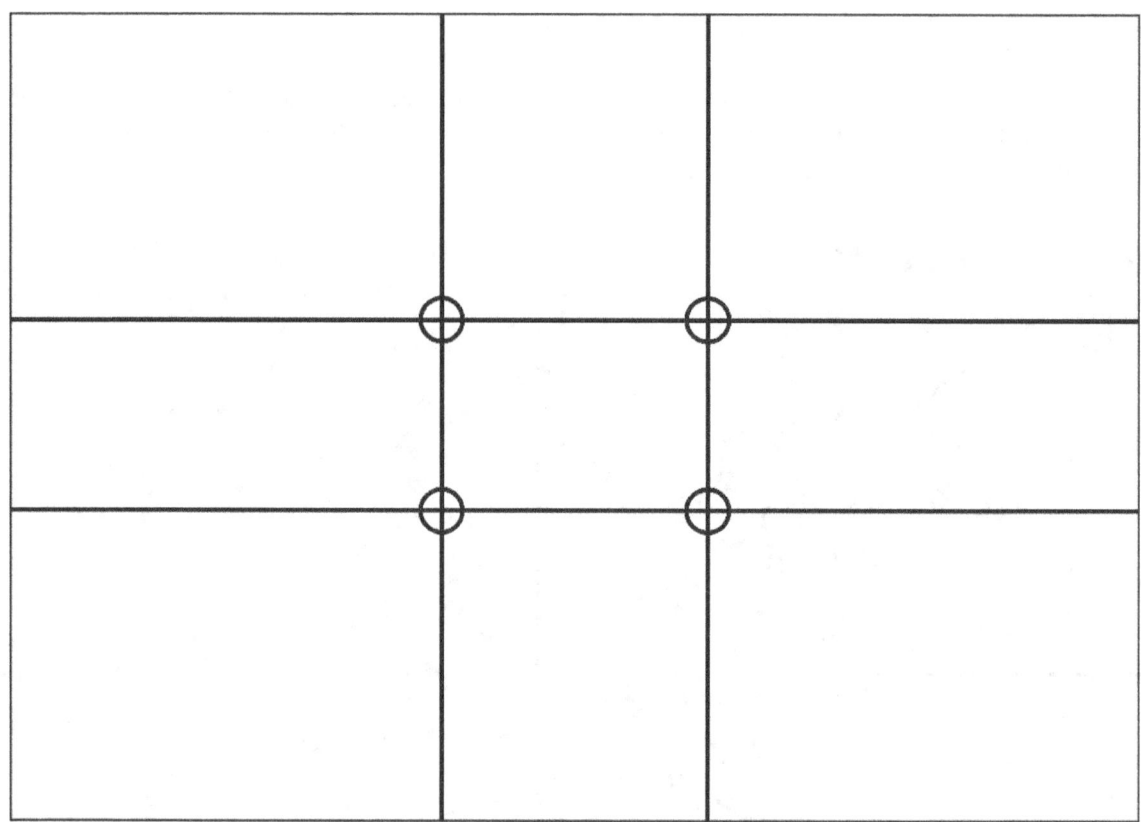

Golden ratio with intersections

Orientation according to these lines and intersections can help to create a harmonious image composition. However, the golden ratio is never a guarantee for the creation of a good image. It is - among many other design techniques – purely an aid, the use of which also requires experience.

Picture Design and Composition

Applying the Golden Ratio

Subdivision according to the principle of the golden ratio ensues by means of the following formula:

$$\frac{a+b}{a} = \frac{a}{b} \quad \text{or} \quad \frac{a}{a+b} = \frac{b}{a}$$

If we consider the overall length of a side to be 100%, then the individual lengths of a=61.8% and b=38.2% are what emerge.

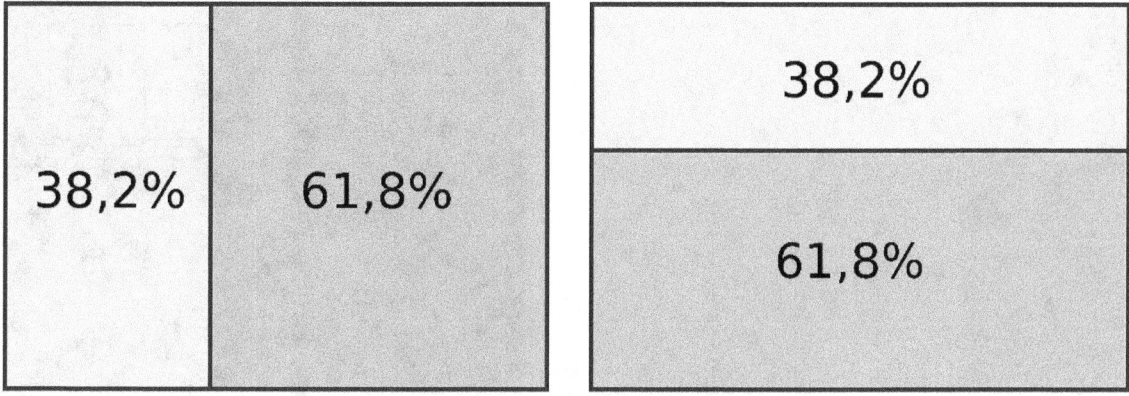

Segmentation according to the golden ratio

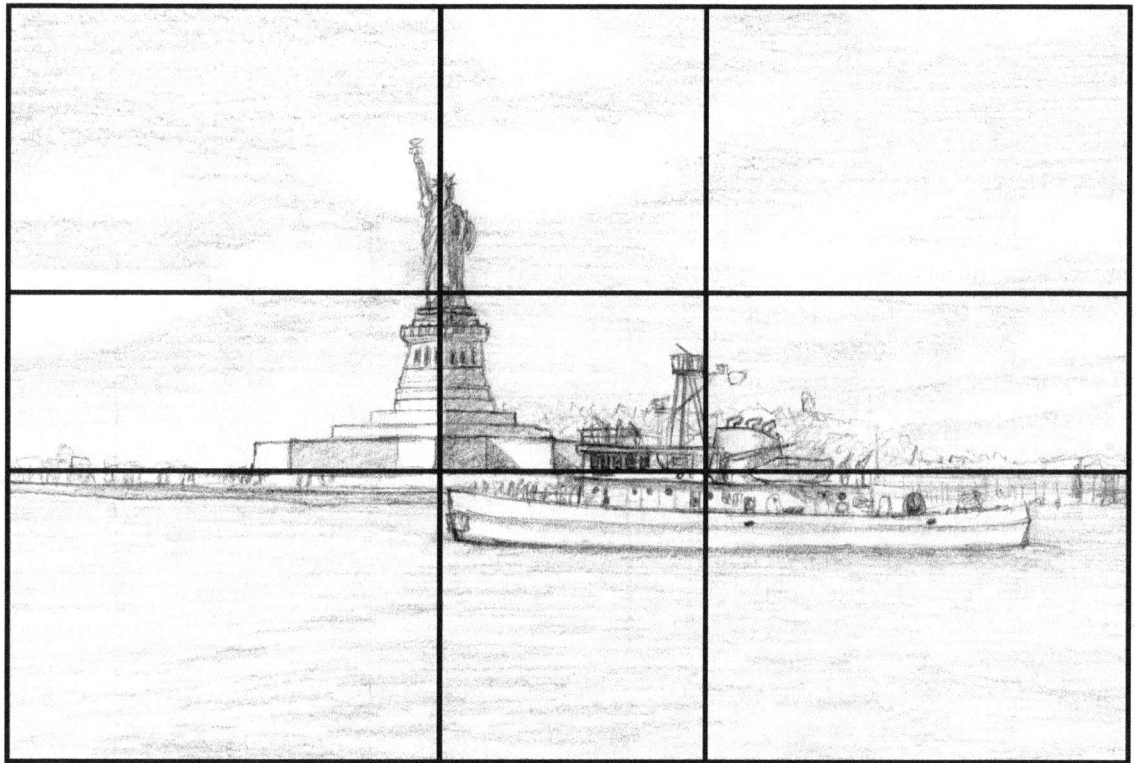

Landscape drawing with the golden ratio as orientation

It is noteworthy that the orientation according to the relationship of the golden ratio comes from nature and can be found again and again in natural forms. This is probably the reason why division according to the golden ratio is perceived as particularly harmonious by humans.

Examples of the occurrence of the golden ratio in nature are the dimensions of an ivy leaf or the arrangement of leaves in various plants. This is also referred to as the golden angle, which is about 137.5°.

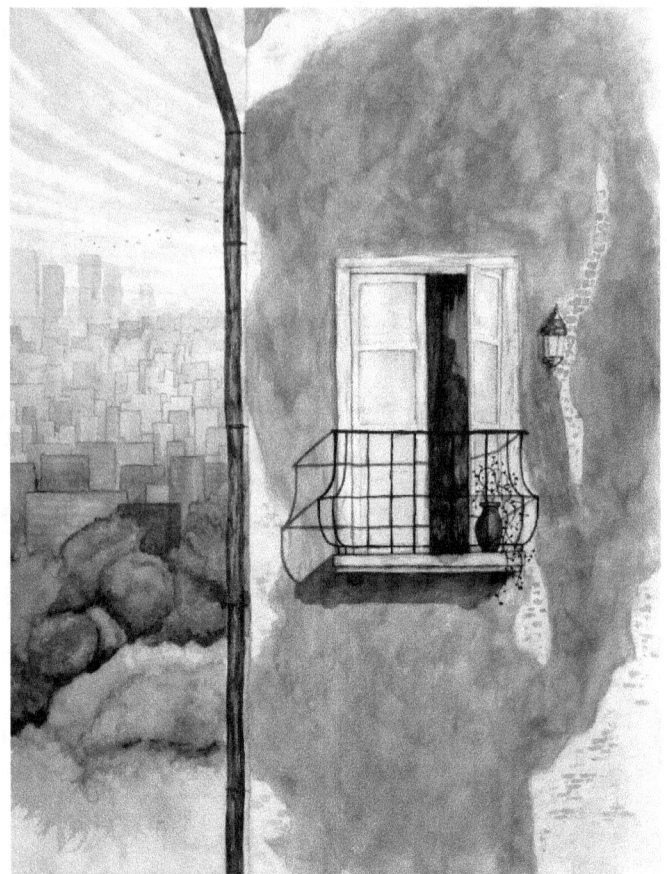

Picture composition with the aid of the golden ratio

The Rule of Thirds

The "rule of thirds" is a composition aid based on the subdivision of pictures according to the rules of the golden ratio. The rule of thirds is mainly known from photography, but also plays an important role in other areas of the visual arts. Like the golden ratio, it is one of the most popular design methods.

As the name suggests, the picture is imaginarily divided into three equal parts. This division into thirds can take place both horizontally and vertically. Alternatively, it is usual to divide the picture directly into nine equal fields, which are very helpful for the design.

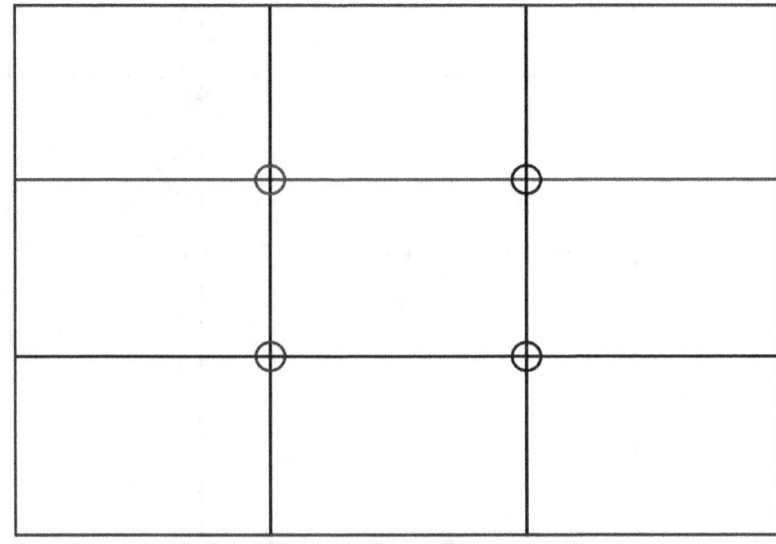

Subdividing into thirds with intersections

There are intersections between the subdivision lines which can also be used as composition aids. Often good images are created by placing the main motif on one of these intersections. With these aids it is possible to create harmonious compositions and to bind the viewer to the optical design.

When applying the rule of thirds, however, be aware that the rule of thirds - contrary to what the name may promise - is not a fixed rule, but rather a design aid. The use of this method does not guarantee an appealing composition. The aim of the rule of thirds is above all to prevent the main motif from being placed in the center of the image, as this is usually boring and static.

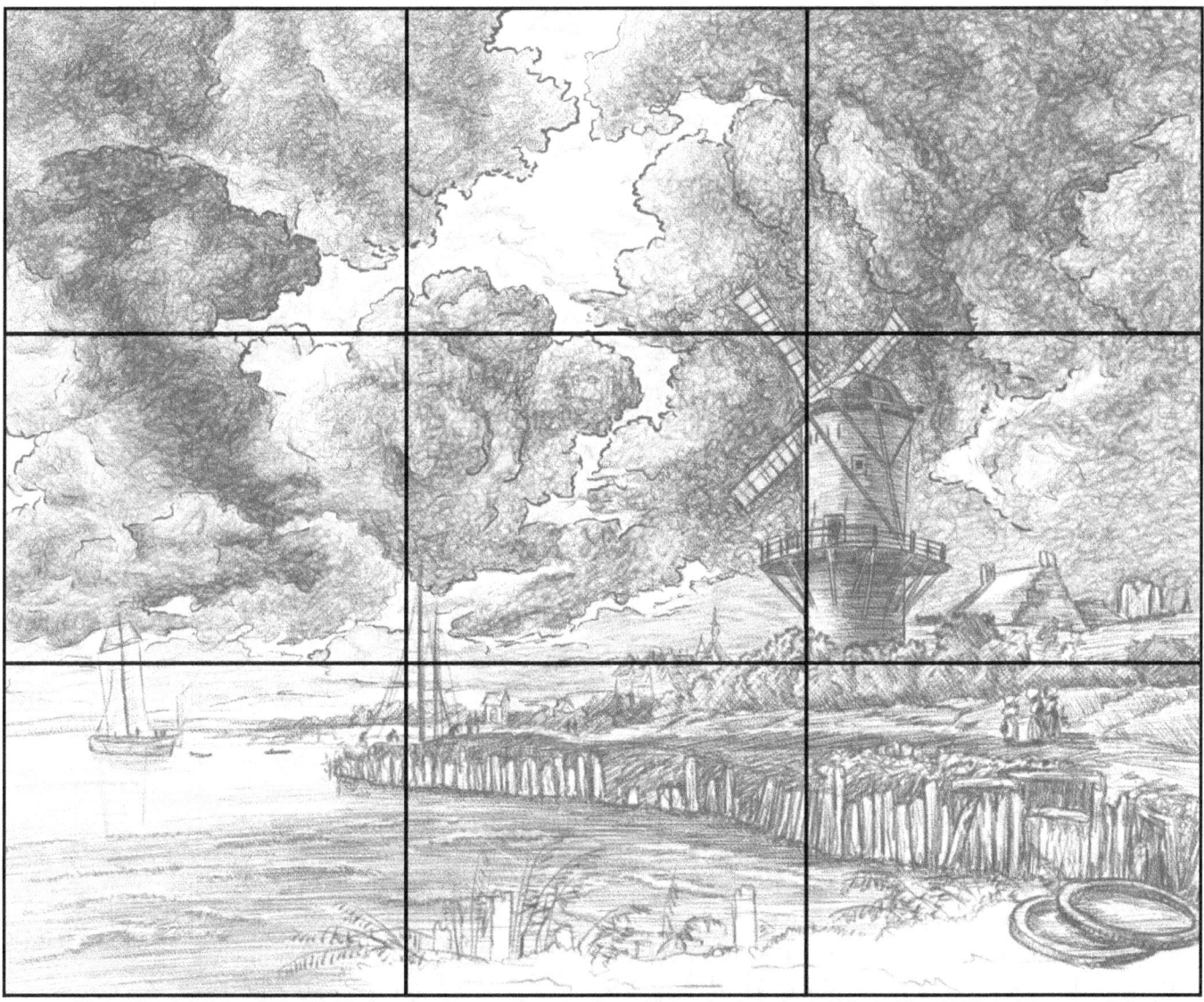

The rule of thirds recognizable in a landscape sketch of a painting by Ruisdael „Windmill at Wijk bei Duurstede"

You can use the rule of thirds without any further aids. If you like, you can also sketch the subdivision lines on paper beforehand. However, the image is usually divided into nine parts rather than three. With this help you will orient yourself to the subdivision lines when positioning your motif. You can skip the center, or place elements there that do not flow, or only subordinately flow, into the picture design.

Make sure that you move the most important design elements to the side. However, it is important not to push them too far to the edge. As already mentioned, you can also use the four intersection points to create the picture. Often it is very appealing if striking elements of the picture composition are positioned at these points.

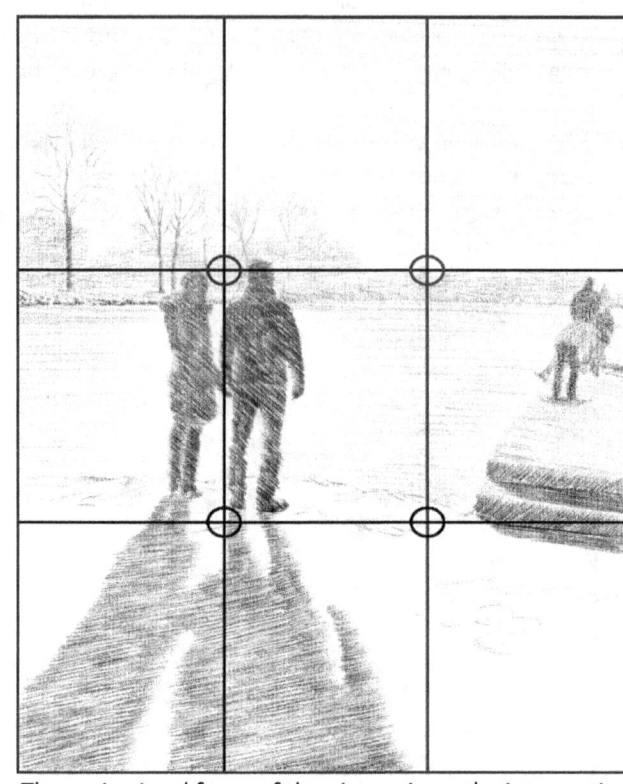

The main visual focus of the picture is on the intersection at the top left

Subdivision of Image Levels

The rule of thirds is often used to divide the composition into three picture levels: foreground, midground and background. This composition technique is therefore an ideal means of creating landscapes.

The three levels represent the near area, the far area and the sky. In landscape paintings, for example, one often sees a subdivision in which either two thirds of the earth and one third of the sky are visible, or vice versa, one third of the earth and two thirds of the sky. The pictures in this chapter are very good examples.

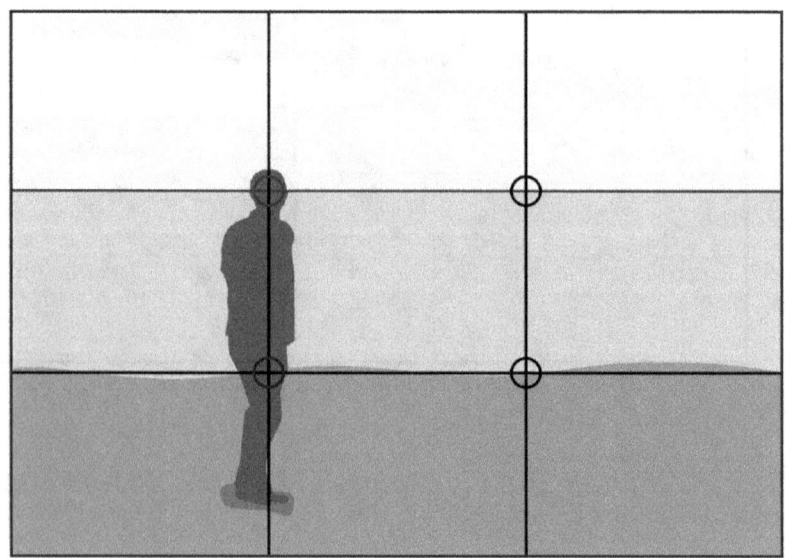

Subdivision in thirds: fore-, mid- and background

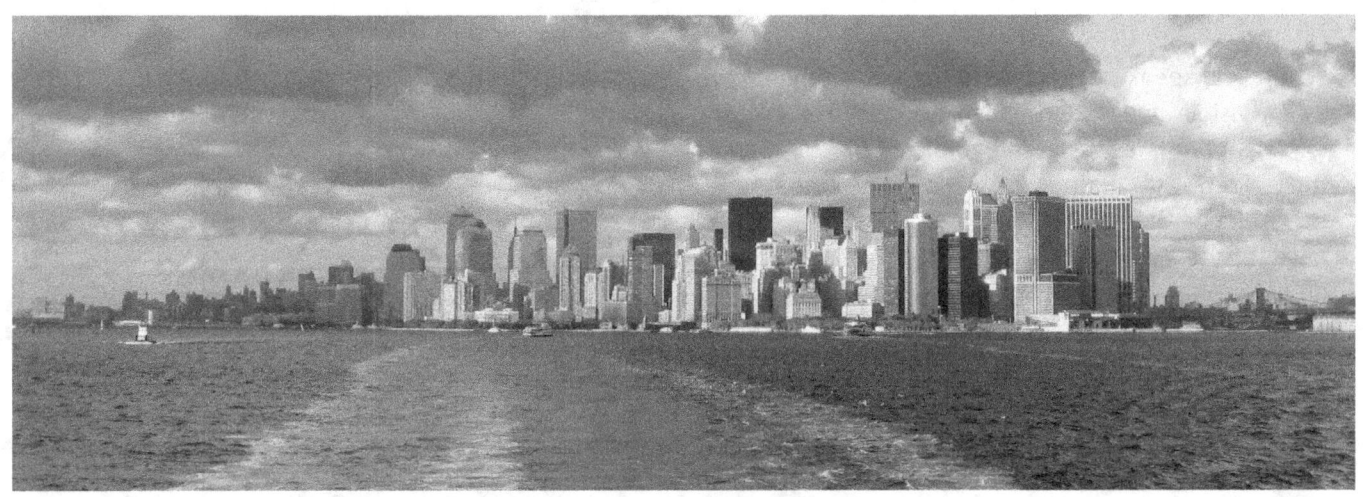

Landscape picture – skyline of New York

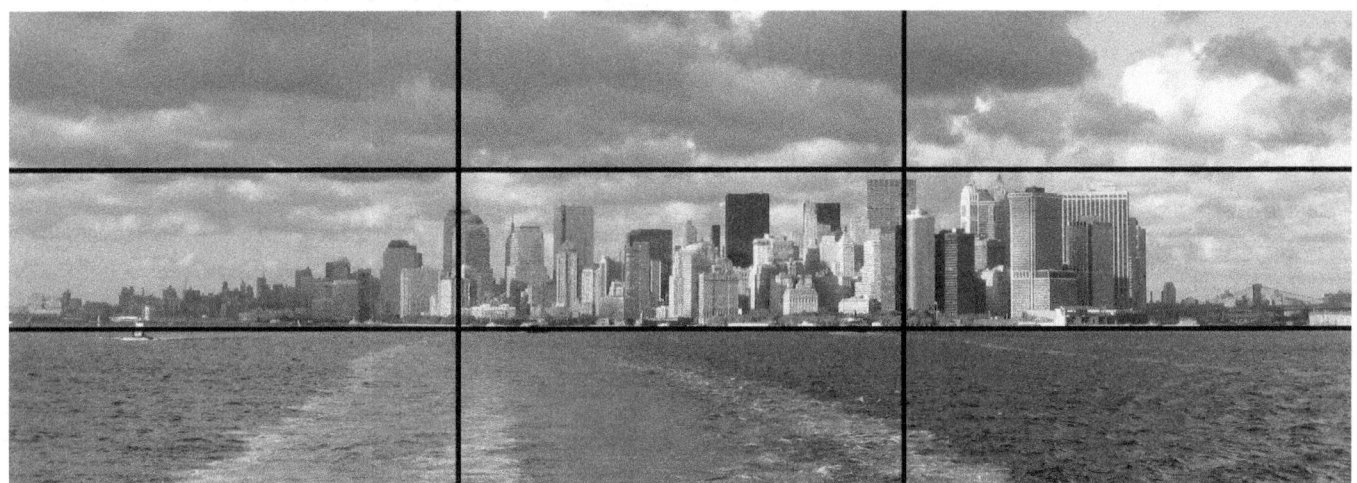

The same image subdivided into thirds

5.2 Lines as an Element of Design

When we speak of lines as a design element, we mean visible lines in an image. So here we are not talking about lines that serve to align objects, such as the golden ratio. Rather, it is about lines created by the objects themselves and the effect these lines have on the viewer. On the one hand, this effect can be emotional, for example by conveying feelings such as stability, narrowness or dynamism. Dynamic features, such as movement in a certain direction, can also be visualized by lines. On the other hand, lines often guide the viewer's gaze through the picture, which is of great importance for a successful picture composition.

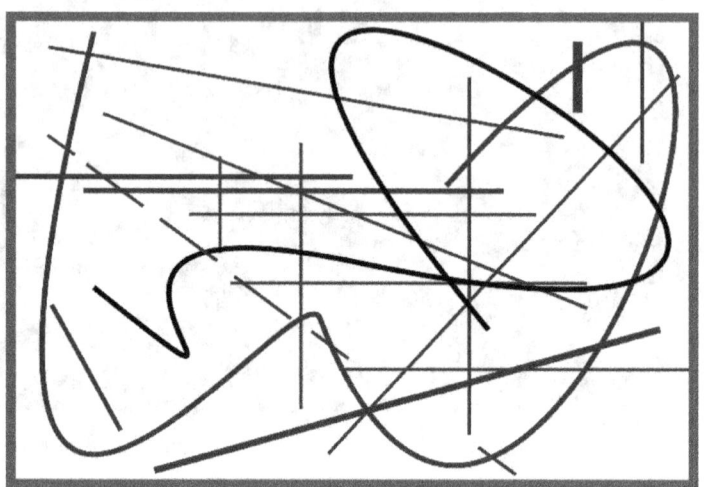

Lines in different directions

Lines can be created by copying a concrete line. This technique is often used in drawings and illustrations. On the other hand, lines can also be created by boundaries, for example in places where light and shadow separate, where surfaces with different tonal values adjoin each other, or where different patterns or structures meet. In this way, lines emerge, especially in paintings and photographs.

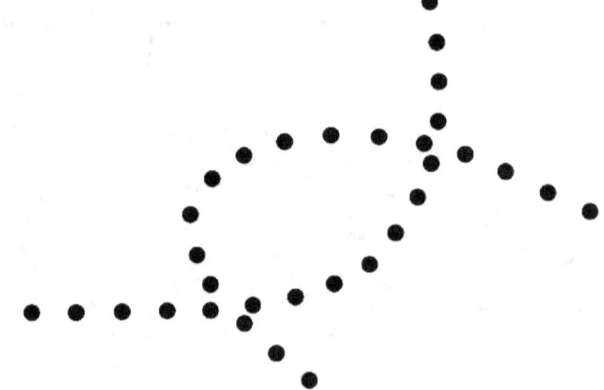

Dots become two lines

A series of dots can also be mentally completed to form a line by the viewer if the dots are close enough to each other and describe a continuous line. One thinks here of the Gestalt (form) law of proximity or also the law of good continuation.

Picture Design and Composition

Horizontal Lines

A picture inevitably contains at least two horizontal lines: The upper and lower sides of the frame. The third horizontal line in many pictures is the horizon. Especially in landscape paintings the horizon is the basis for the composition. It represents the reference lines for all contained objects and conveys the feeling of gravity in the pictorial world.

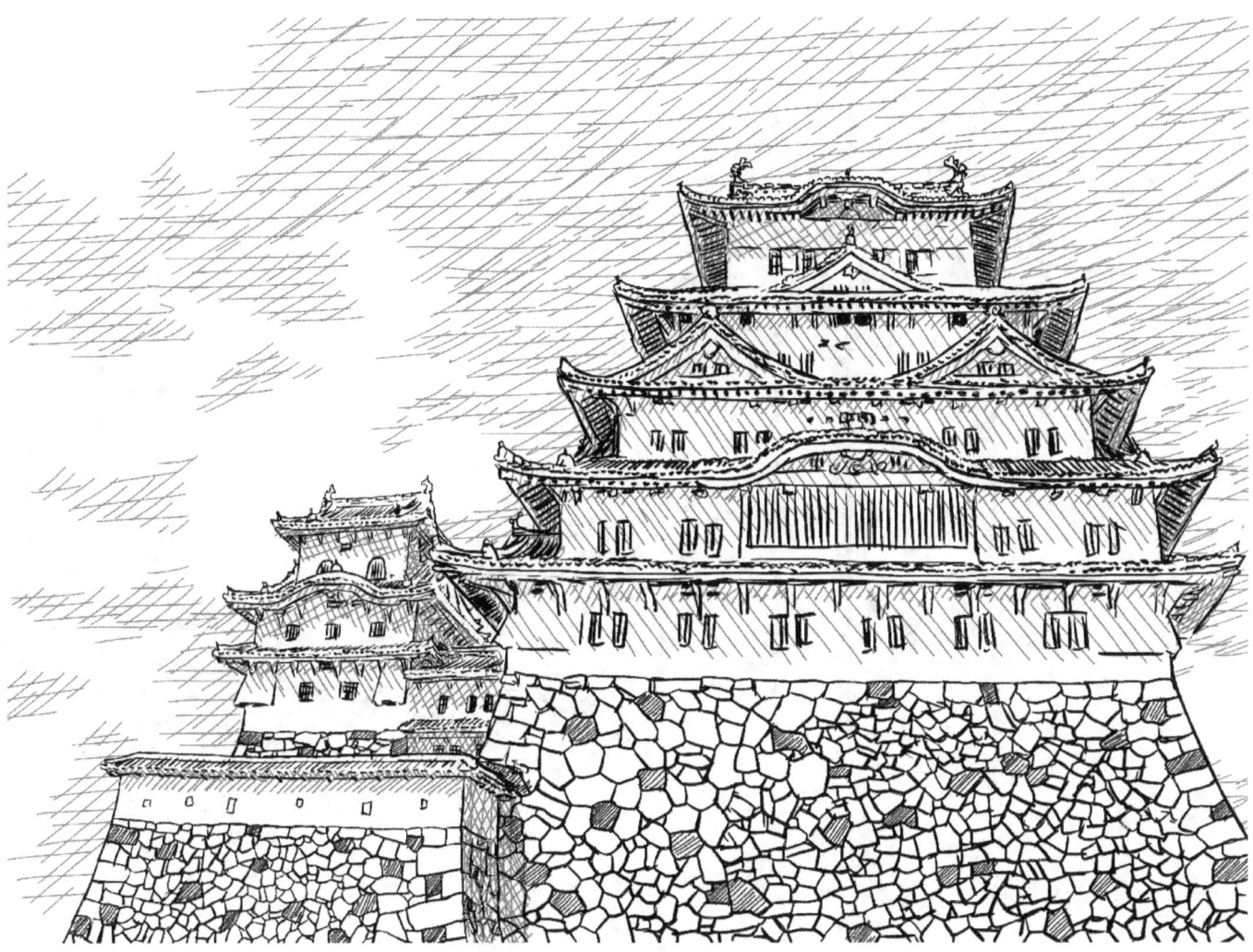

Drawing of the castle Himeji – roofs allow horizontal lines to emerge

What the viewer associates with horizontal lines are properties such as stability and tranquillity. Our field of vision is aligned horizontally, so horizontal lines can be used to create the effect of space and depth. However, these lines are not very dynamic and bring little movement into the composition.

Vertical Lines

As with horizontal lines, there are automatically at least two vertical lines in an image that are created by the image frame. If you allow more vertical lines to appear in the image, they can create a certain visual balance together with horizontal lines. With both line types, however, one should make sure that they actually run parallel to the picture frame, as angle deviations in comparison to the frame are very easily noticeable. Typical objects that correspond to vertical lines are trees, people, street lamps and the like.

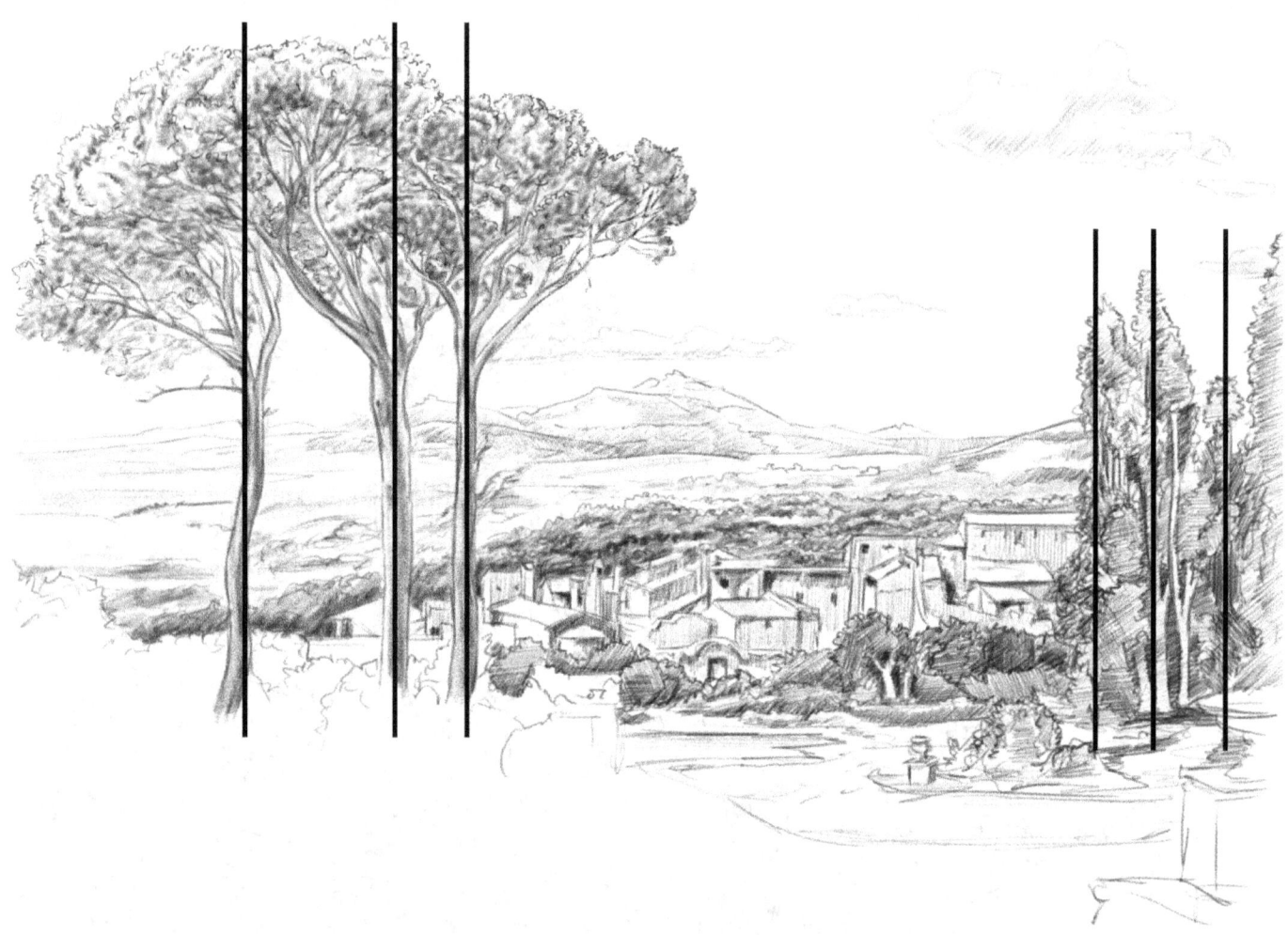

Trees in the foreground and middleground correspond to vertical lines
Image: Drawing after the painting "Tivoli – View to the Villa d'Este" by Carl Rottmann 1826

Vertical lines are more likely to represent speed and motion than horizontal lines. However, if used awkwardly, they can act as a barrier or grid. In addition, vertical lines can quickly lead the viewer's gaze out of the image if the gaze is not recaptured by other design elements. At the edge of the picture, on the other hand, they can serve as blockades that keep the gaze in the picture. Portrait is the best format for displaying a single vertical line in an image. The landscape format is ideal for compositions in which several vertical lines are represented that form a horizontal structure.

Picture Design and Composition

Diagonal Lines

The image design can be made more dynamic with diagonal lines, which are more interesting and effective. While horizontal and vertical lines appear rather static, diagonal lines create a high degree of dynamics. With diagonal lines the viewer suggests movement and speed. Additional tension can be created by displaying diagonals at different angles. The higher the difference in the angle of the various lines the greater the resulting contrast. A single diagonal is sufficient, since each diagonal line creates a contrast with the vertical and horizontal lines of the picture frame. The maximum contrast is created by diagonals at a 45° angle.

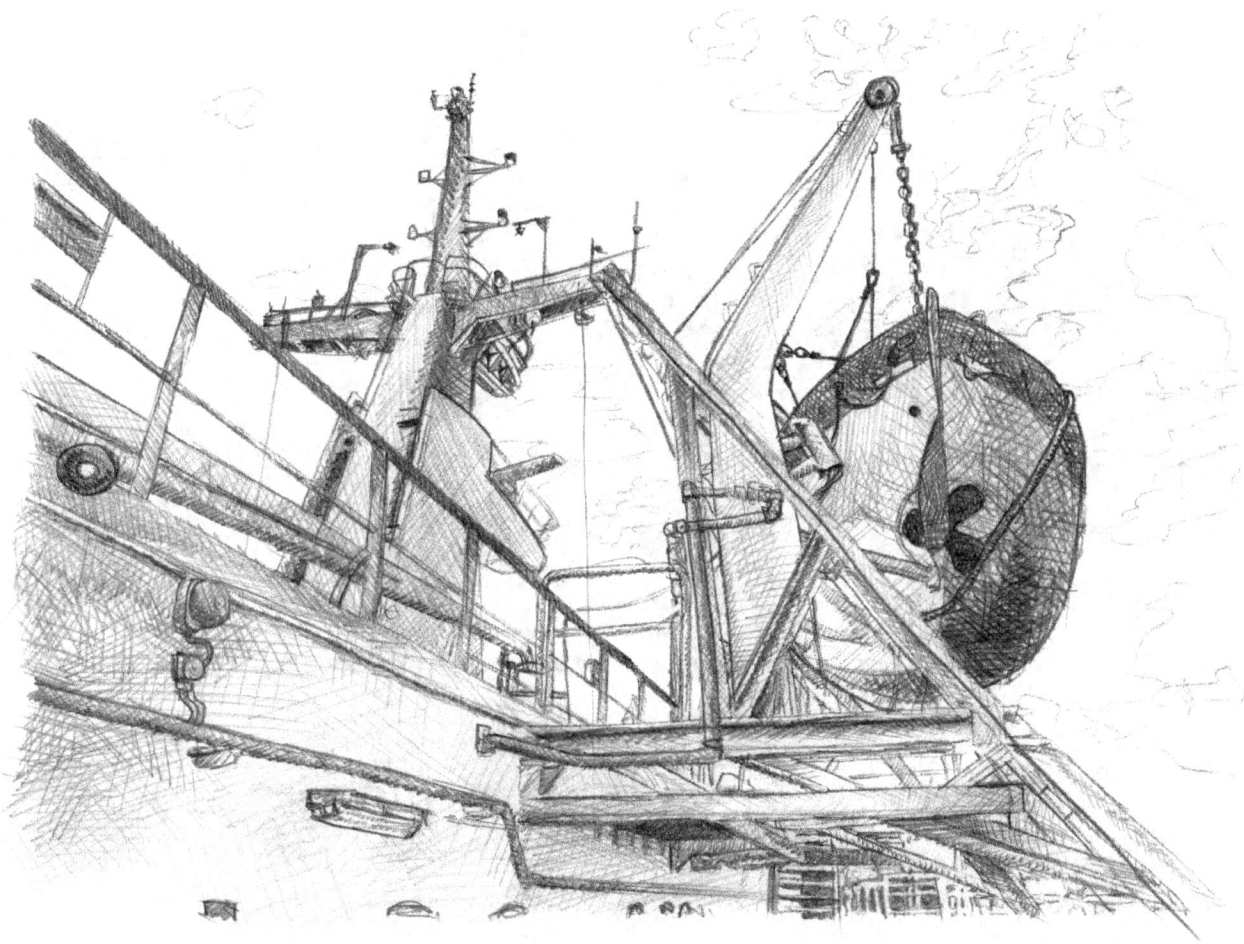

Lines help to create tension and depth in this picture composition

Another special feature of diagonal lines is that they can convey an impression of space and depth. This makes them perfect for landscape drawings. Only diagonal lines can make the perspective effect visible. The depth effect can unfold particularly intensively when an oblique point of view is displayed on picture objects. In general, diagonals are often a product of the viewing angle, since most scenes and objects actually consist primarily of horizontal and vertical lines. From a drawing point of view, the objects are then depicted in so-called two-point perspective.

Example Image: Kajikazawa in the Province Kai

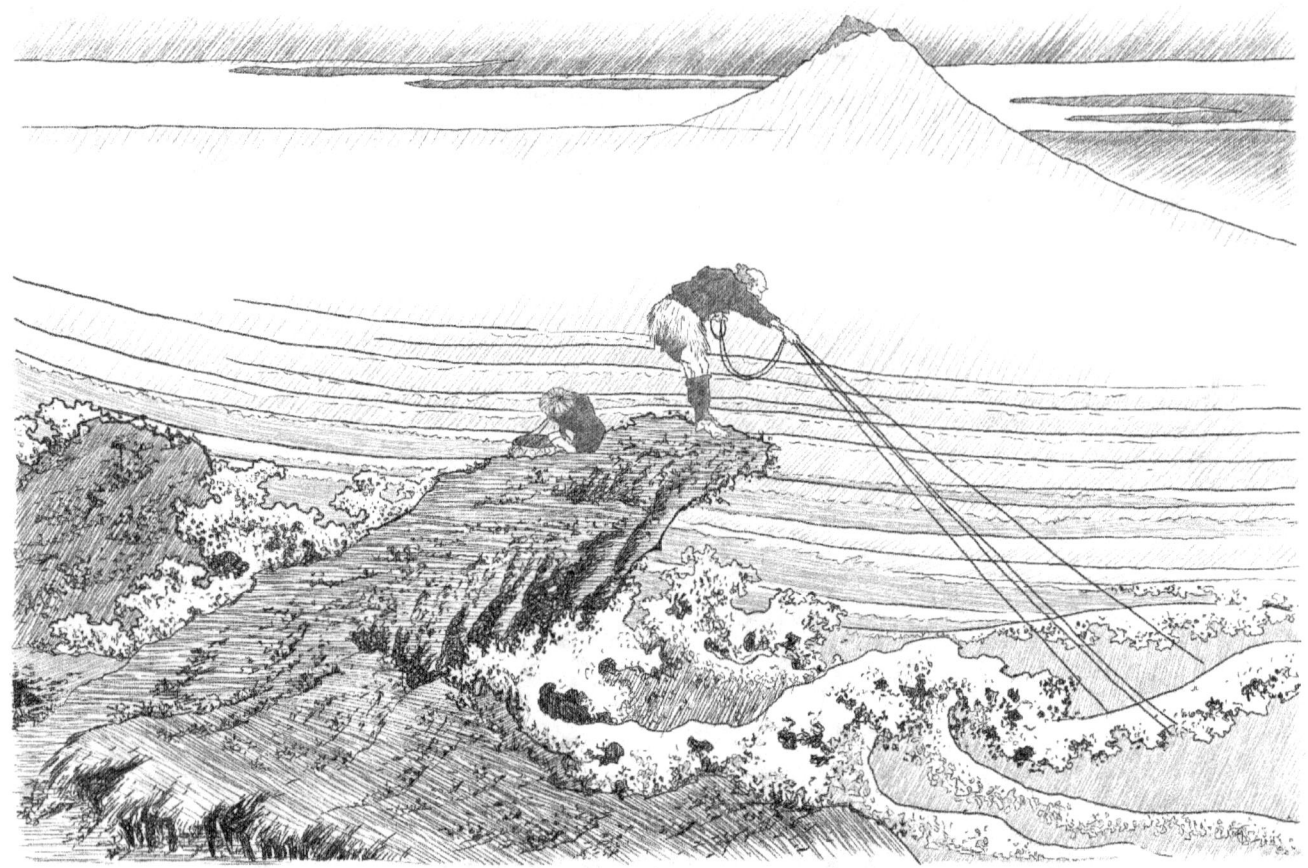

Kajikazawa in the Province Kai
Drawing after the colored woodcut by Katsushika Hokusai, 1831

In the drawing, which was drawn from a woodblock print by the artist Katsushika Hokusai, diagonal lines are visible that spread out like a fan. In contrast to this, there are further diagonals which spread in opposite directions and cross the other lines.

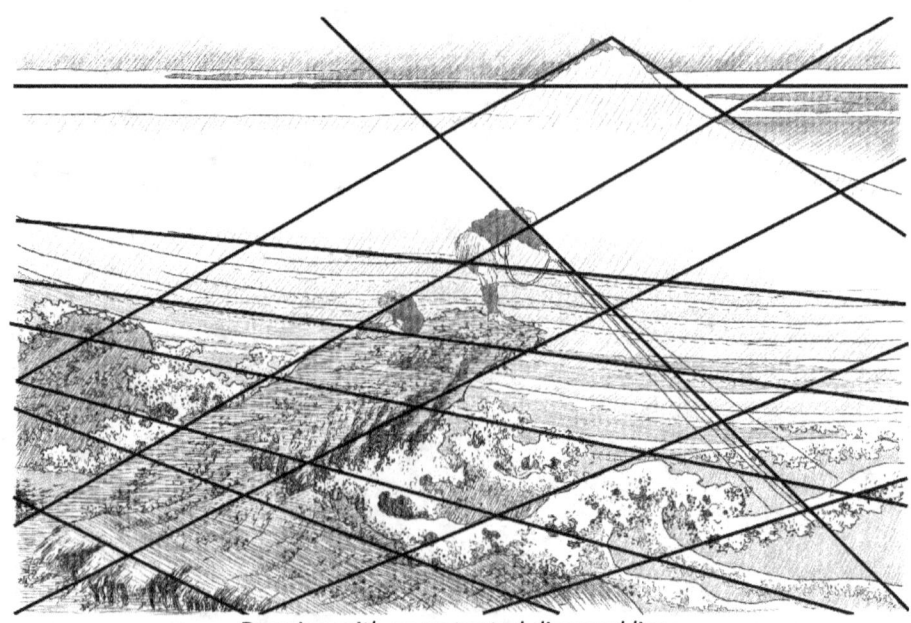

Drawing with accentuated diagonal lines

Picture Design and Composition

Several More Tricks Using Diagonals

Diagonal lines can contribute to the viewer's gaze staying in the picture. While vertical lines can cause the viewer to look out of the image, oblique lines can cause the viewer to look from one side of the image to the other.

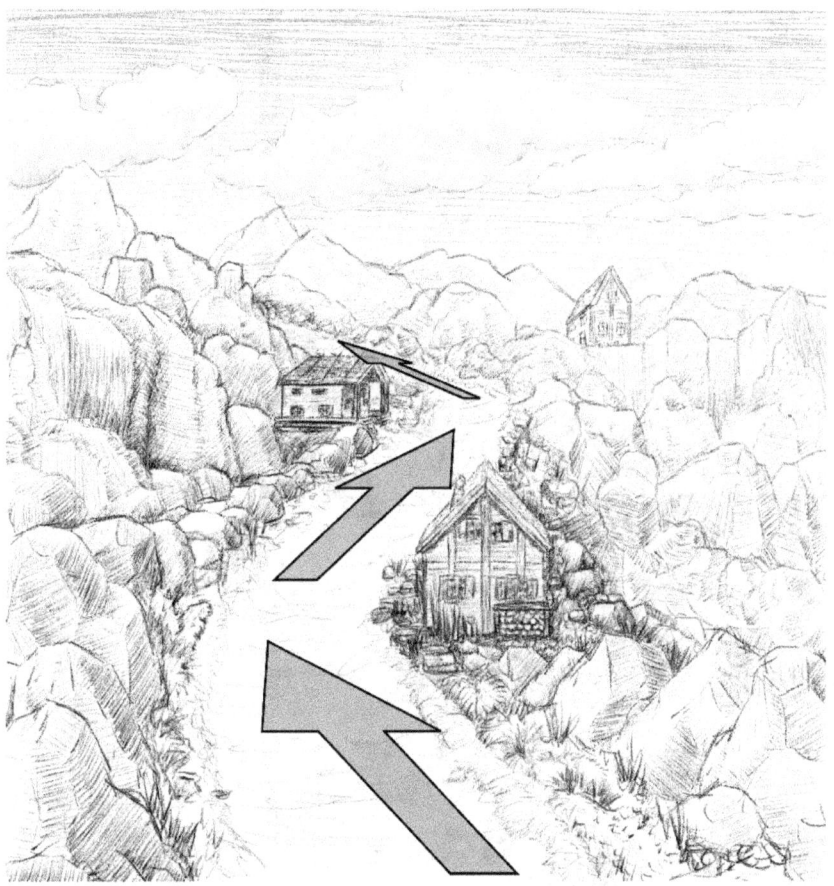
Road with zigzag course guides the viewer's gaze through the picture

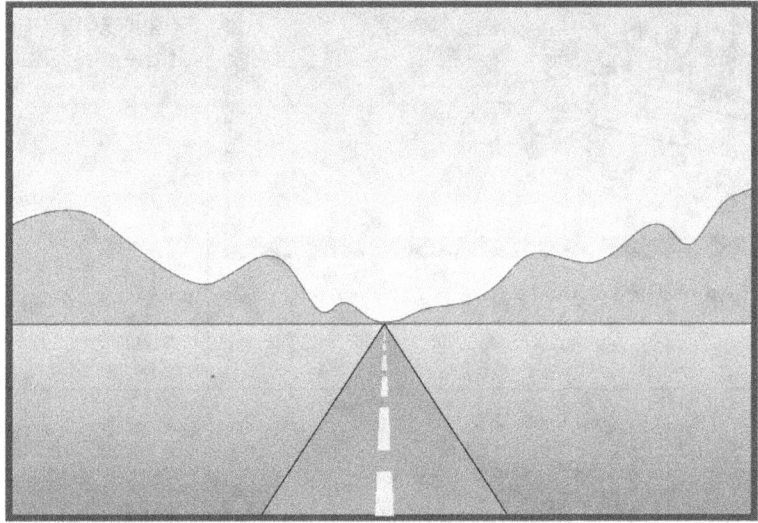
A vertically positioned road quickly guides our view out of the picture

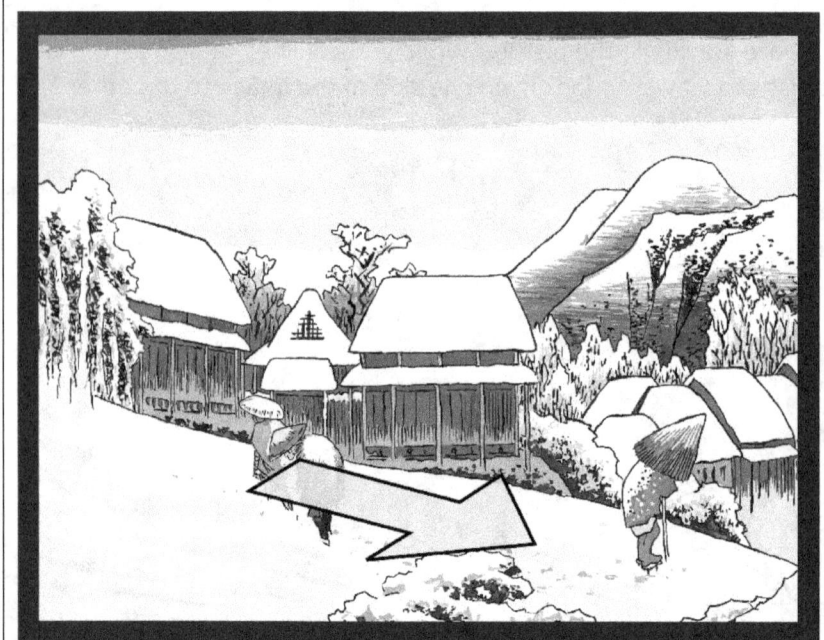

Descending Diagonals

Ascending and descending diagonals are often used to create certain image effects. One speaks of ascending diagonals if the line runs from the lower left to the upper right, whereas one speaks of descending diagonals if the line runs from the upper left to the lower right.

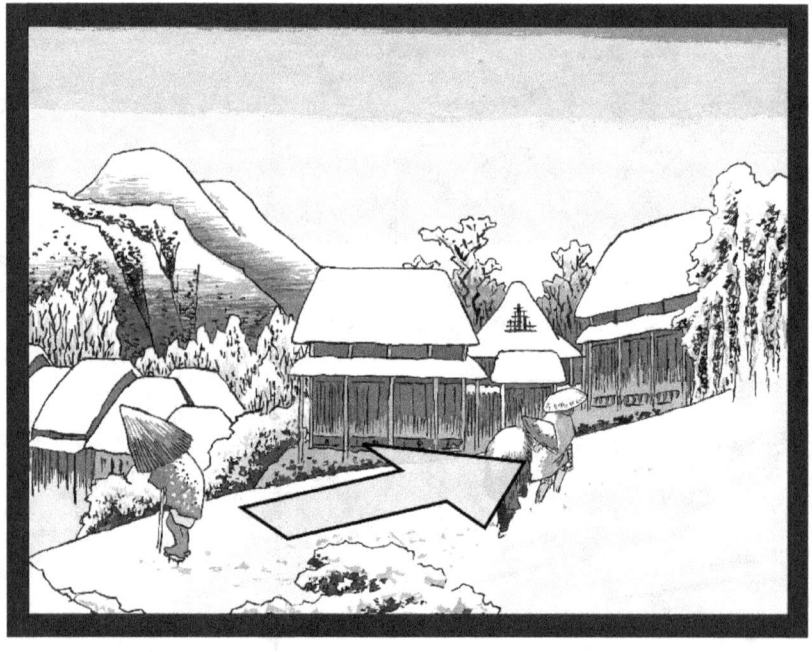

Ascending Diagonals

Descending lines are rather suggestive of negative feelings and can contribute to guiding the viewer's gaze out of the picture. In addition, the viewer spends less time with the details along the diagonals. In contrast, ascending diagonals are more associated with positive feelings and seem more aesthetic for some people. The viewer's gaze is held longer in the picture and lingers longer on the details in the area of the diagonals.

5.3 Light-Dark Contrast

The light-dark contrast results from the different brightness of elements. This tonal value contrast can occur with the uncolored colors black, white and gray, but is also found with the primary and secondary colors to the same extent. In the case of chromatic colors, one speaks of the color brightness.

Light-dark contrast is used very frequently and very specifically in image design. It can be used to add depth to an image or to draw attention to certain elements. For example, surfaces with the same brightness appear to be on the same plane. Strong tonal contrast, on the other hand, creates plasticity. Bright elements appear as if they are further in the foreground, while dark elements recede into the background. Painters and draughtsmen consciously use the light-dark contrast to clearly separate light and shadow. In the motif depicted, the contours become more recognizable, which leads to an impression of corporeality and three-dimensionality.

Strong contrasts are also a tool for directing the viewer's gaze to the most important areas of the picture. Display the elements of your drawing that you want to focus on with the strongest contrast. Dragging the less important areas with low contrast will take away the attraction.

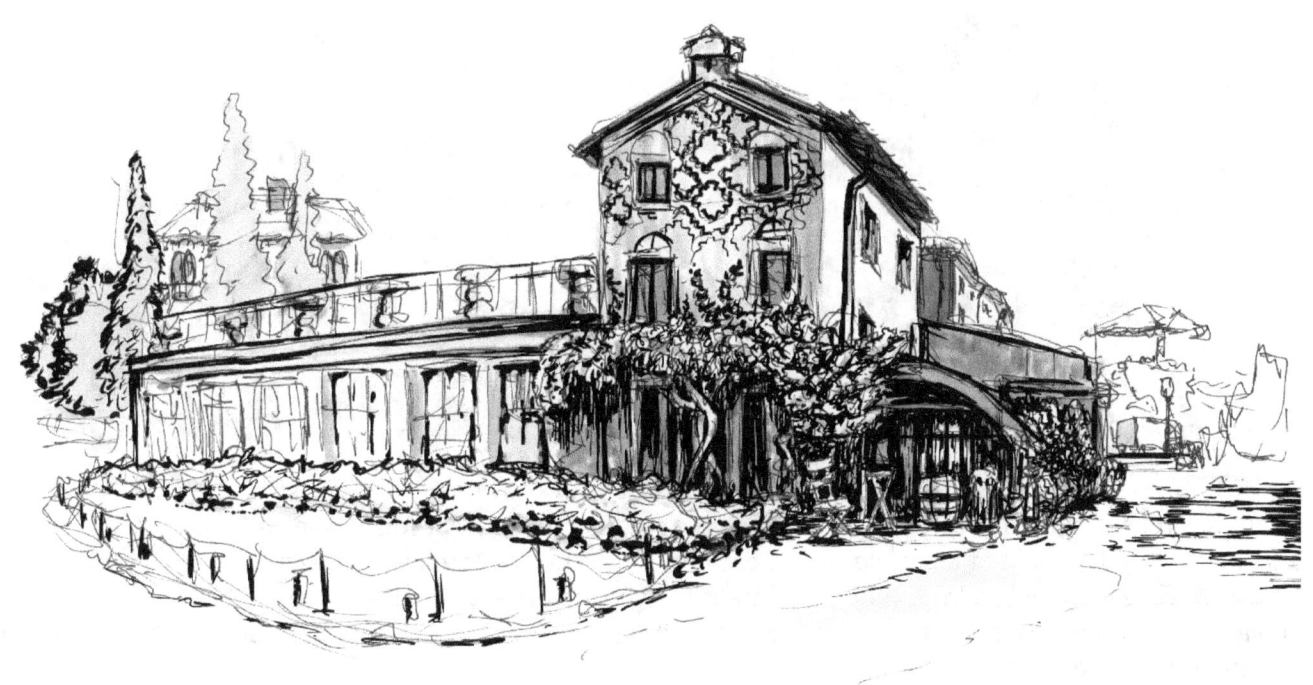

Stronger light-dark contrasts in a drawing lead one's attention directly to the most important aspect in the picture

The other effect of light-dark contrast is the weighting of picture elements or picture areas. Because bright elements attract the viewer's attention, they appear more important than things that lie in the dark. This method can be found in countless pictures of different artists from different epochs in art history. Again and again it can be seen that the significant elements are depicted in a bright light, while things that the viewer is not supposed to deal with any further are obscured in the darkness and disappear.

Using Contrast to Depict Weather

With the help of contrast you can give the viewer information about the weather in landscape pictures. Depending on the weather conditions, the light can be direct or diffuse and thus cause stronger or weaker contrasts.

If, for example, the sun hits an object directly on a cloudless day, it is very strongly illuminated on the side facing the light. The opposite side disappears almost in the shade and is slightly brightened by the small amount of light scattered in the atmosphere. This hard light creates very strong tonal contrasts. This type of light quality is called direct or directional light.

direct light   diffuse light

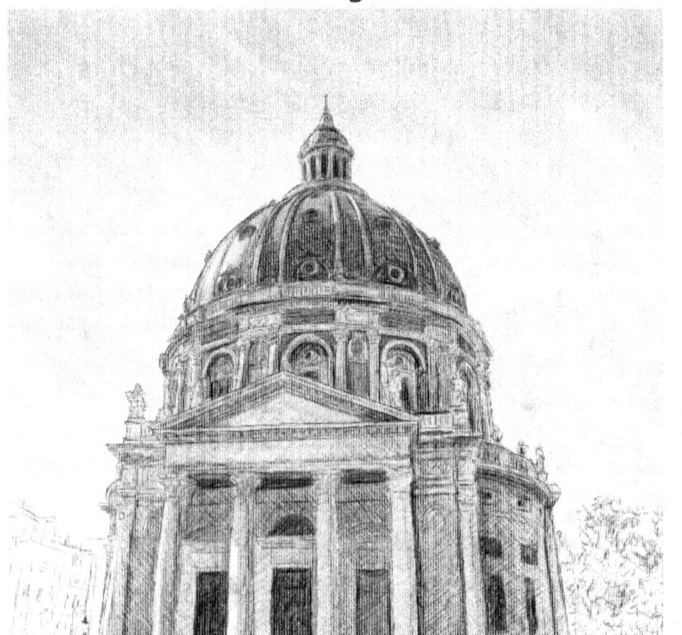
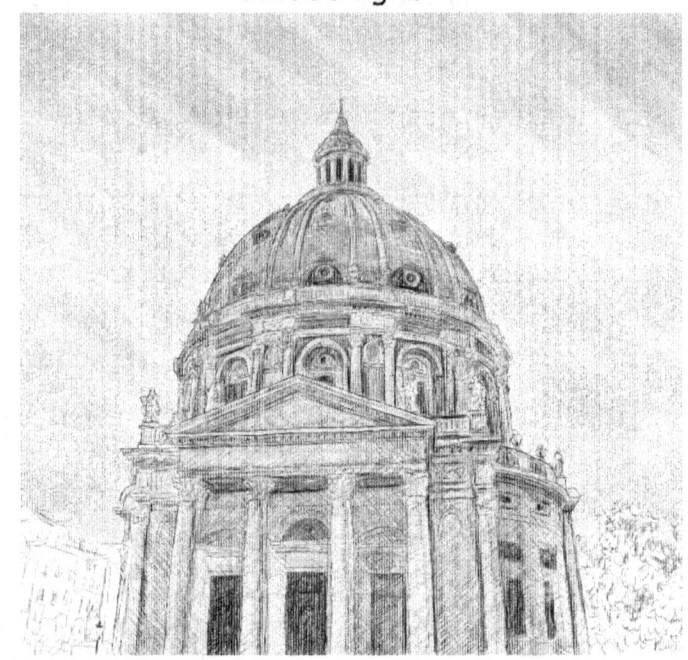

Comparison between direct and diffuse light

Diffuse, soft light is produced, for example, when the weather is cloudy or foggy. The sun's rays are then scattered by the increased amount of molecules in the air, resulting in much more indirect light. As a result, the sunny side of the object experiences a lower luminous intensity, while the shady side is brightened by an increased amount of light. In extreme cases, hardly any or even no visible shadows occur. The tonal value contrast in this lighting situation is correspondingly low.

Picture Design and Composition

5.4 Perspective and Space

The term perspective refers to the angle from which the artist depicts the motif. Conversely, it is also the point of view from which the viewer sees the scene. The perspective changes automatically when the artist moves - be it up, down, left, right, forwards or backwards. Every inclination or new orientation of the vista also changes the perspective.

Perspective is a particularly powerful instrument of image design, as it can be used to directly influence the effect of the image and to create targeted effects. The view from above (bird's eye view), for example, creates a completely different impression than the view from a low point of view - even if nothing else changes in the motif.

A perfect example of this are 17th century landscapes, where the viewer's point of view is particularly low, whereas in the centuries before it was rather a view from above on the landscape.

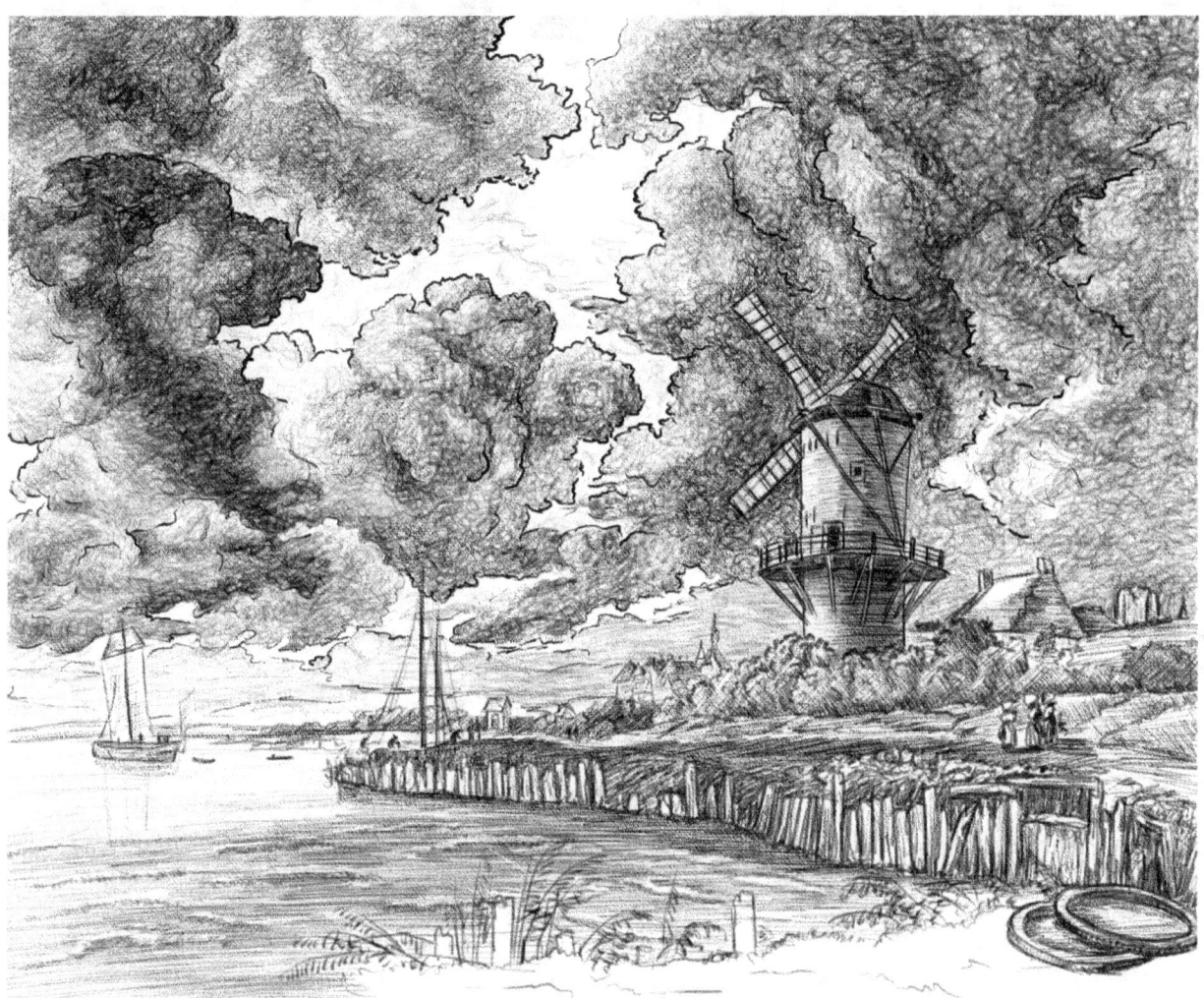

Low viewer's point of view to a landscape drawing with considerable emphasis on the sky
Drawing after the painting "The Mill at Wijk bij Duurstede" by Jacob van Ruisdael

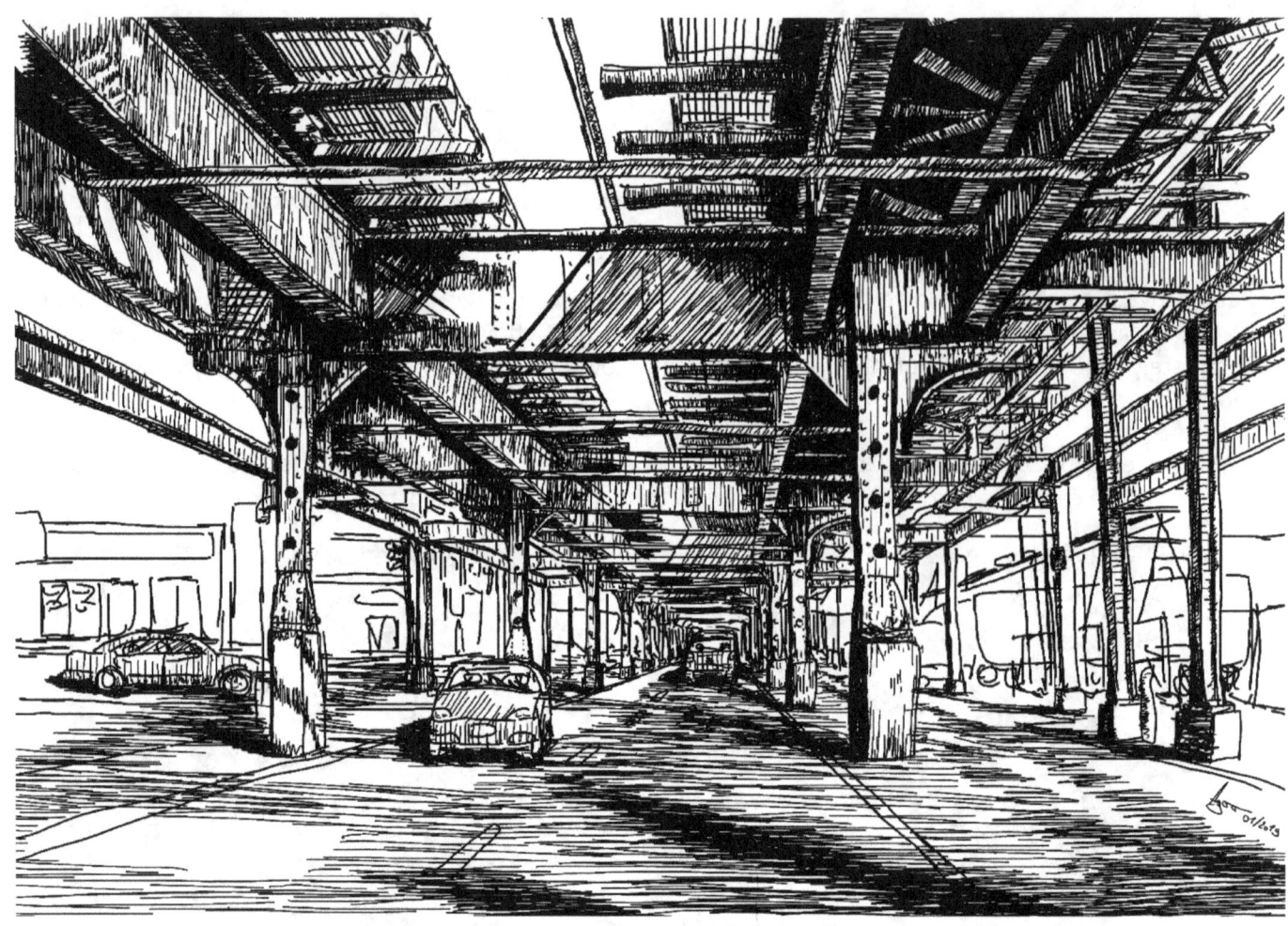

Central perspective in this city scene draws the viewer's gaze into the depth of the picture

Example Image: Art and Science

The picture in this example shows a replica of Carl Spitzweg's "Art and Science". In the painting from the Biedermeier period several techniques of spatial representation are used. The scene is set in a free space in front of a building with a view of its front. Objects in the foreground, such as the fountain and the doves, convey an awareness of the three-dimensionality of this surface. The people stand on the floor in the lower part of the picture, while the houses tower above them. A sign hanging on the left of the building creates an additional spatial effect, as do the shadows cast by the buildings. The painter also offers the viewer a look into the distance - in the upper right corner. This view unfolds its full effect only by means of the tower further away, whereby the painter makes use of the air perspective here. The gate on the right, which is partially concealed, also contributes to a sense of depth.

Picture Design and Composition

And to return once again to the contrast theme of the previous chapter: Note the pictures and linen sheets near the two people. They form particularly bright image areas and thus attract the viewer's attention. The same applies to the collar, the cuffs and the book of the main actor.

The man on the right, with his dark coat in front of the light linen cloth, stands out particularly well. In contrast, the man to his left wears a lighter coat, which creates a strong contrast to the dark gate in the background.

There would be even more to note in this painting, but the examples already mentioned show how the painter Carl Spitzweg purposefully used the most diverse design techniques to create appealing picture compositions.

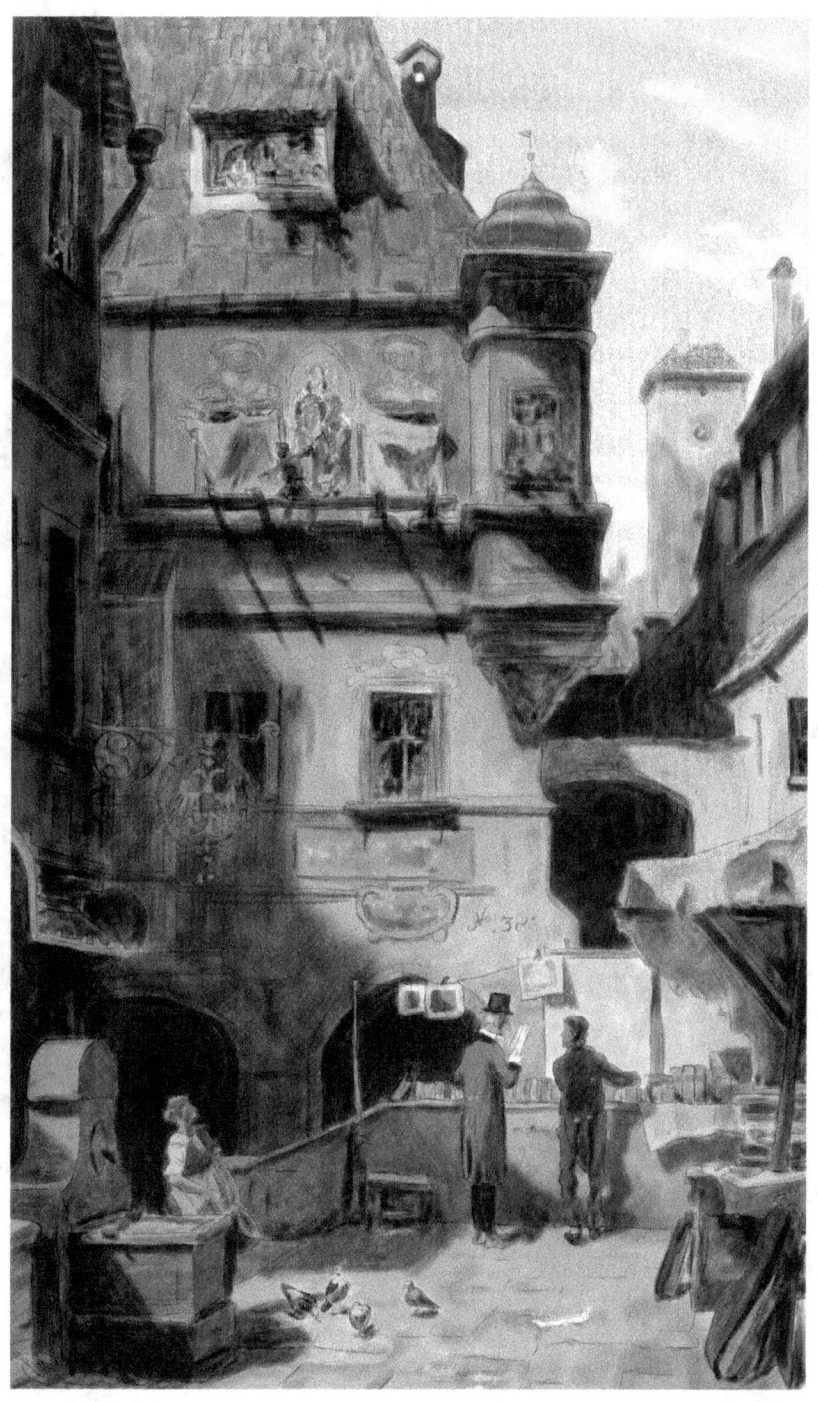

City scene with an example of spatial effect:
"Art and Science" (Replica)
Original: Carl Spitzweg, 1880

Conveying Spatiality through Light and Shadow

Through the targeted use of light and shadow, the spatial effect of objects can be increased. Light and shadow describe the shape of both small and large bodies, which also works at a greater distance. The vanishing point perspective is also a suitable instrument for perfecting the representation. The vanishing point perspective can thus be used to construct shadows correctly.

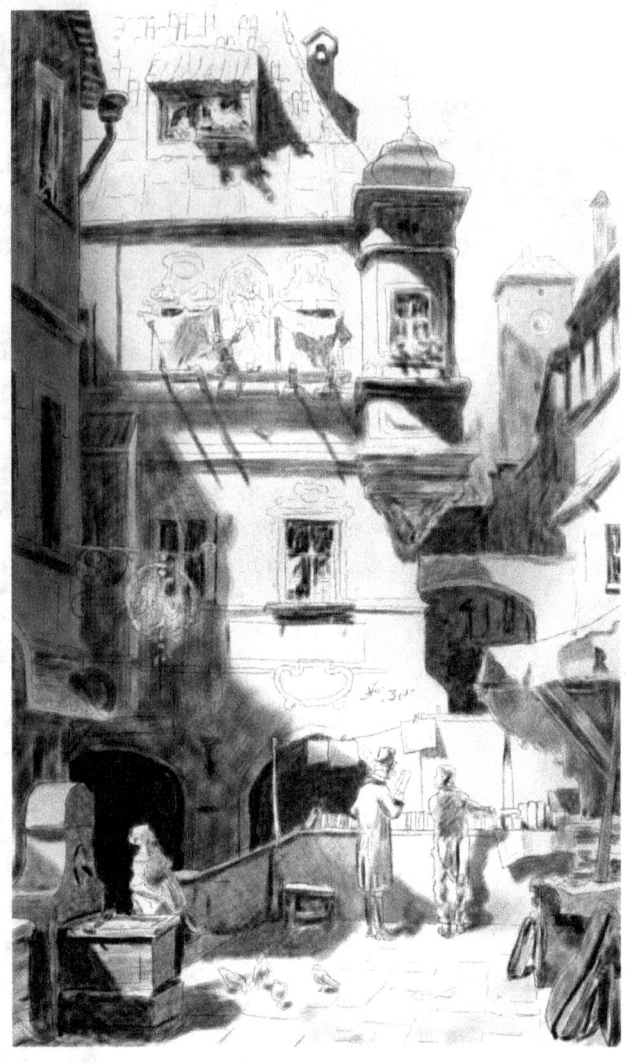

Spatiality of a city scene by means of light and shadow
Picture: "Art and Science" (Replica) reduced to shadows
Original: Carl Spitzweg, 1880

For a good light and shadow composition, landscape painters often adjust the ideal time of day to find a good shadow cast according to the position of the sun. In some landscape paintings it can also be seen that a suitable cloud constellation creates a play of light and shadow that additionally supports the illusion of a deep space.

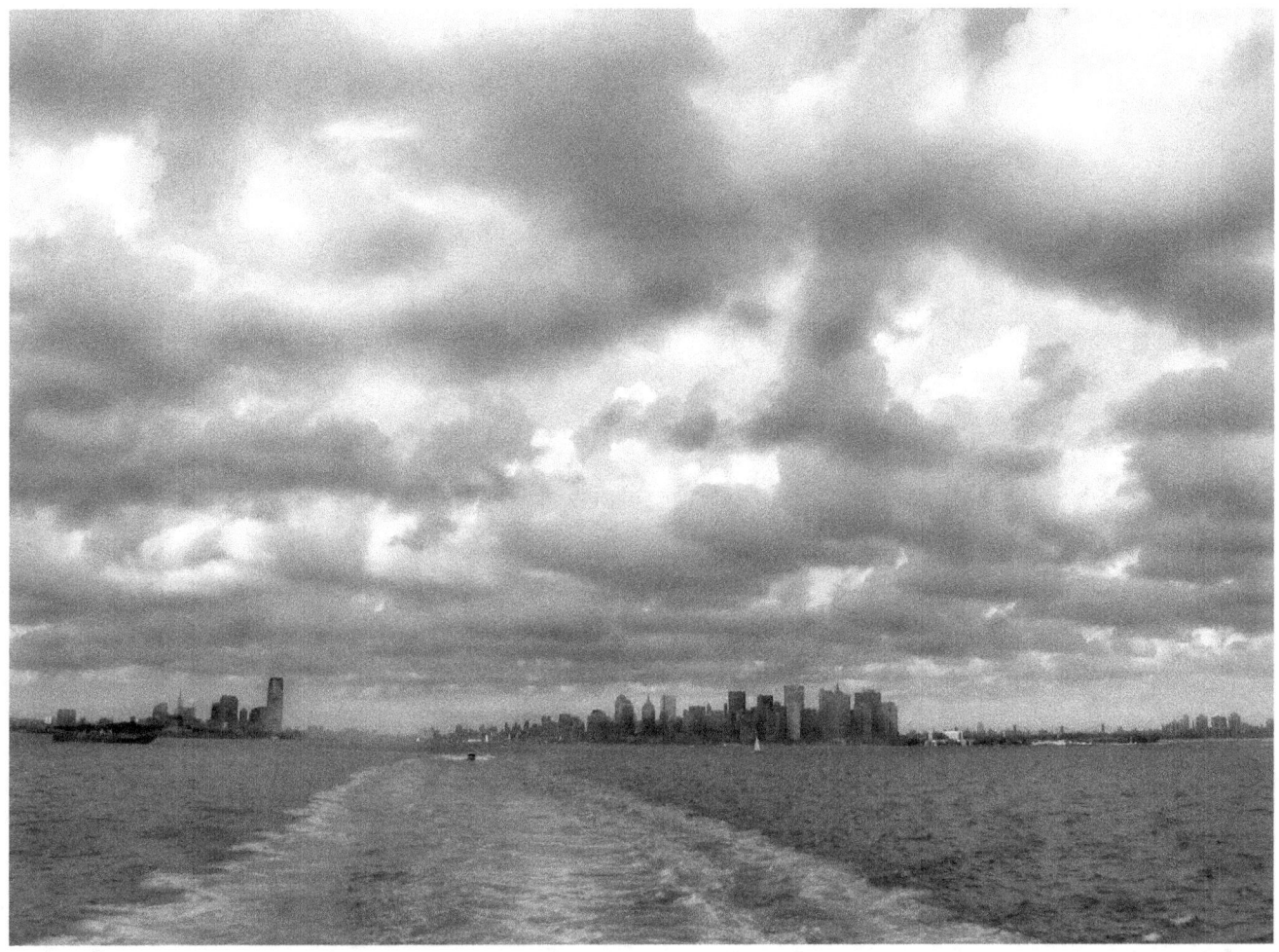

The cloud constellation in this picture conveys a better impression of the depth

And another little trick, which can be implemented with the representation of drop shadows: If you show the shadows of objects that cannot be seen in the picture, you expand the space spiritually. The artist conveys to the viewer the feeling that the true space goes beyond the visible part of the picture.

Studies – Drawing Landscapes

*» The artist is nothing without talent, but
talent is nothing without work. «*

- Émile Zola -

6 Studies – Drawing Landscapes

In this chapter the theory will again be put into practice. You have learned a lot in the meantime, from the basics of drawing to image design. In the following exercises you can improve your drawing skills, deepen your knowledge about spatial representation and learn more about image design using practical examples.

6.1 Small Landscape Sketches

Small sketches of landscapes are a perfect exercise for starting, which also loosens up possible mental blocks. Just draw what you can think of. A sunset, a city, a piece of woodland or sketches with different screen layouts.

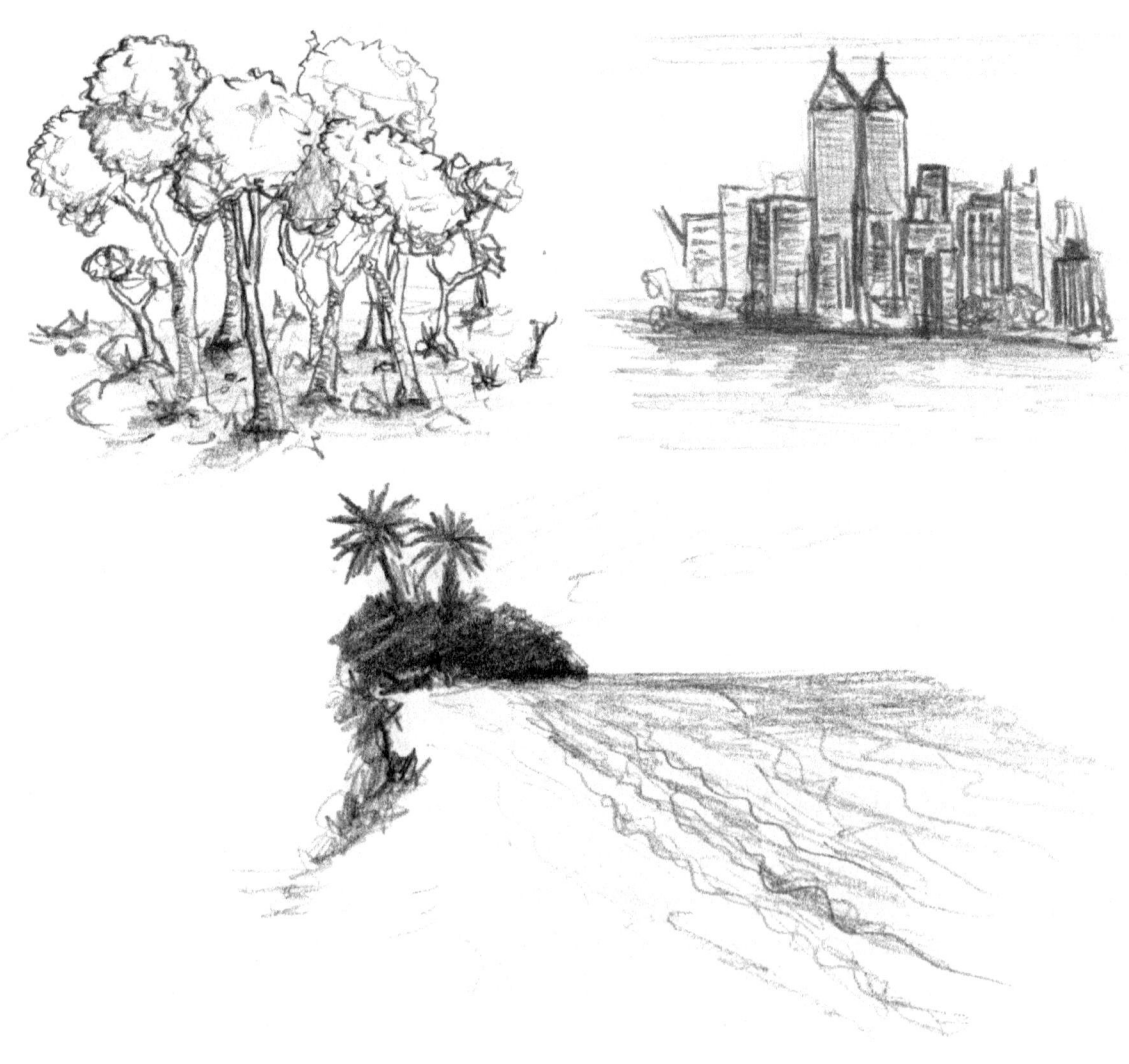

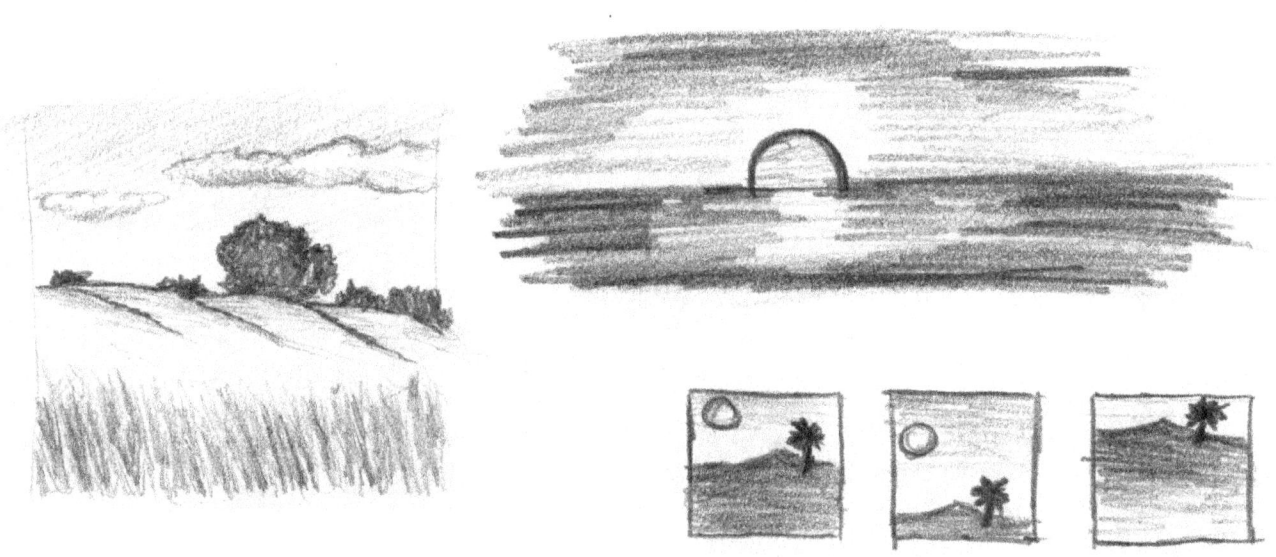

6.2 A Simple Landscape with Bush and Field

This step-by-step exercise is mainly about showing a bush and trees in the background. You start with a rough sketch of the landscape. In this first step it is about dividing the paper and defining the positions as well as the proportions of the image objects.

Now that you have defined positions and proportions, you can sketch the contours more precisely. But you don't have to draw every little detail here.

Now you can start drawing shadows and textures. The forest in the background is drawn with few details and lower tonal contrast. The bush, which is further in the foreground, should be drawn in more detail and should receive stronger contrasts, especially in the dark area.

In this step, apply the knowledge from the previous chapter which showed how to draw trees. For a bush, the techniques are equally applicable.

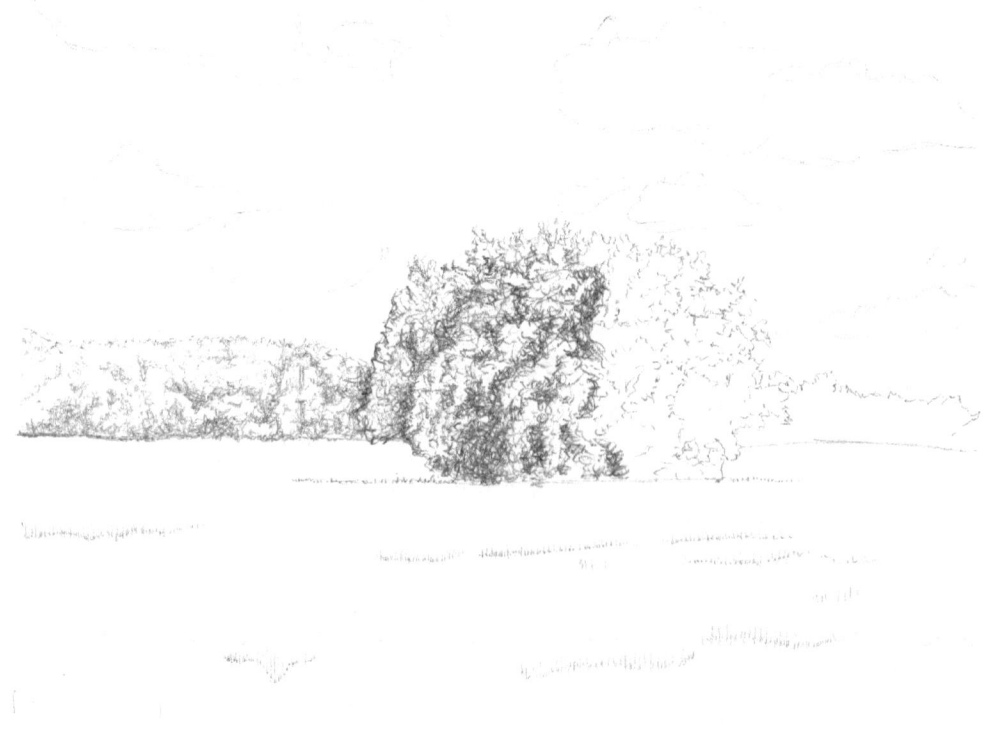

One shades now bit by bit the bush and background. You can first draw the lighter tones and then the darker ones. In this way you can gradually work out the shape of your motifs.

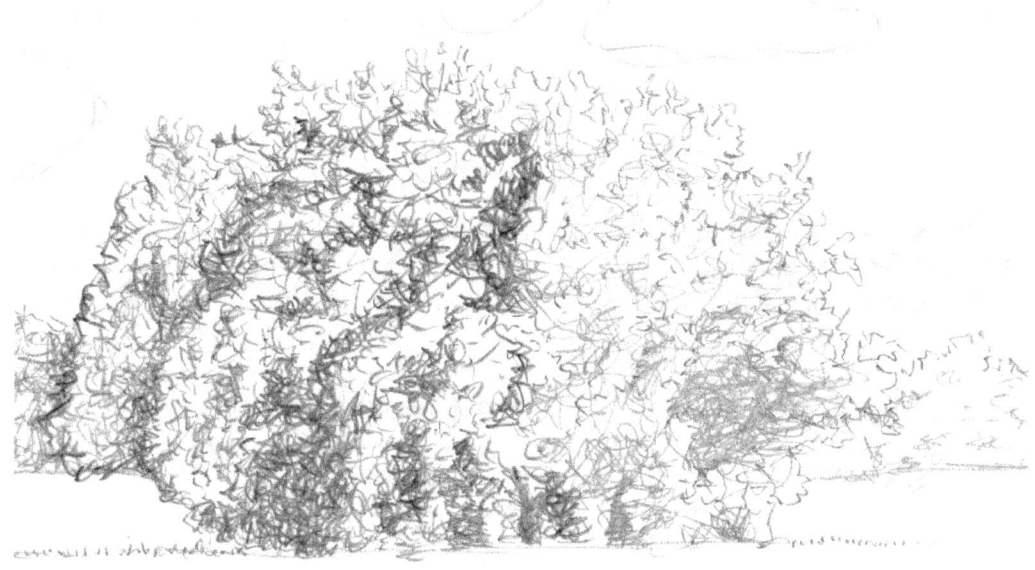

Once the bush and trees are finished, you can give the clouds soft shadows. The cornfield in which the bush stands can be indicated with a few lines. Then the picture is finished.

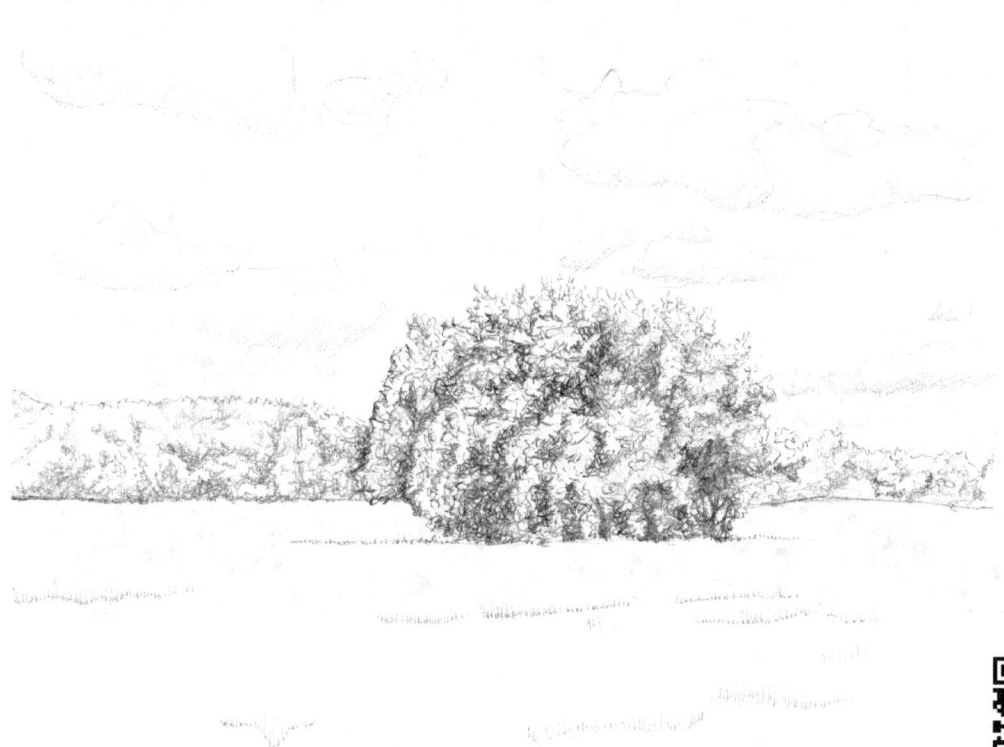

6.3 Copying Photos Using the Grid Method

If you draw landscapes from photos, you can use the so-called grid method. With this method, you can display the outlines faster and more accurately.

This is How the Grid Method Works

With this drawing method, you draw a chessboard-like grid on the photo and the same grid on the paper. The dimensions of the grid on the paper may be smaller or larger than those on the photo. However, the height-width ratio of the boxes must be the same; otherwise the image will be distorted. The number of boxes in height and width must also be the same.

The grid lines now serve as an orientation. It's a matter of taste how tight you draw the grid - but you shouldn't draw it too tight.

In the following pictures, implementation of the grid method is shown:

1. Rastering of the Photo Template

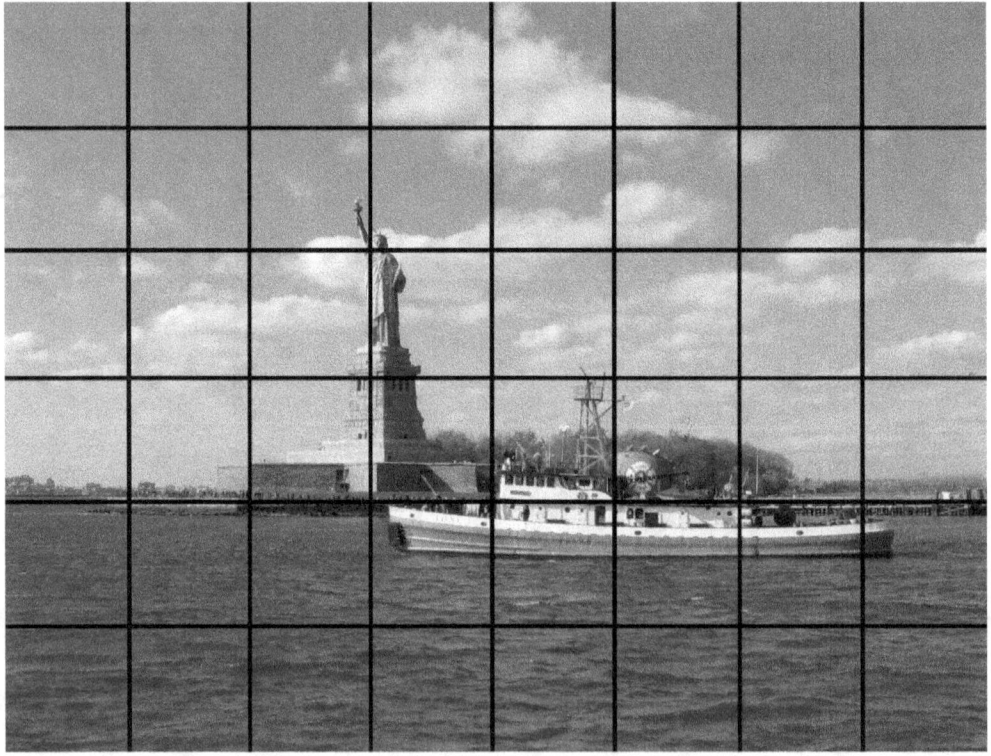

2. Rastering the Drawing Field

3. Marking and rough sketches of the most important contours corresponding to the photo template

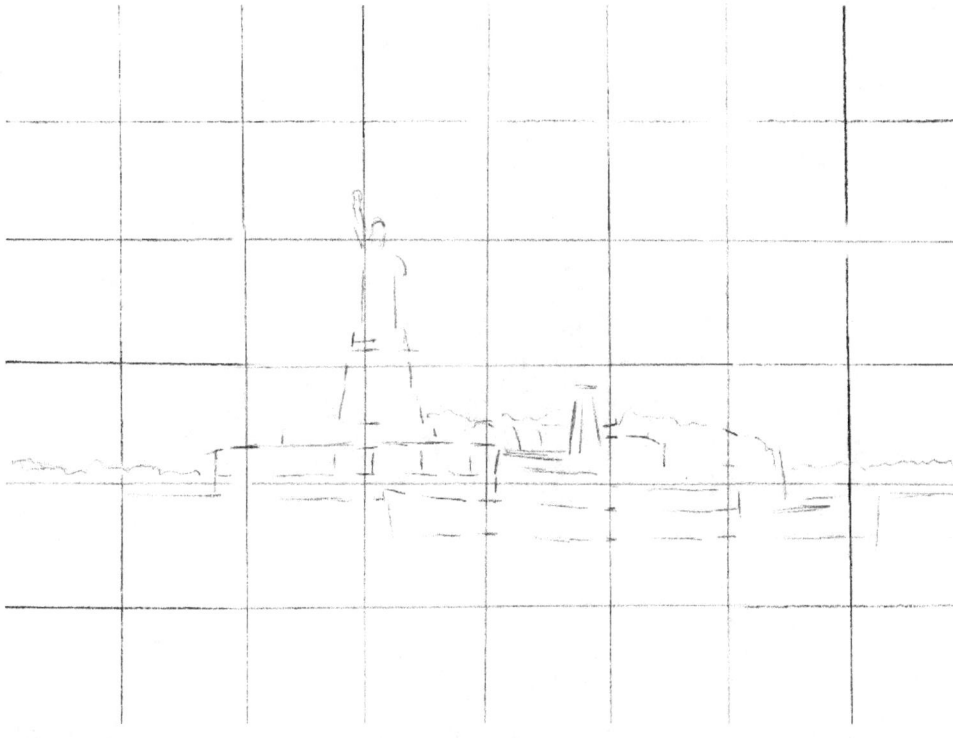

4. Erasing the Grid and Detailing the Drawing

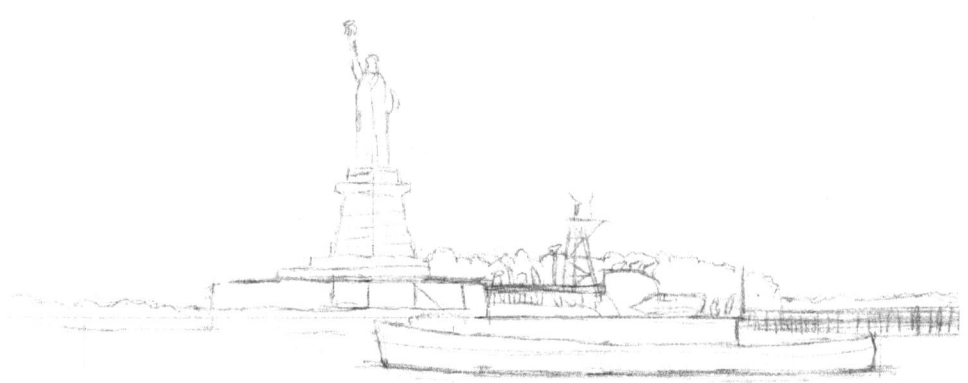

5. Erasing the Grid and Shading the Drawing

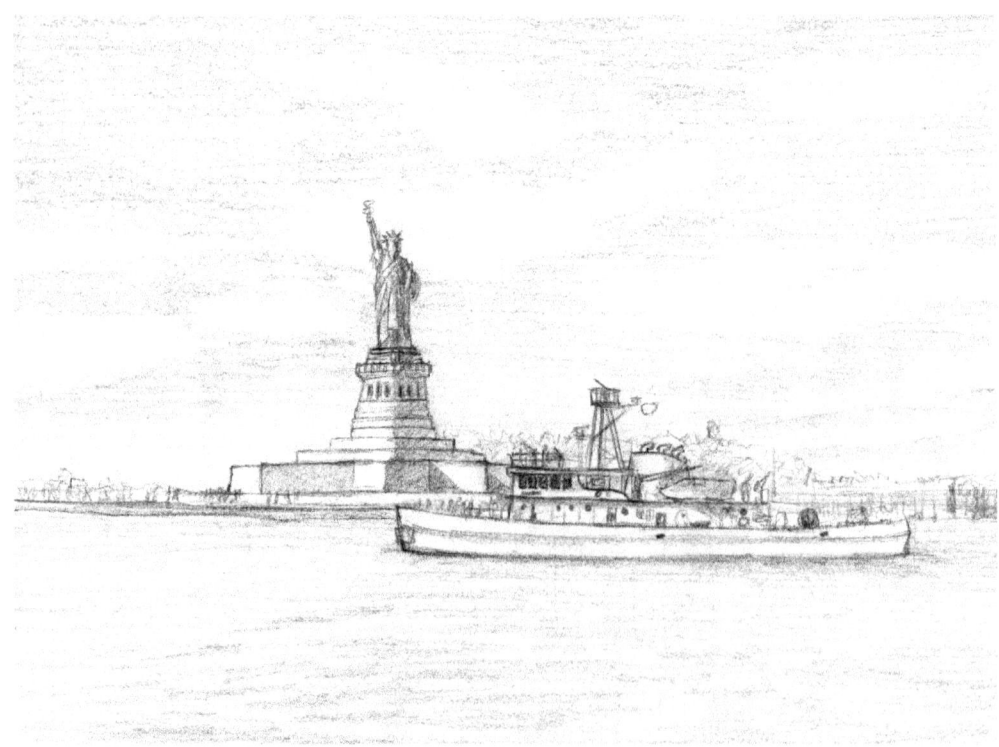

The drawing in this example was also shaded with the drawing technique shading. The picture shows the Statue of Liberty in New York together with a fireboat.

Studies – Drawing Landscapes

6.4 Trees and City

In the drawing for this study, a city is to be depicted that is a little farther away from the viewer. In the foreground there are three trees that attract the eye. The picture shows a view from the Villa d'Este to the Italian city of Tivoli.

This drawing is based on a watercolour by Carl Rottmann. Carl Anton Joseph Rottmann (* January 11, 1797 in Handschuhsheim; † July 7, 1850 in Munich) is a German landscape painter who belonged to the circle of artists of the Bavarian King Ludwig I.

Let's get started

It is best to start with a rough sketch that divides the pictorial space and determines the proportions of the motifs. If you want to use the original painting as a template, you can best find the picture on the Internet under the following title:

"Tivoli - View from Villa d'Este, 1826"

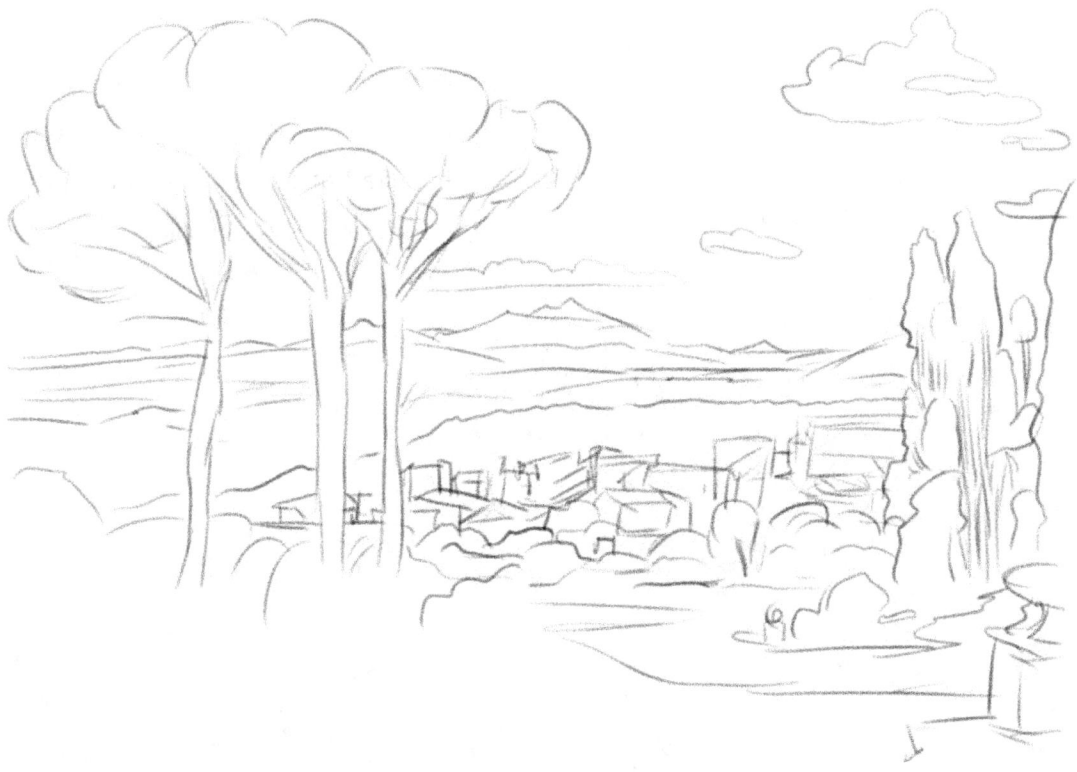

In the next step the preliminary drawing is detailed. You should carefully erase the previous sketch so that you can just recognize the lines.

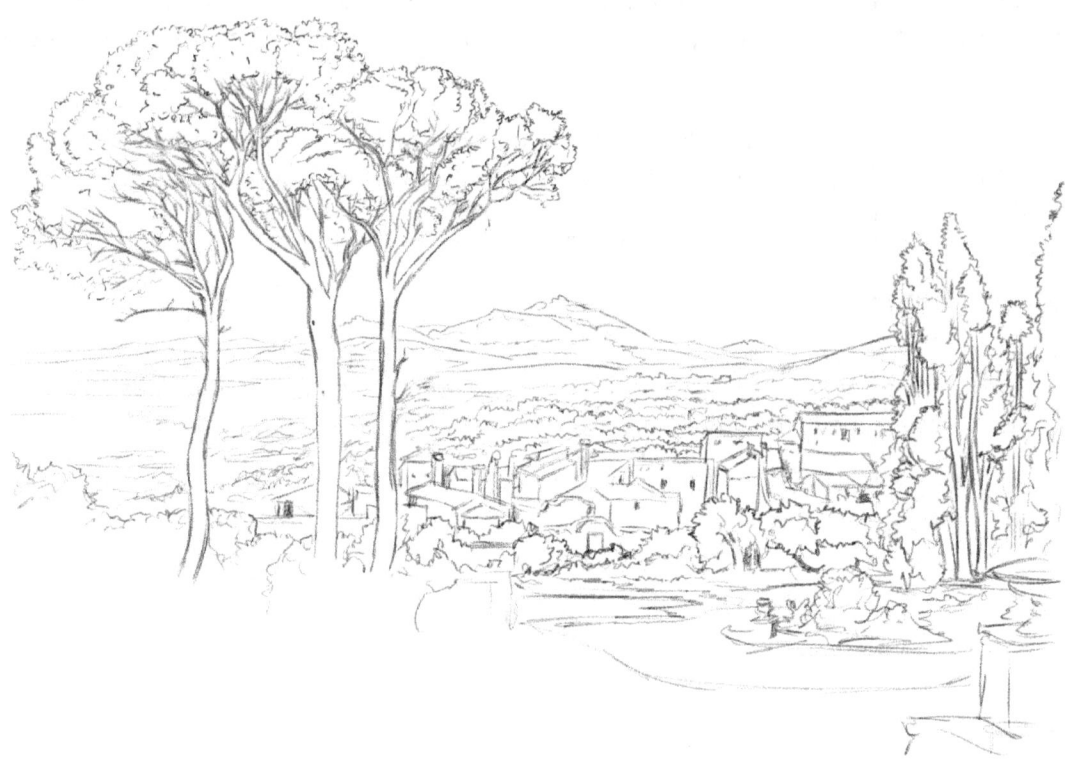

Now you start shading. If you are right-handed, it makes sense to start at the left side of the picture, so that you don't smear the drawing with your arm.

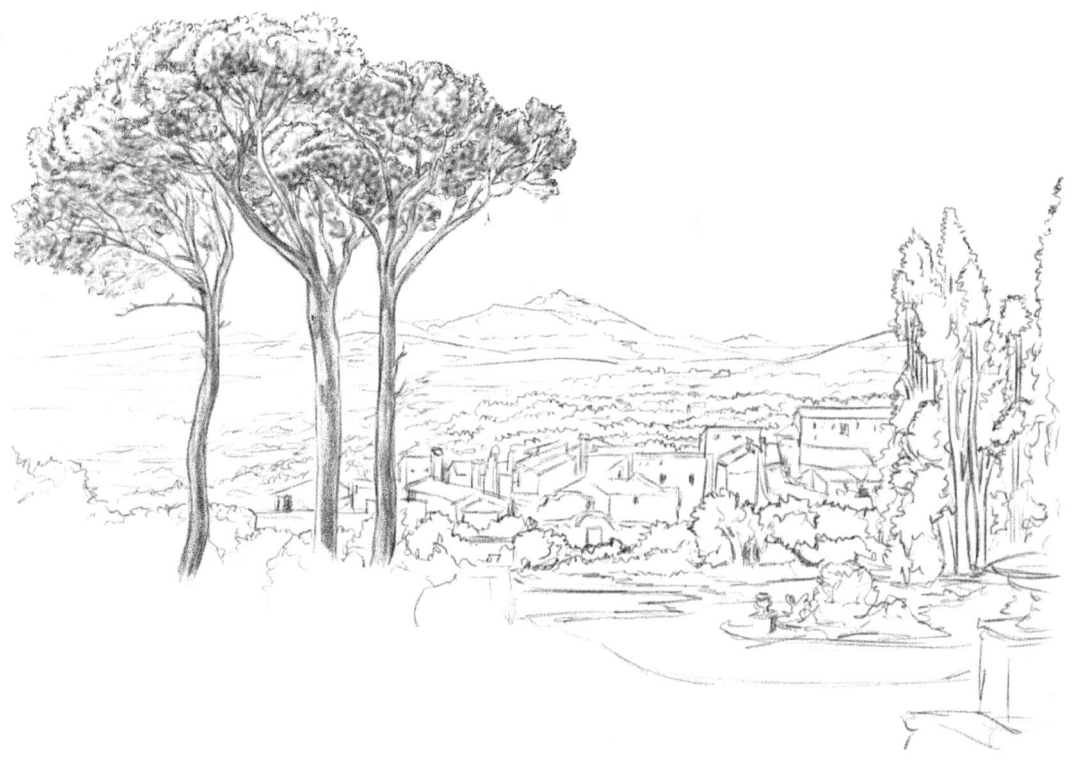

You can continue with the middle ground. Shade the city and the trees on the right.

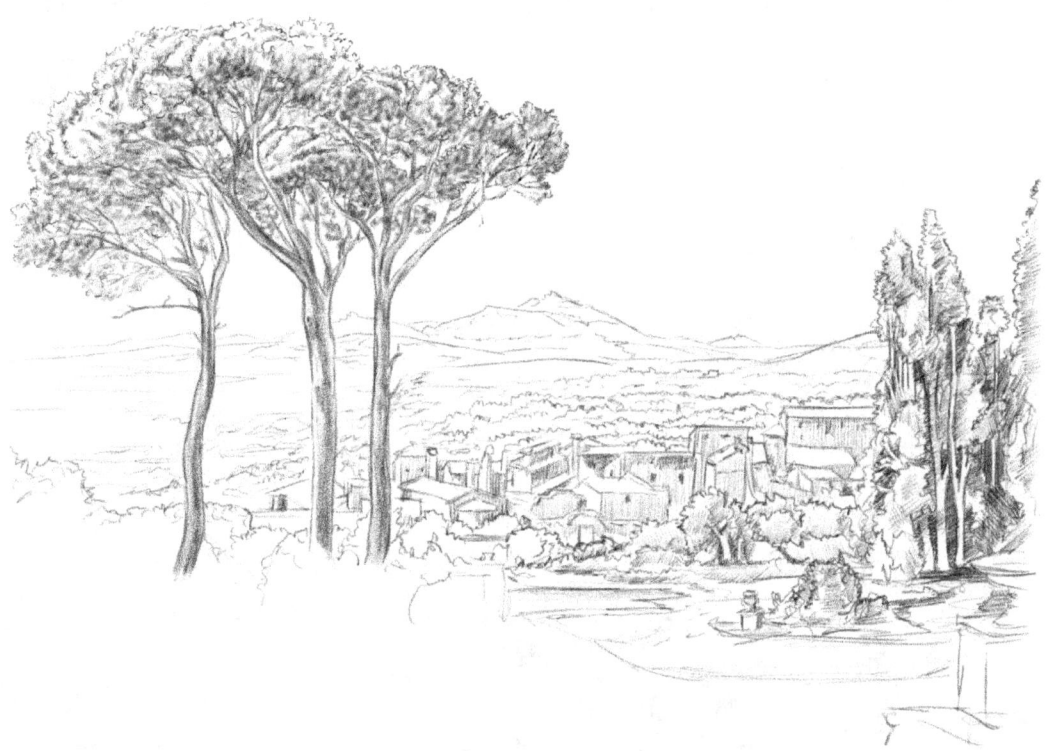

Now try to increase the contrast of the city by setting dark accents. Shadows cast from the roofs onto the walls can be drawn very dark, as can windows. However, only small, very dark areas should be created. The group of trees and the bushes in front of the city will be darkened even more to create a contrast to the lighter houses.

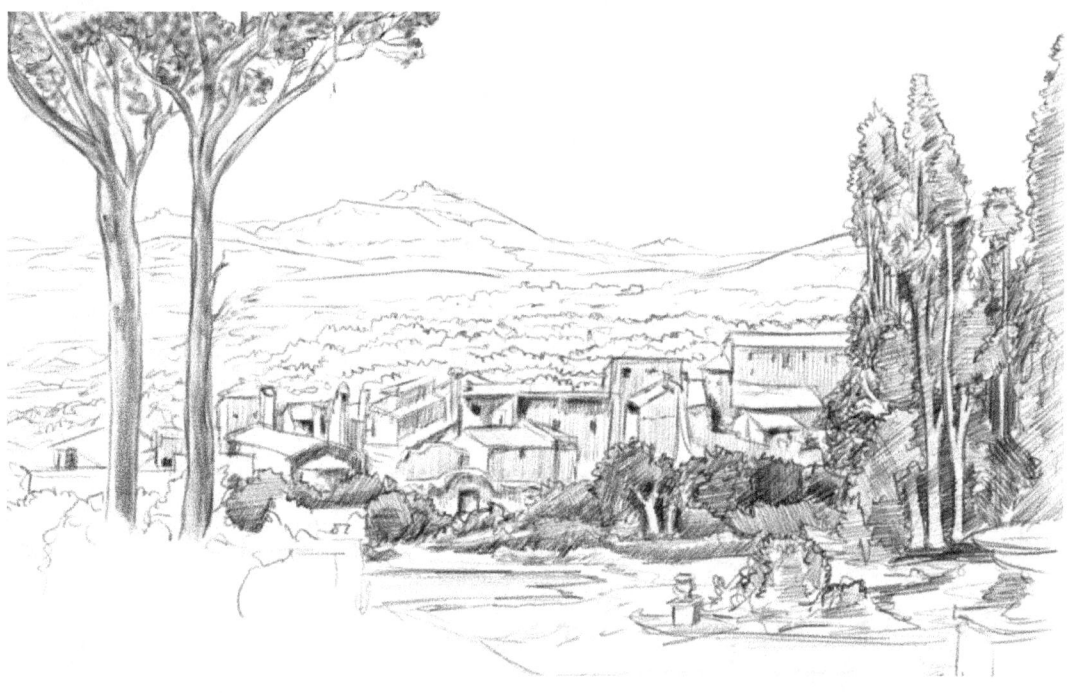

Now you can display the background and the clouds. The trees behind the city should be hatched relatively darkly. The houses of the city stand out optically because they are surrounded by darker trees and bushes. Also some dark dots, which are created by windows and shadows, create strong light-dark contrasts in this step.

Then compare your drawing with the original. Make corrections where necessary. Then the drawing is finished.

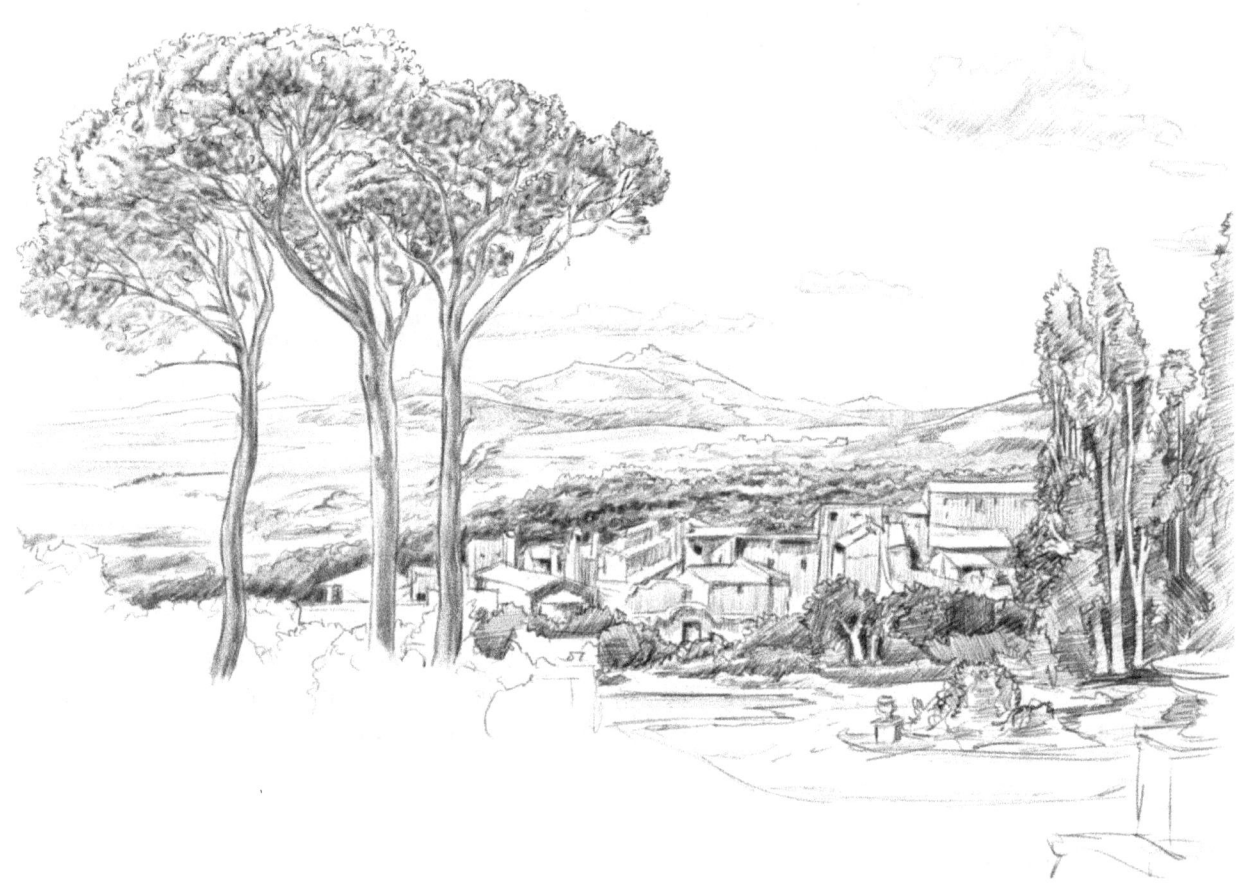

Template for quick practice:

6.5 Drawing a Dominant Sky

While in the earlier landscape paintings the distribution of the picture surface showed 2/3 land and 1/3 sky, in the 17th century the Dutch painters reversed this weighting. More and more often landscape pictures now showed the sky with 2/3 of the picture surface.

A very good and extremely well-known example of this is the painting "The Windmill at Wijk bij Duurstede" by Jacob van Ruisdael. Van Ruisdael was a Dutch baroque landscape painter who was born in Haarlem, Holland, in 1628/29. The windmill is one of his most important works.
The main focus of the painting is on the sky with its dramatic cloud constellation. But also the whole composition is remarkable. Use your knowledge from the chapter on pictorial design and composition to decipher van Ruisdael's methods.

Let's get started

Start your drawing with a reasonably detailed preliminary drawing. Of course, you can approach it slowly and start with a gentle sketch of the rough outlines or use the grid method if you use the original image as a template.

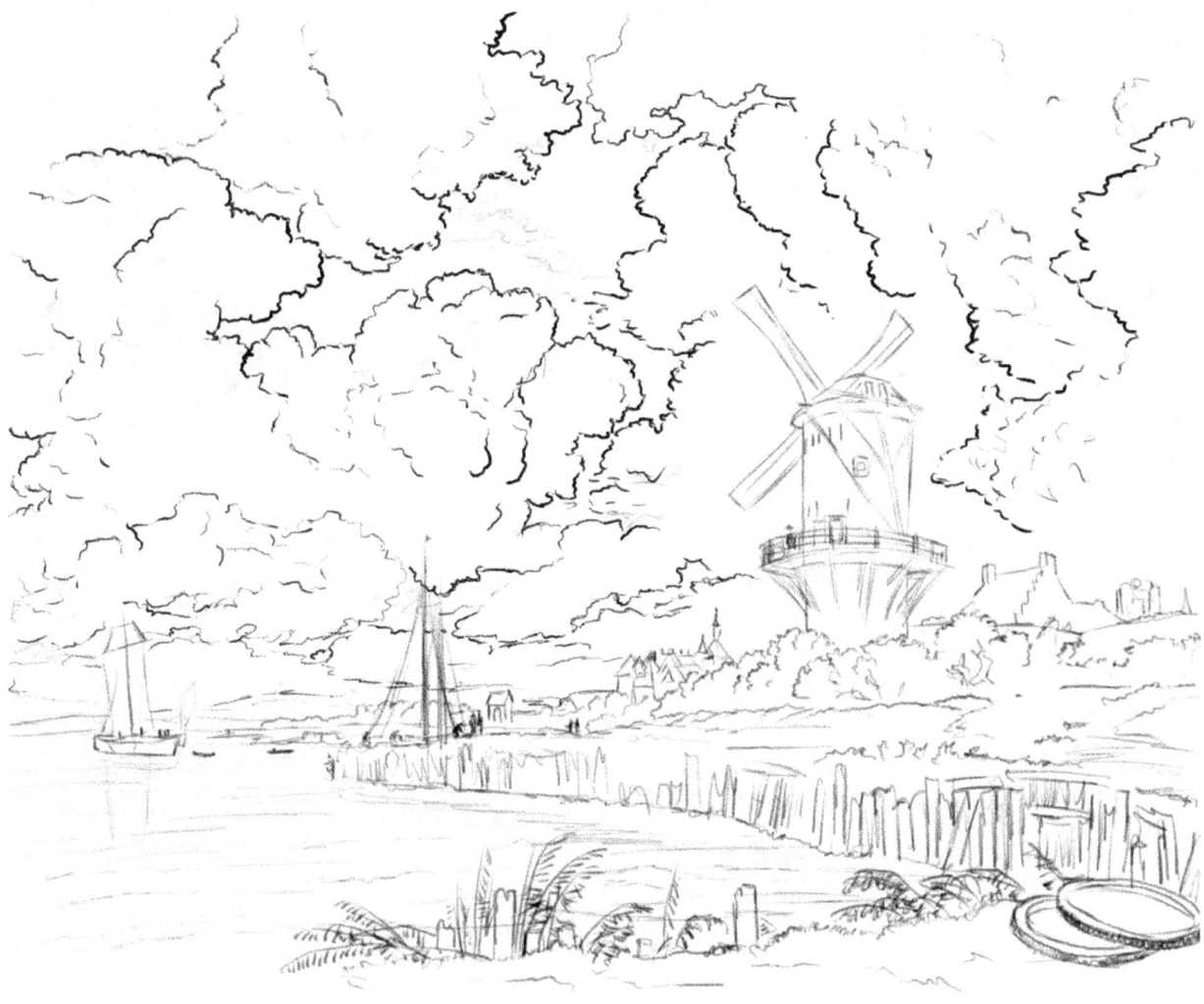

Now draw the shading of the clouds with the pencil. You can use small semicircles for hatching, but also other hatching techniques.

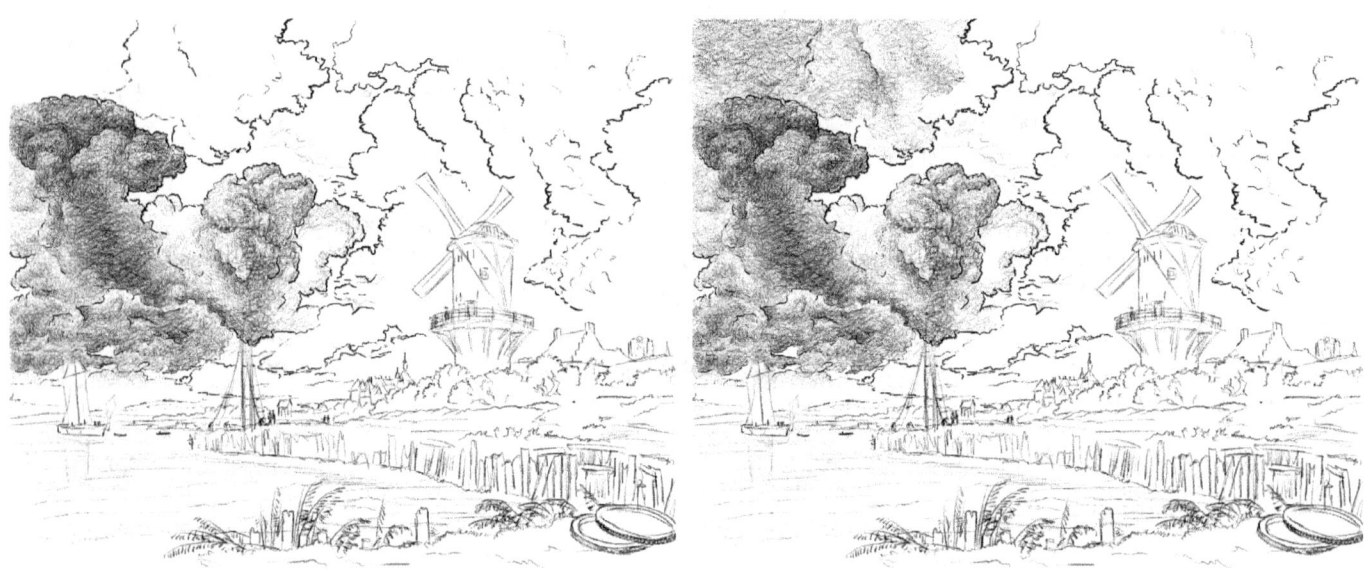

Gradually the sky is filled with clouds. If you want to draw in detail, you will be busy for an hour or two. If you want to work faster, you can do that as well. However, the effect of the image will be more like a sketch. This is by no means worse, but only different.

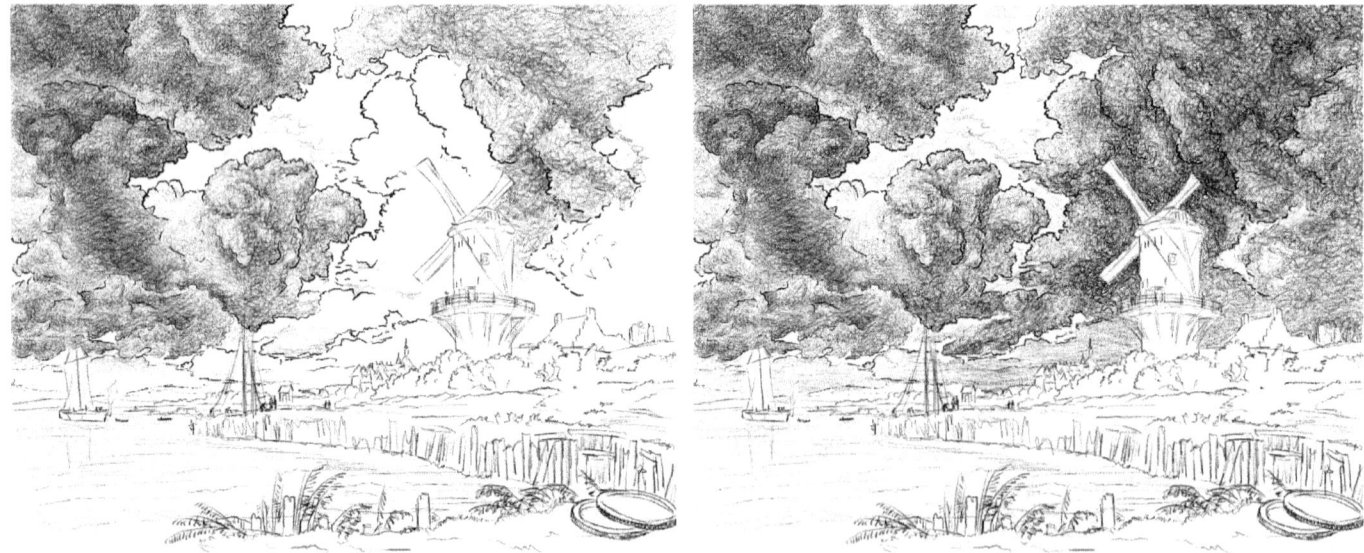

In the end, your work with the clouds should be critically viewed once again, but this time in its entirety. Compare your drawing with the original image and make corrections where necessary. For example, I have made some parts even darker.

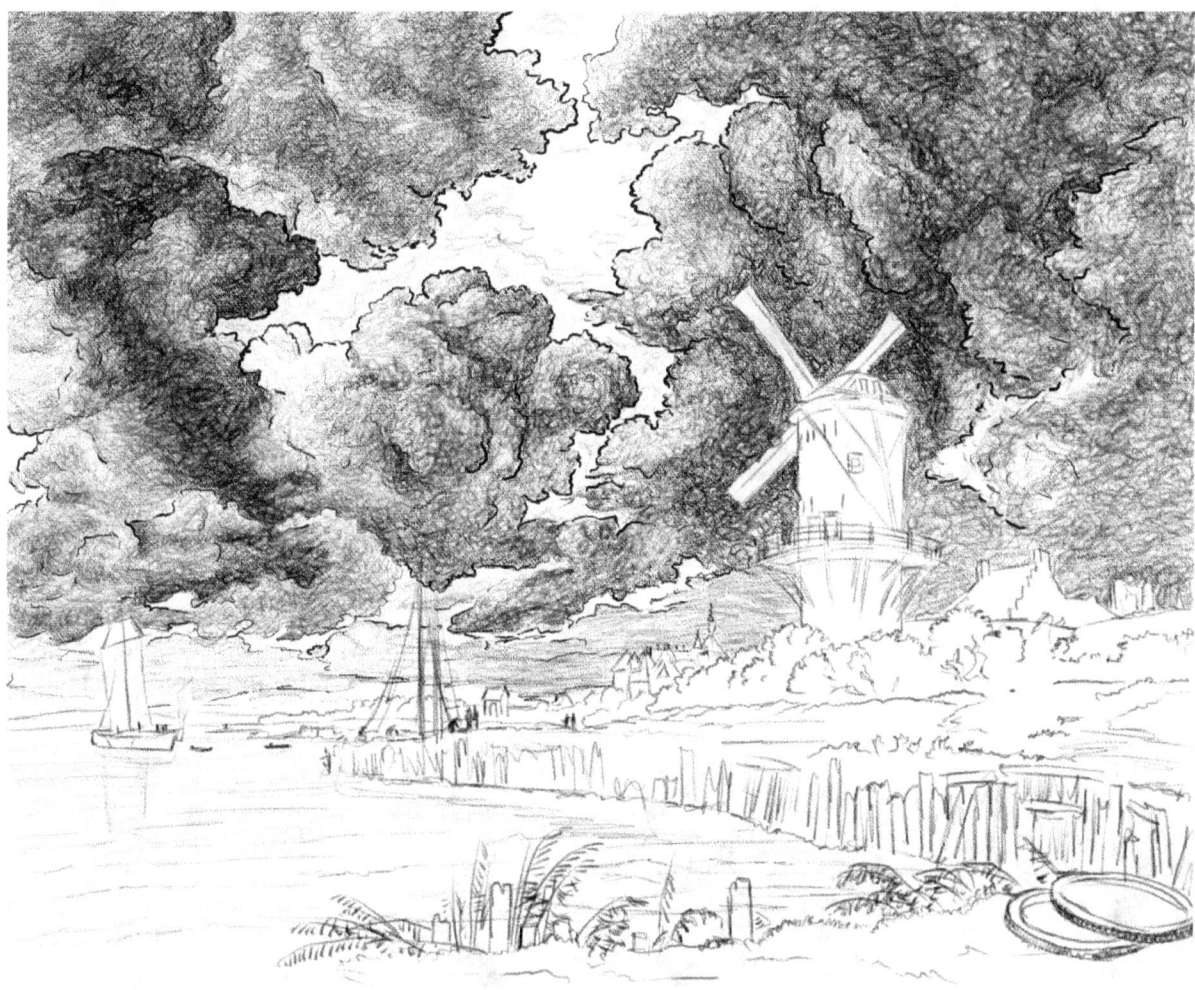

We continue now with all motifs that are on the ground. Regarding the mill, you should make sure that it is set off from the sky. Therefore, try to make the wings of the windmill bright in order to create a tonal contrast to the dark clouds behind them.

The same applies to the house to the right of the windmill. You draw the bushes the way you have previously learned.

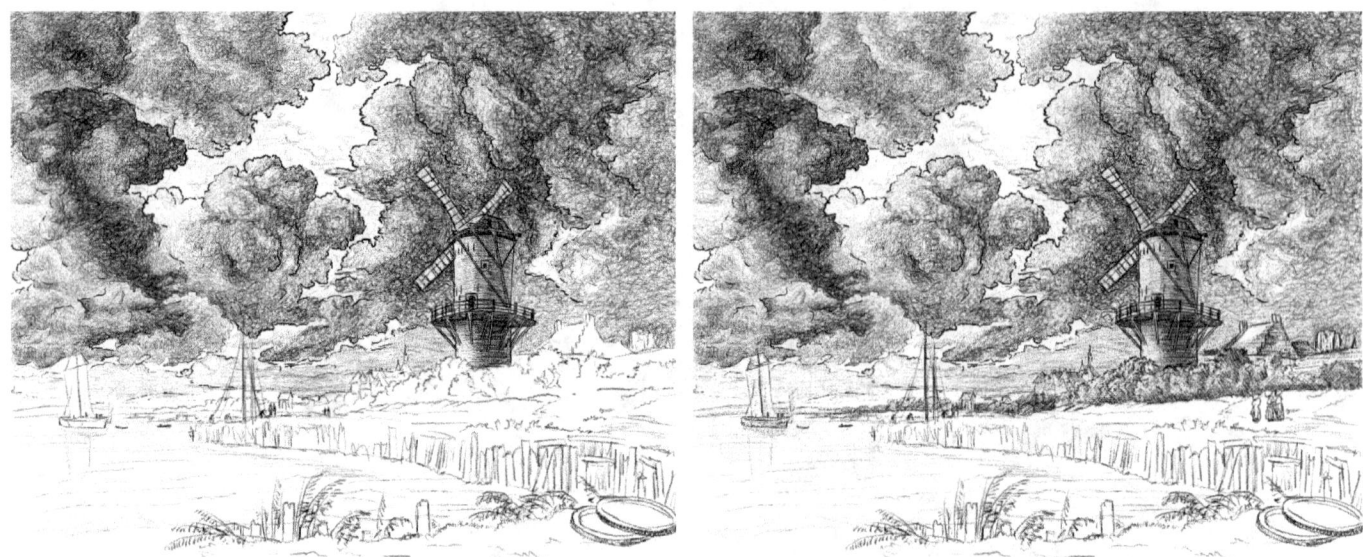

Now the next step involves the meadow and the bank reinforcement. Pay attention as well here to the people in the picture. Some are closer, while others are very far away and can only be recognized as small black silhouettes. You can use your knowledge about the representation of wooden structures to reinforce the banks. Then the water is next.

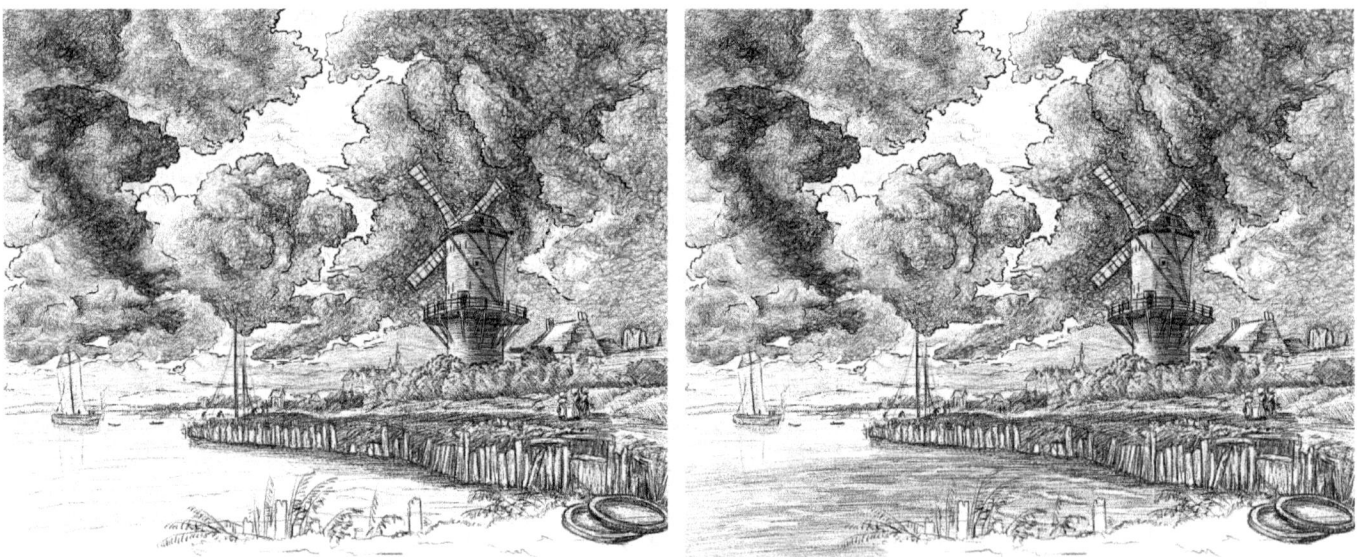

In this last step, I have included small waves on the surface of the water. Their light edges can also be created with the help of an eraser pencil, if they have not already been planned in advance.

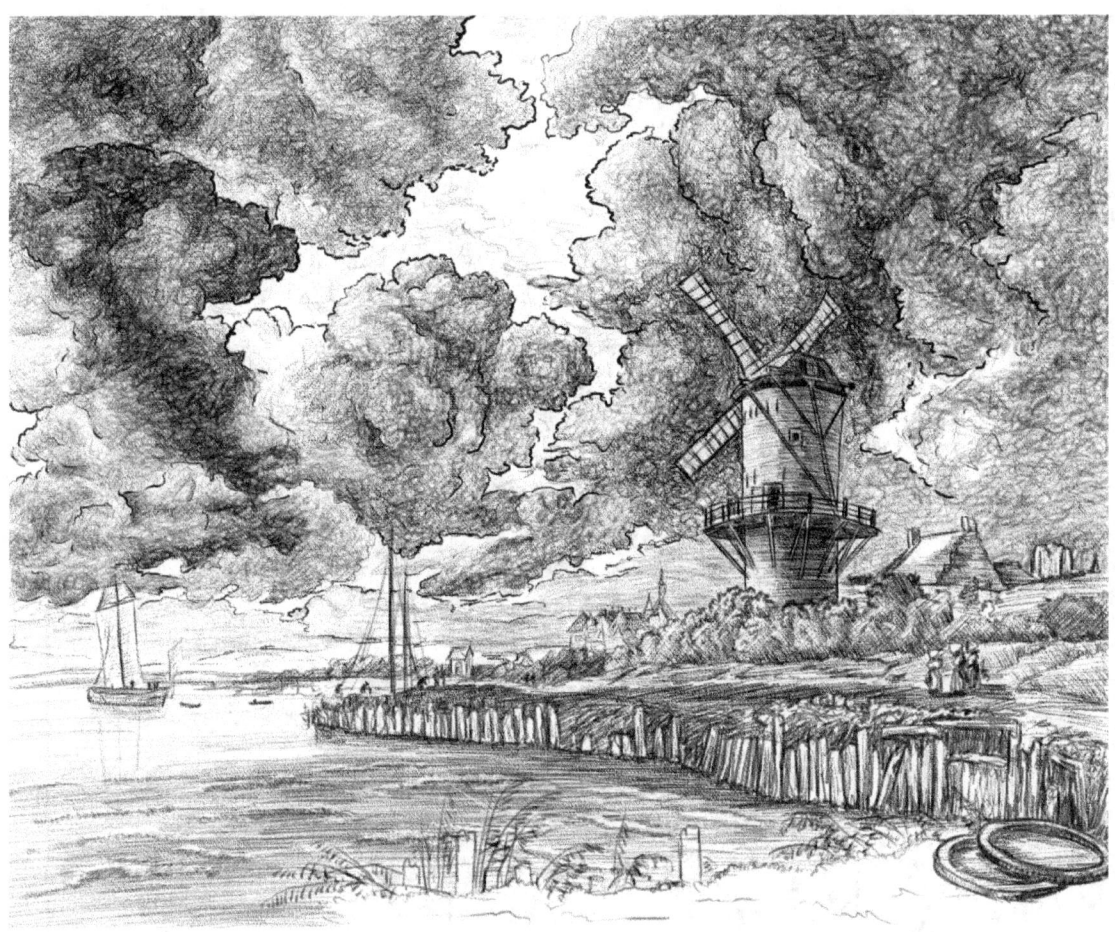

Picture Composition

When you copy a picture, always pause for a while and examine the composition of the work. The composition of Wijk bij Duurstede's windmill, for example, is very well thought out. The room layout corresponds approximately to the rule of thirds, with about 2/3 being occupied by the sky. The windmill penetrates the space of the sky and extends into the second third. Several diagonals appear in the form of the bank, the windmill wheels and the clouds. They open the space and direct our gaze through the picture. Persons who are at different distances also direct us through the picture at the level of the horizon. The impressive cloud constellation also creates very strong dynamics.

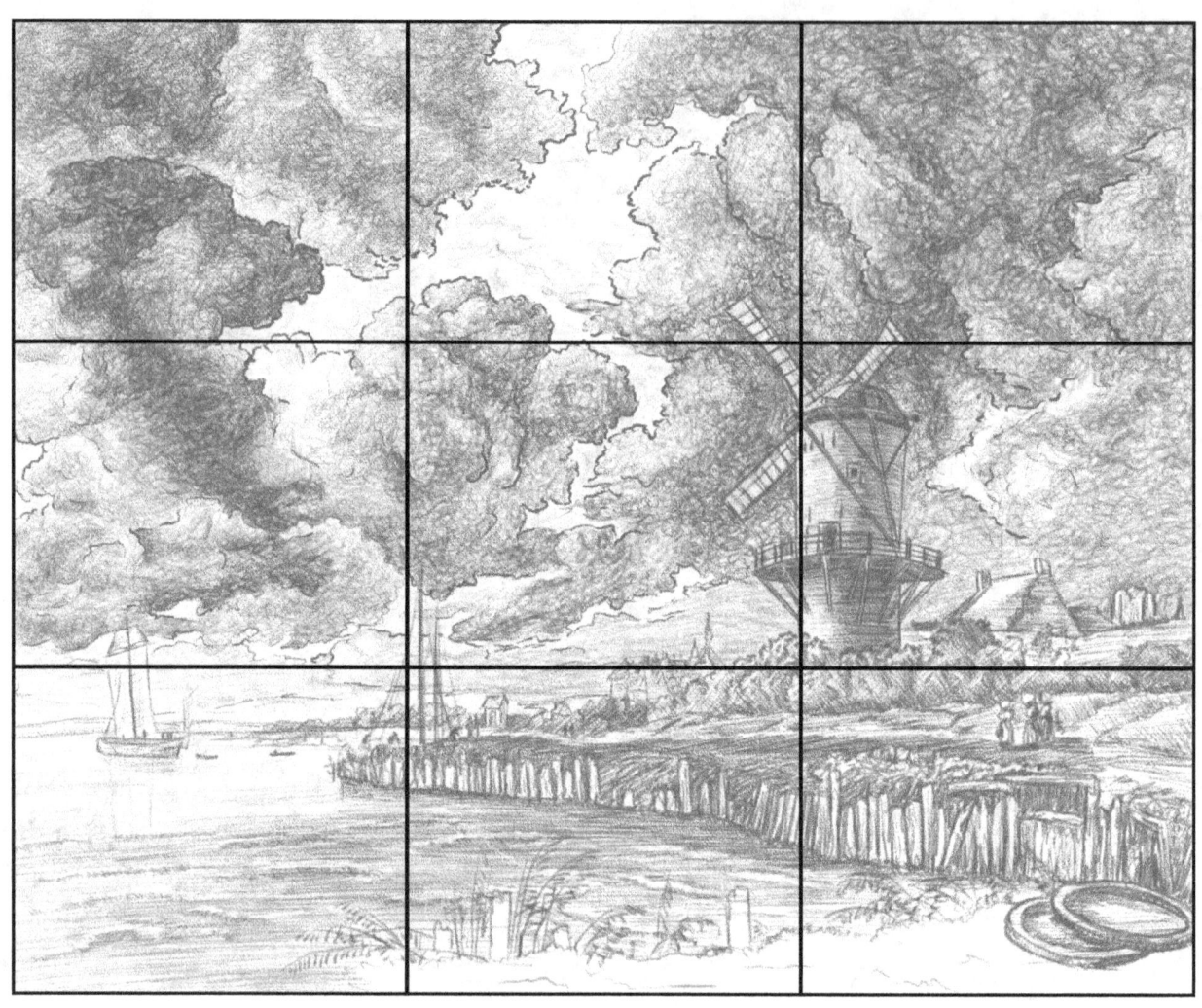
Subdivision of the picture using the rule of thirds

6.6 Architecture in Indian Ink

The drawing in this exercise corresponds in style to Urban Sketching - a drawing style in which urban scenes are quickly sketched and then colored with colors or monochrome shading. The drawing tool used in this case was an ink pencil for the first sketch. The shading was done with a brush and ink.

Do not be afraid to try out other drawing tools. Especially with ink you can create fascinating and very contrasting pictures. The line with ink and ink is strong and clear and creates characteristic drawings.

Let's get started

Try to sketch loosely in this example. Strokes don't have to be straight and don't have to lead to perfect shapes. The loose stroke only makes the drawing appear more alive.

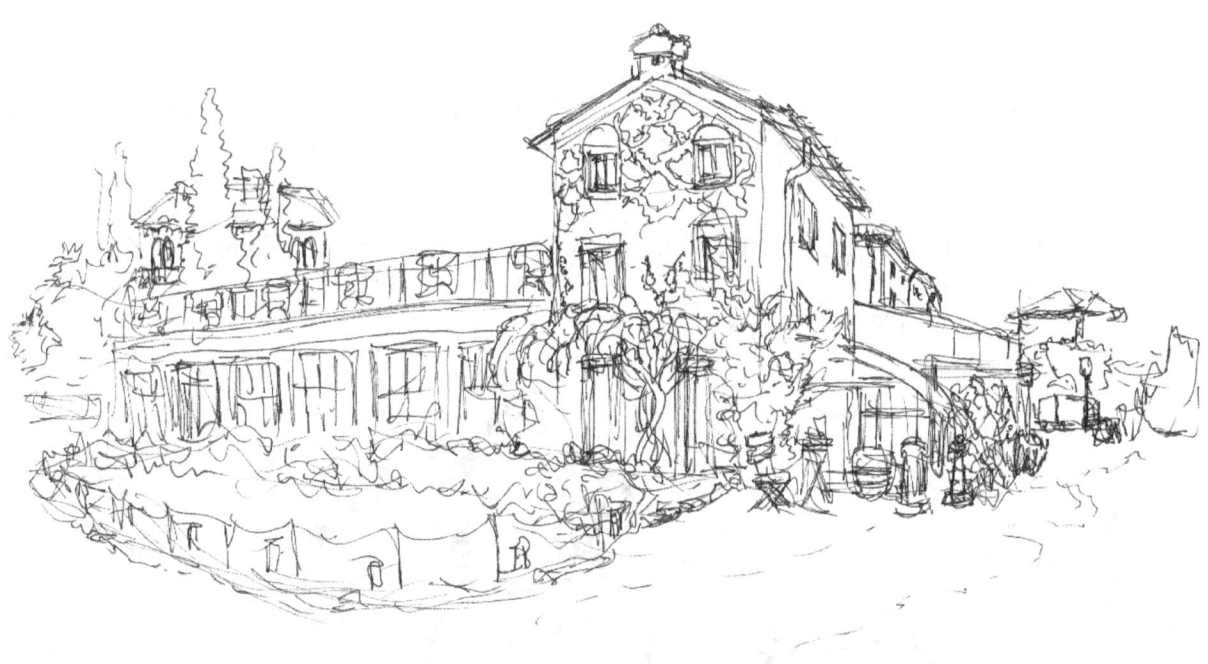

Let's start by inserting the initial light application of shadow. Use a brush and apply the ink diluted with water carefully onto the paper.

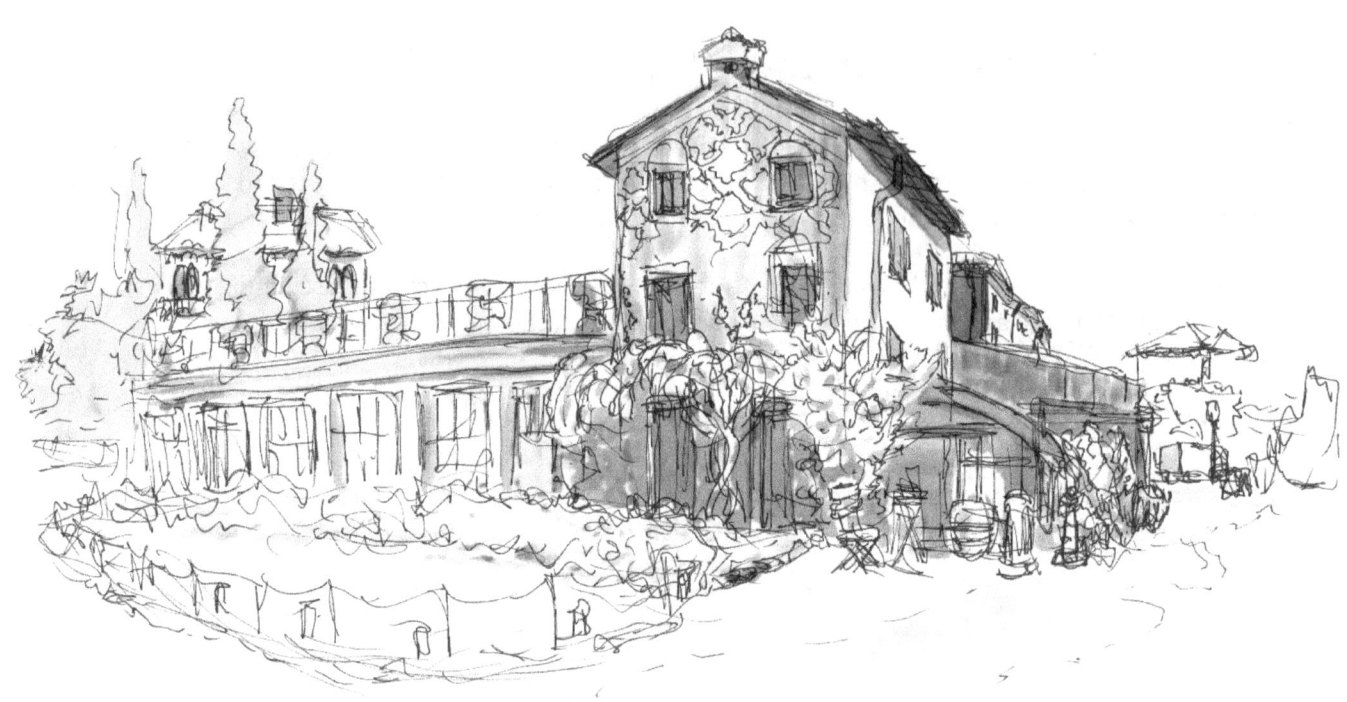

When designing the drawing, it is important to set accents through strong contrasts. Strong contrasts attract the viewer's attention and should therefore be placed precisely where the compositional center of the picture should be.

Try not to copy the motif exactly. It is better to take advantage of your artistic freedom and use the methods of image design. For example, contrasts can be weakened or intensified, parts of the picture can be left as pure line drawings and objects can be moved, removed or added.

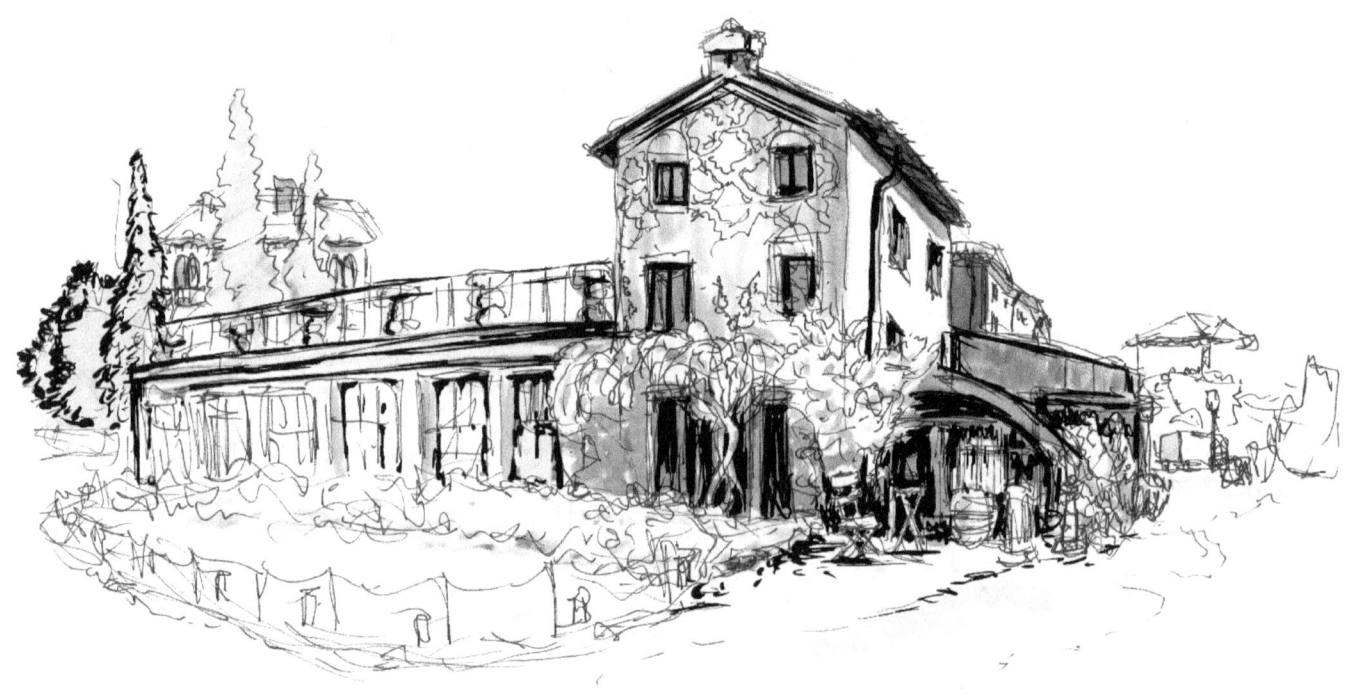

Finally, the drawing is given the final touch by adding details. I drew the patterns on the house and the texture of the plants in this step. On the right side I have also drawn the shadow of a tree, which is not visible in the picture. Dark areas at the edges of a picture keep the viewer's gaze in the picture.

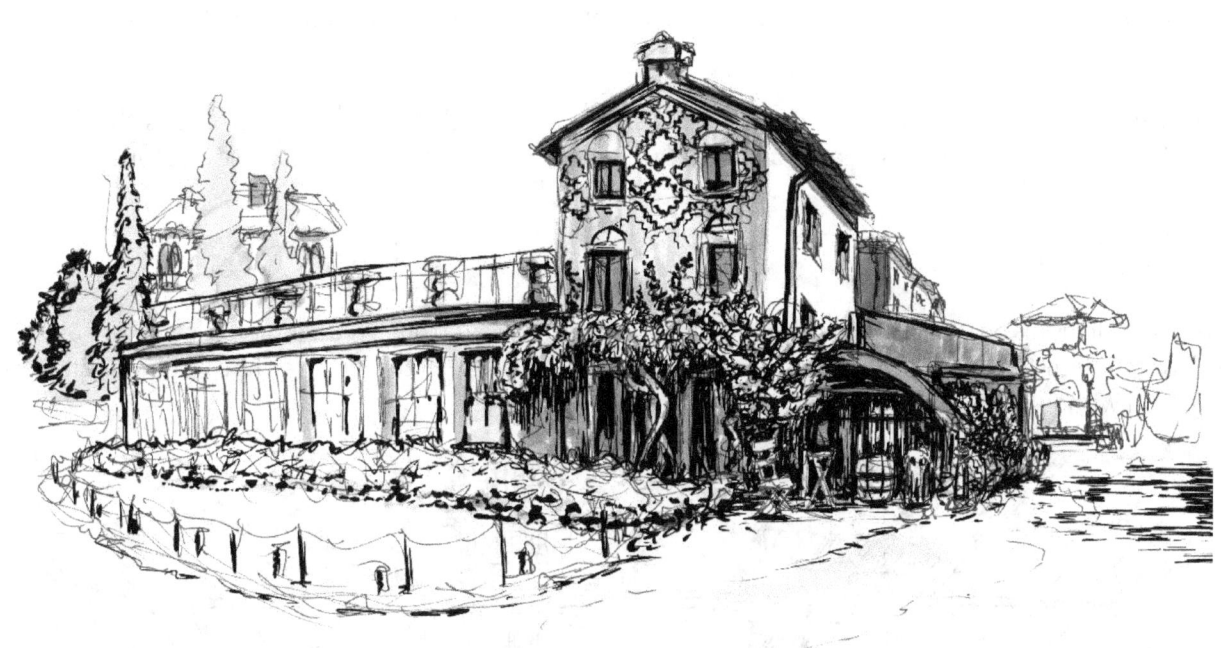

In my drawing I have also shown a restaurant in Bardolino, Italy. I photographed the picture during a holiday and afterwards drew it from the original photo.

Template for quick practice:

6.7 Steel Structures in the City

City views also belong to the field of landscape drawing and at this point we would like to try our hand at such a representation. The aim is to capture an urban scene in which the structures of a steel construction shape the appearance. With this exercise a new aspect is to be introduced and shown regarding the diversity of landscape drawing.

The picture depicts a scene in Chicago (USA). The steel structure that runs over the road is the scaffolding of a tram. The tracks run directly over the road. I created the drawing from a photo I took several years ago.

Let's get started

I used an Indian ink pen as my drawing medium. As with the view from Bardolino, you can start by drawing the basic sketch with loose lines. Also the cars, which are to be seen in the picture, have been depicted relatively simply and without details.

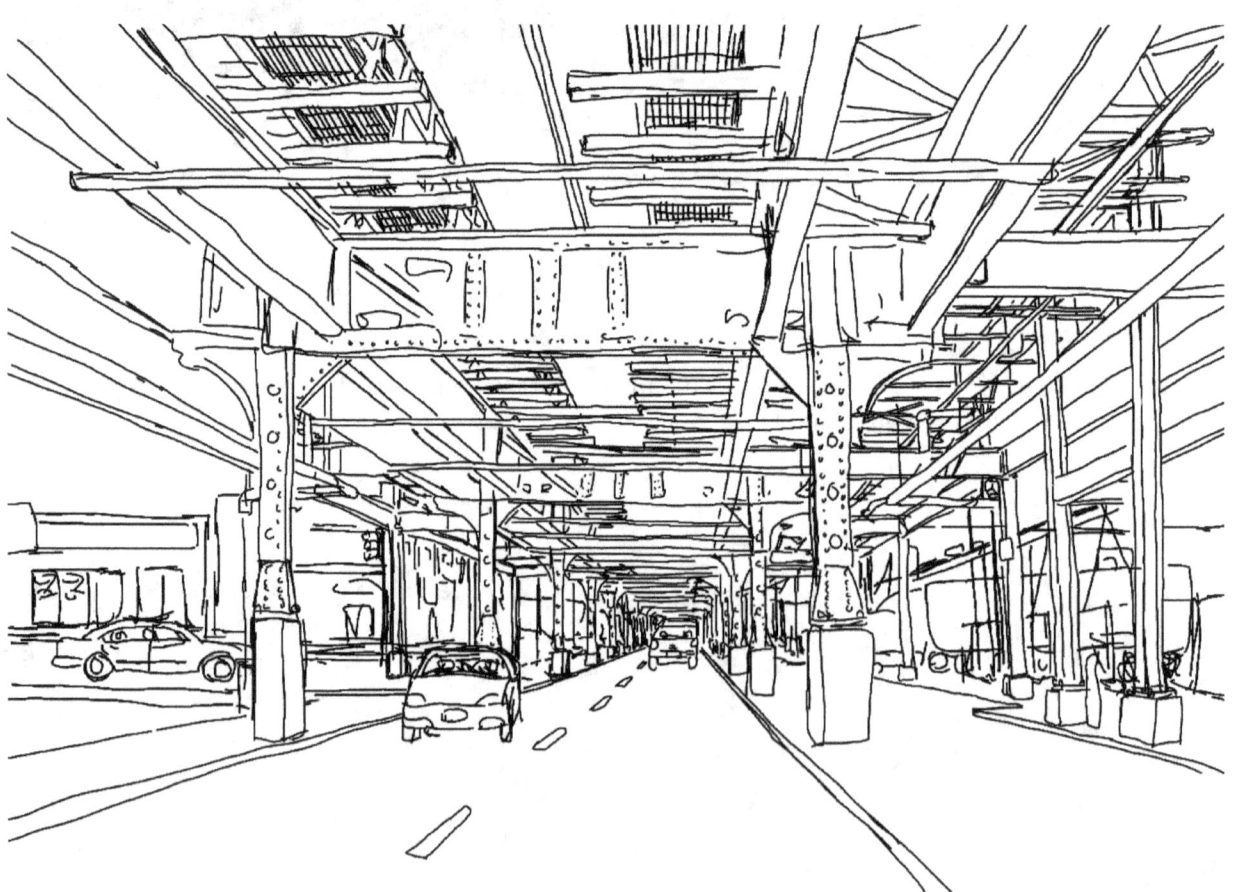

After the preliminary drawing is finished, you can start shading. The technique of my choice was hatching with an Indian ink pen. I chose parallel hatching as the method of hatching. When drawing, you should make sure that you create extremely dark areas as well as areas that remain completely white.

Studies – Drawing Landscapes

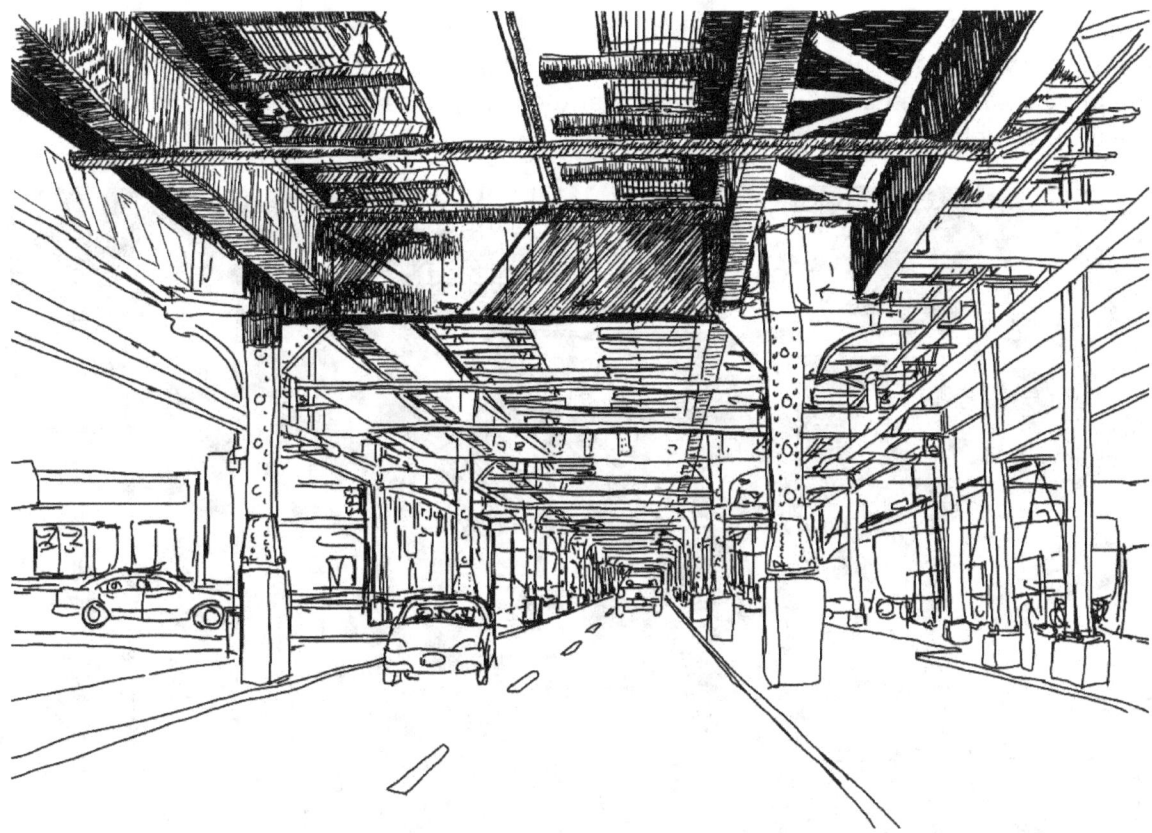

The play of light and shadow makes this drawing particularly interesting. Especially on the large steel beam at the top you can find strong sunlight next to vivid shadows.

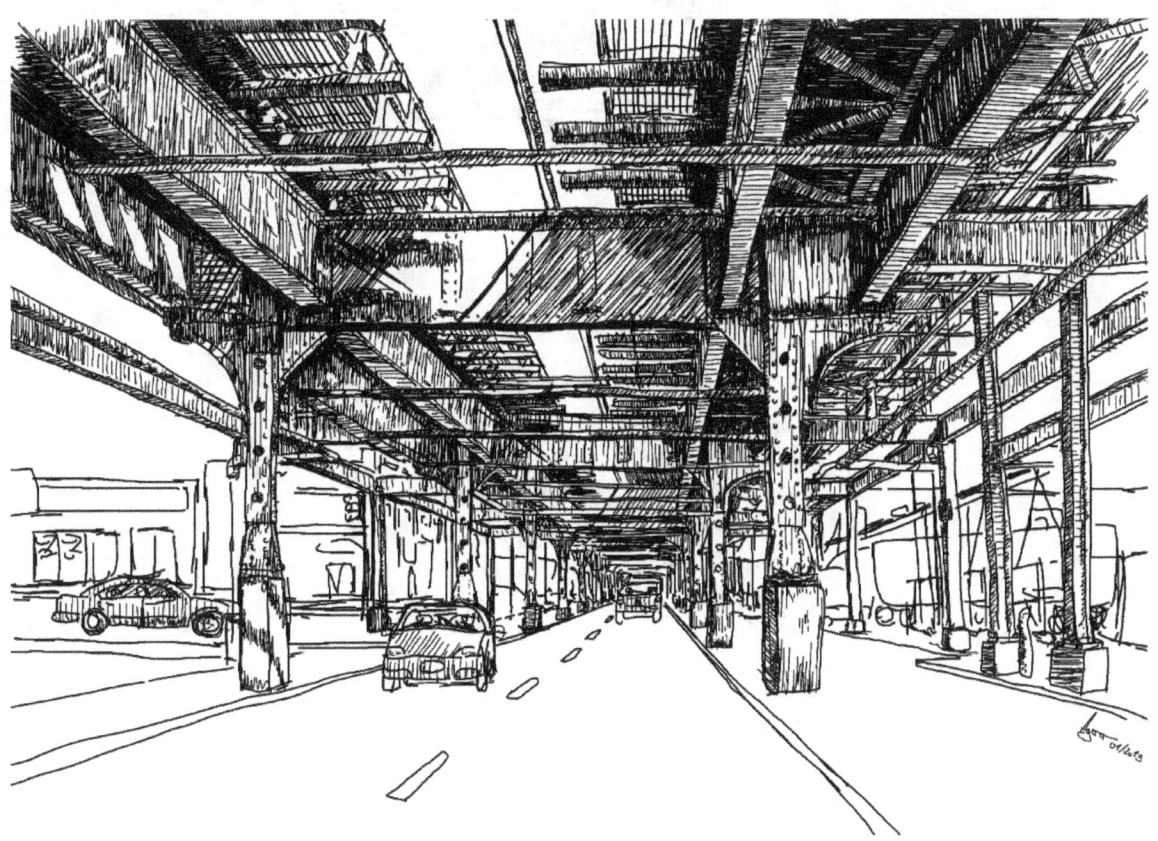

At the end the shadows are hatched, which are cast onto the ground by the steel columns and the superstructure. The sunlight comes from the right, causing the shadows to spread to the left. The background to the left and right can be left as a line drawing so that the drawing is not flooded with hatching. This would only make the picture confusing.

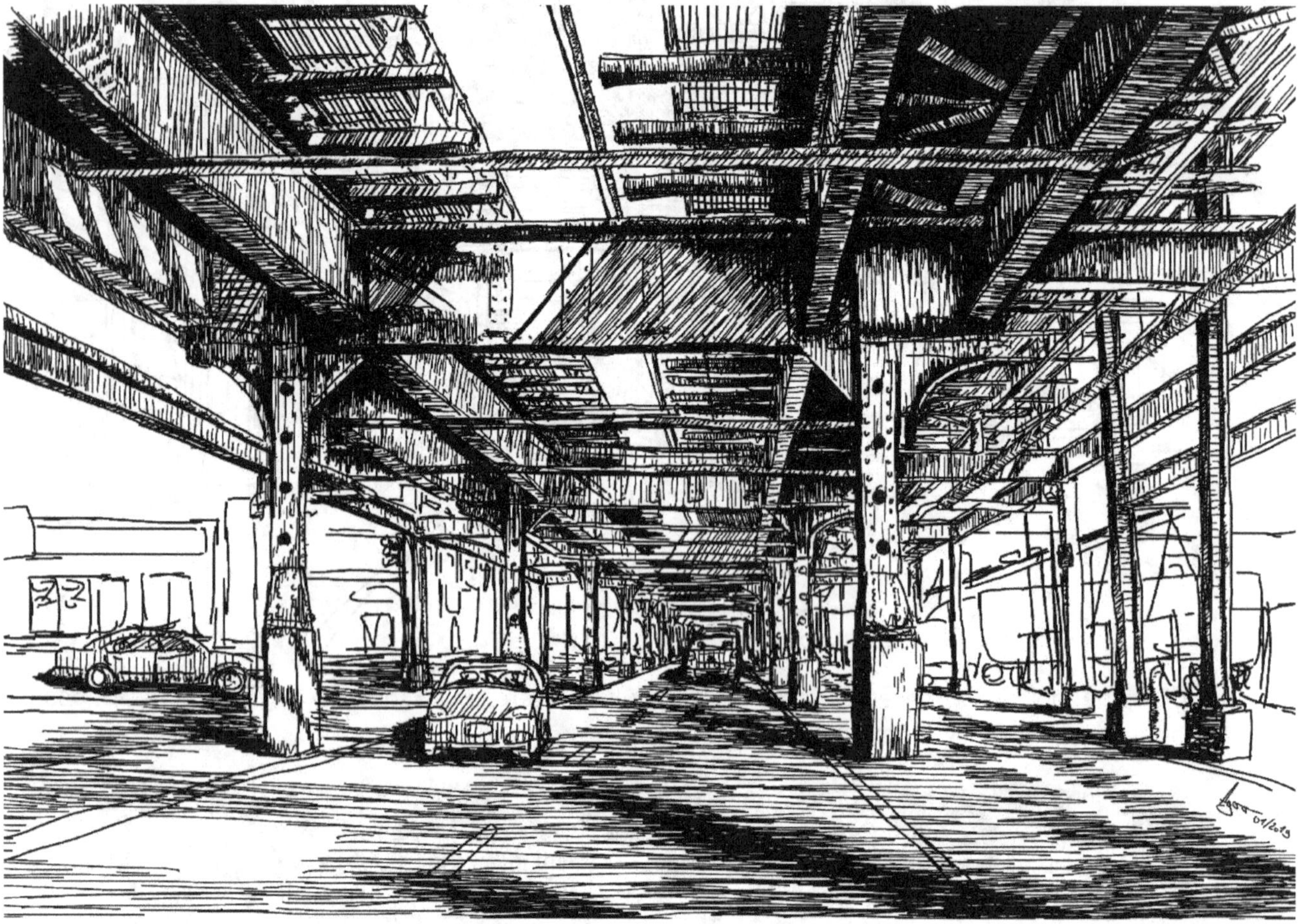

Template for quick practice:

Studies – Drawing Landscapes

6.8 The Elements
Clouds, Mountains, Forests, Water, Rocks

The next exercise includes almost everything a landscape has to offer. You will find a cloudy sky, a mountain, a forest, a lake including reflections, rocks, stones and last but not least a bird standing on a stone.

Like the view of Tivoli, this picture is based on a painting by Carl Rottmann. You can see the Hintersee, which is located in Upper Bavaria.

In my version of the landscape painting I drew with a pencil and did not hold back when it came to creating clear contour lines in order to stress the graphic character of the picture.

Let's get started

In the following picture you can see my preliminary drawing, which is already relatively detailed.

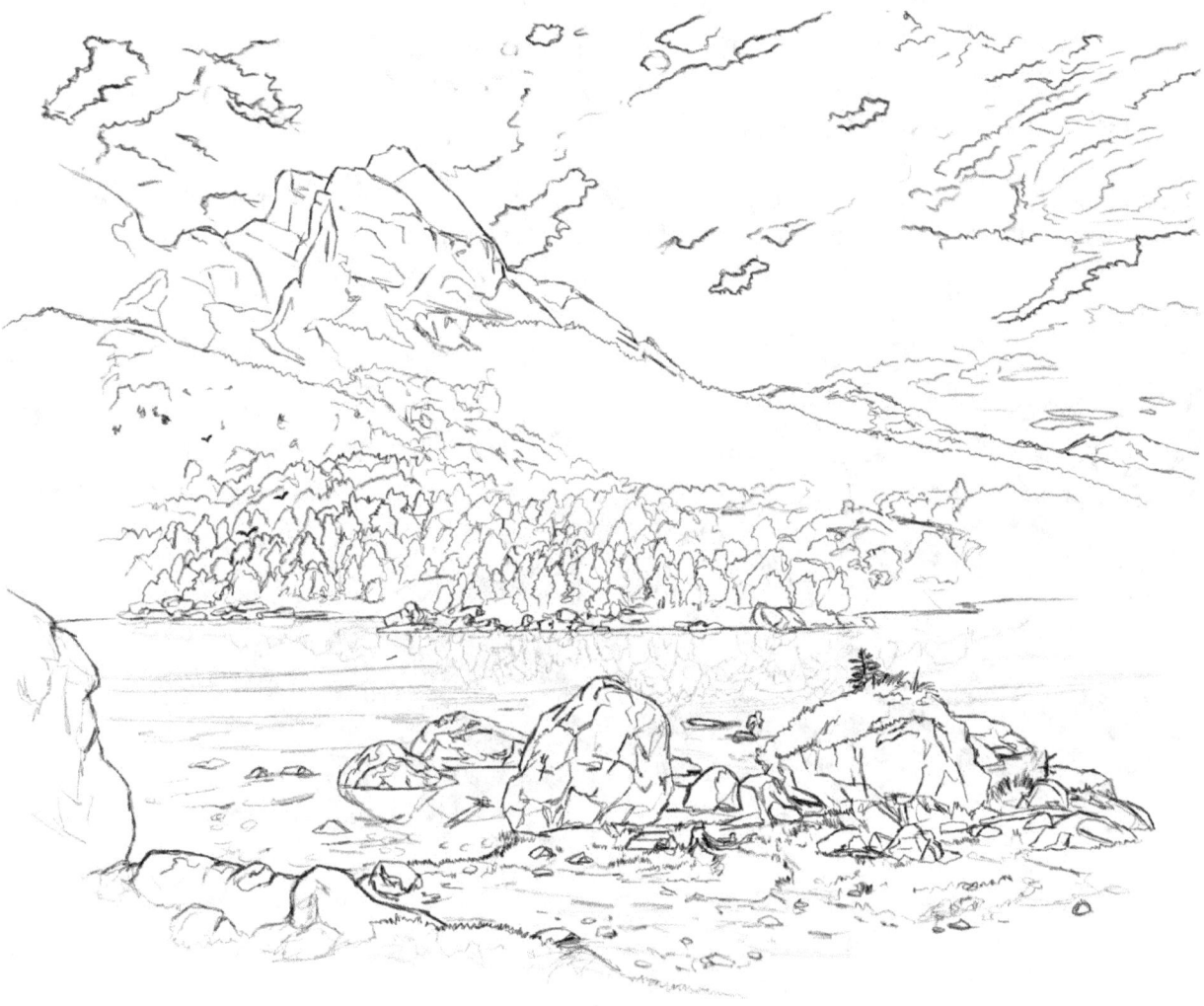

We continue with the top part of the drawing. Draw the sky and the clouds as you learned to do in one of the previous chapters. The same applies to the depiction of the mountain. You can work with parallel hatching of different orientations.

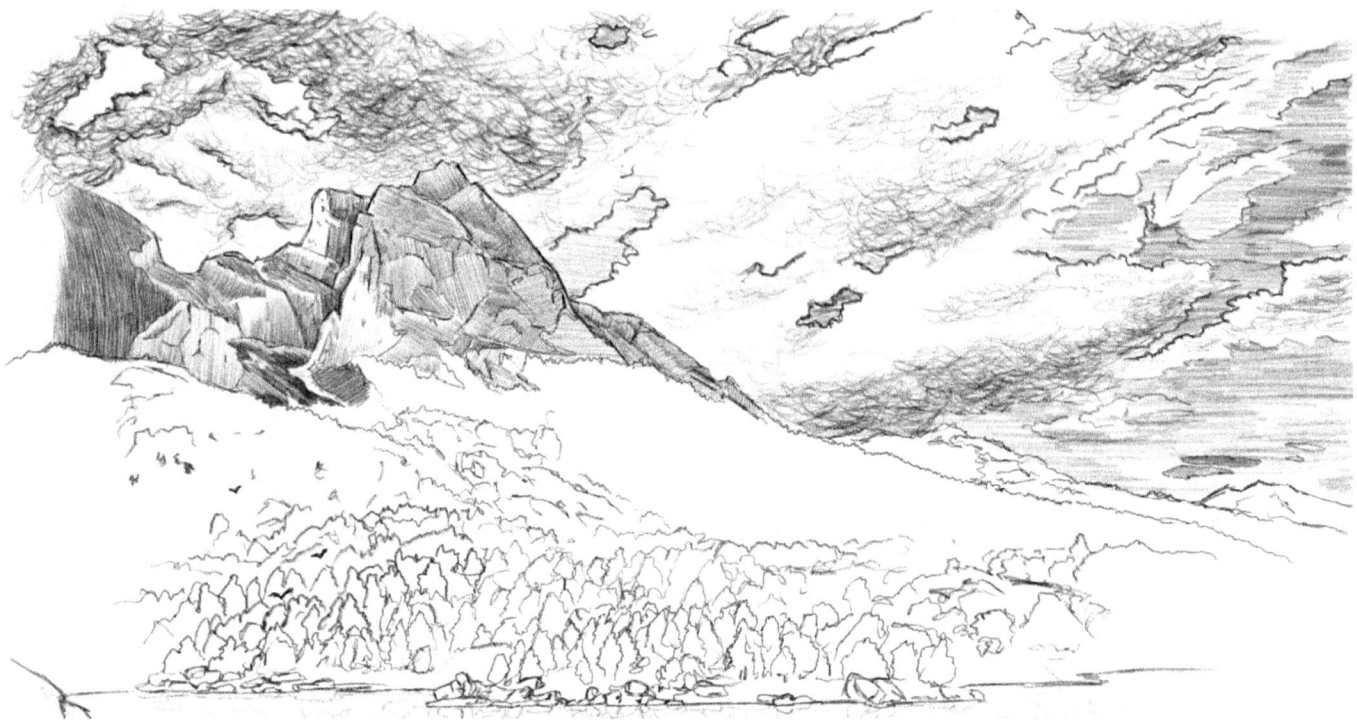

Below the mountain there is a forest. The more distant part is best indicated only schematically. Draw the forest relatively dark, so that later a contrast to other areas of the picture is created.

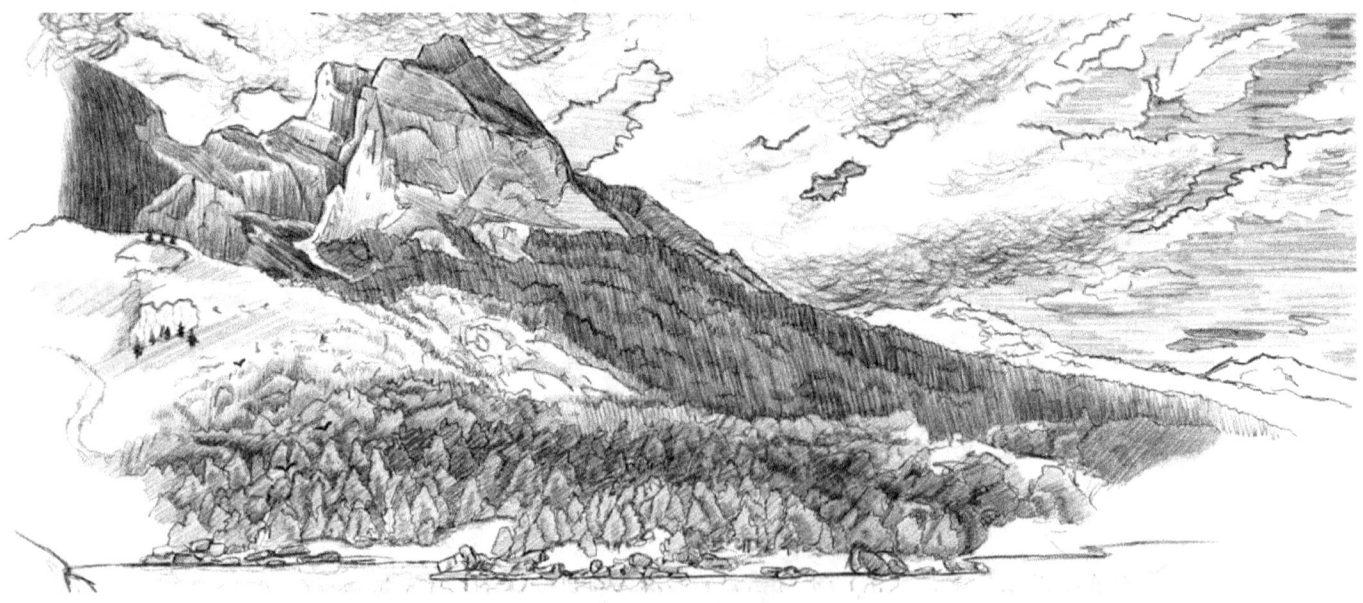

The water surface of the lake is calm and for this reason the trees and rocks near the shore reflect very nicely in the water. The reflection of the first row of trees can still be seen relatively clearly, everything behind it appears weaker and weaker.

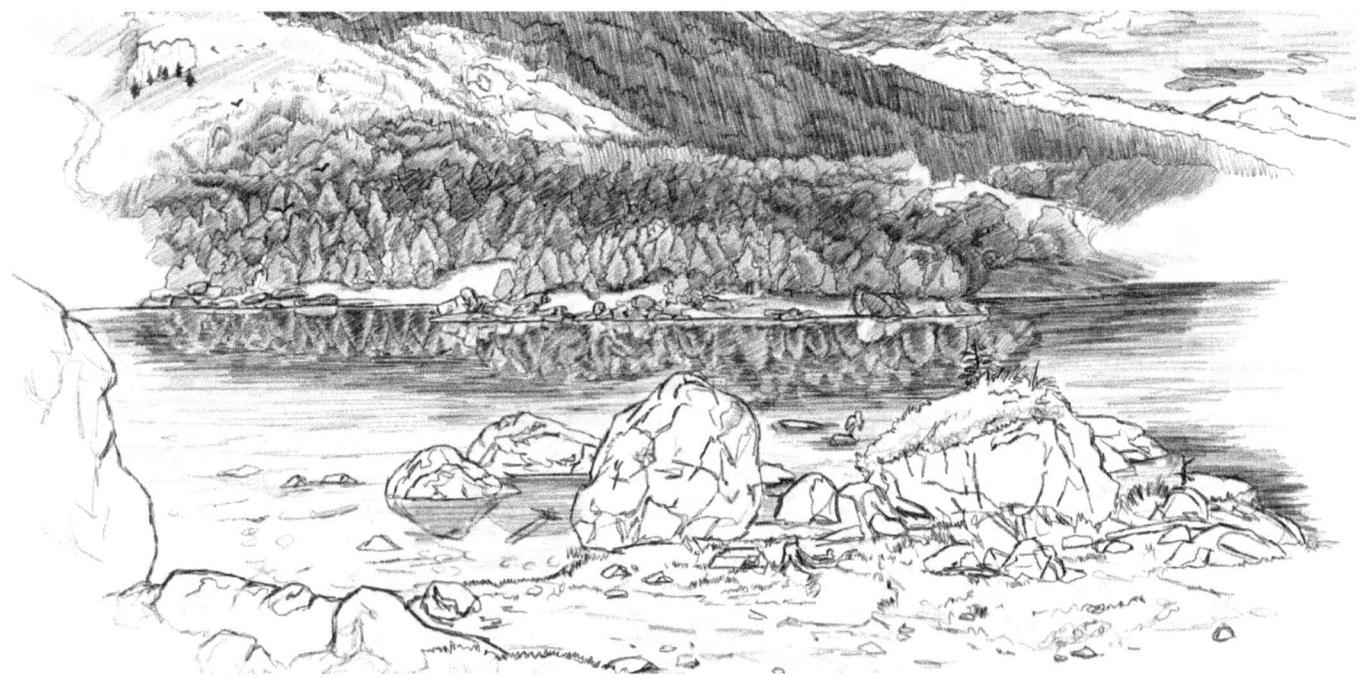

Now we proceed to the rocks in the foreground, which are the eyecatcher of the drawing. Provide the picture with as strong a contrast as possible here. Draw the shadows with the darkest tonal value in the picture. This naturally attracts the viewer's gaze.

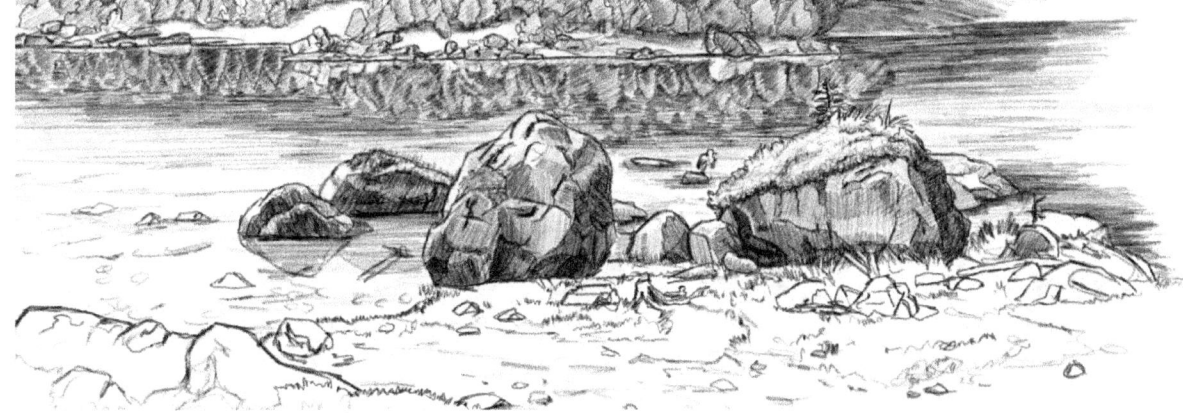

In the last step one draws the shadows of the rocks and a shadow which is thrown from the left side to the ground. Further rocks in the area left and below are only indicated by a line drawing.

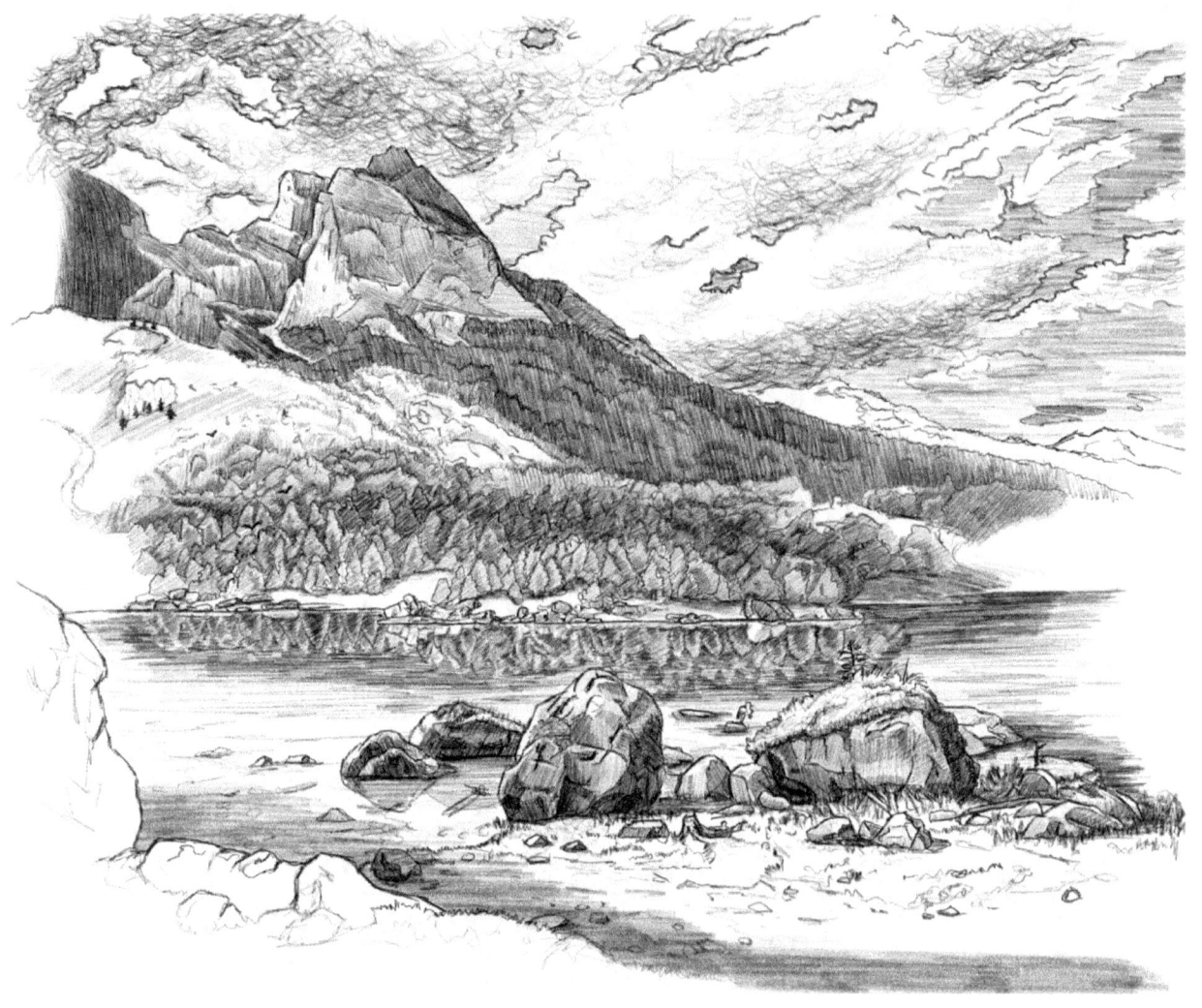

Studies – Drawing Landscapes

6.10 tyscapes

Cityscapes with skyscrapers are one of the most popular themes in landscape drawing today. In this study we want to try our hand at such a city vista. The scene shows a square in Chicago surrounded by a street and skyscrapers.

In addition to the skyscrapers, which provide a backdrop for the picture, the darkly highlighted street lamps are also important elements of the drawing, as they give the picture a structure and guide the viewer's gaze. The persons distributed over the open square are also decisive for the composition of the picture. They fill the room with life and attract the viewer's gaze most strongly.

Let's get started

In the following pictures you can see the origin of the preliminary drawing. The sketching style is loose. Limit yourself to the most important details for all objects. The figures can also be drawn relatively reduced. It is not necessary to depict facial features.

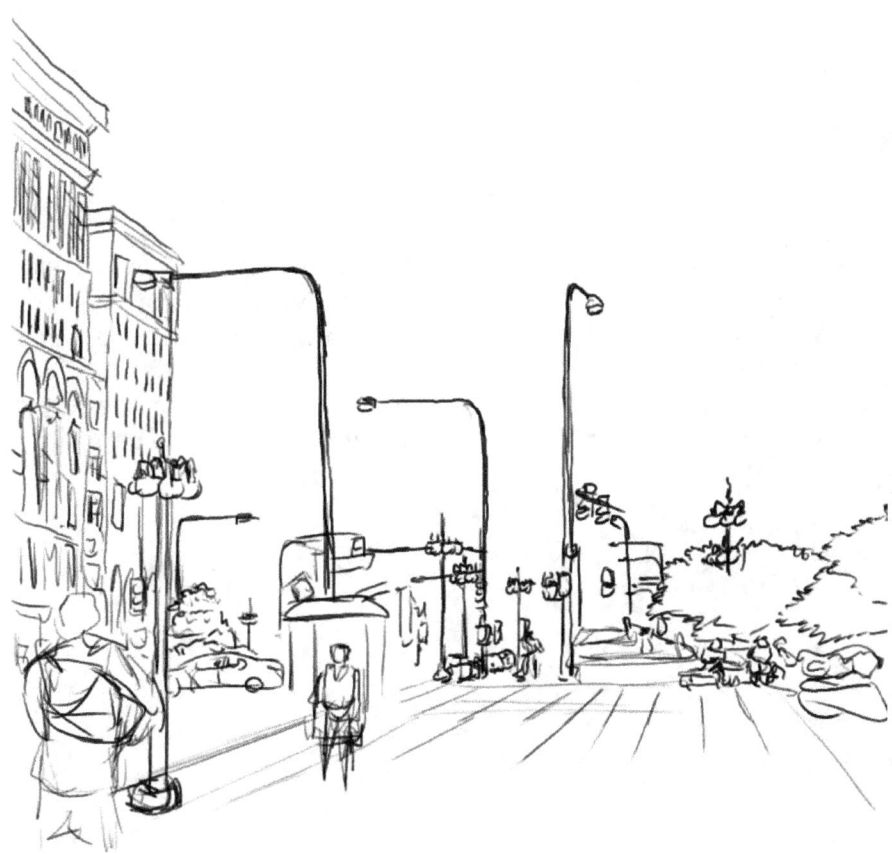

In the second step of the preliminary drawing I added two more persons, because otherwise the free space seemed quite empty. In reality the two persons were never present. I simply added them to make the picture more appealing. For an artist, that's fine.

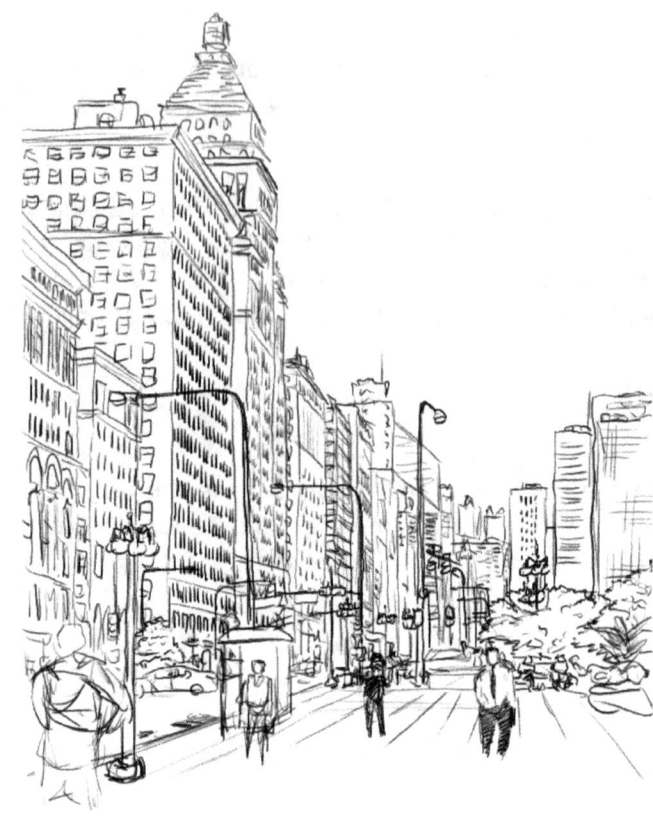

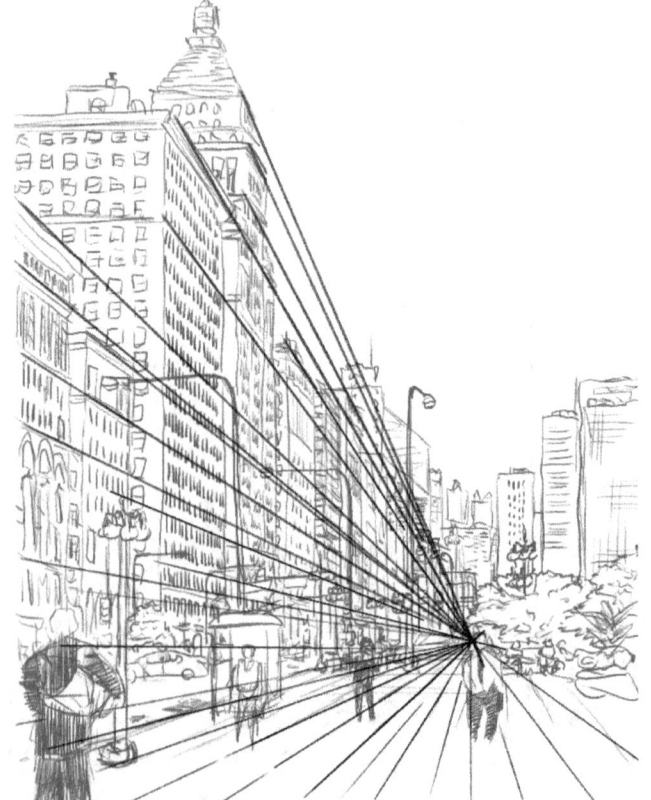

The drawing was also created from a central perspective. You can of course draw in alignment lines as a drawing aid to achieve even better results.

In the drawing you can see several alignment lines that help you to sketch the buildings.

Studies – Drawing Landscapes

When shading, you can start with the darkest tonal values to give the drawing structure from the very beginning.

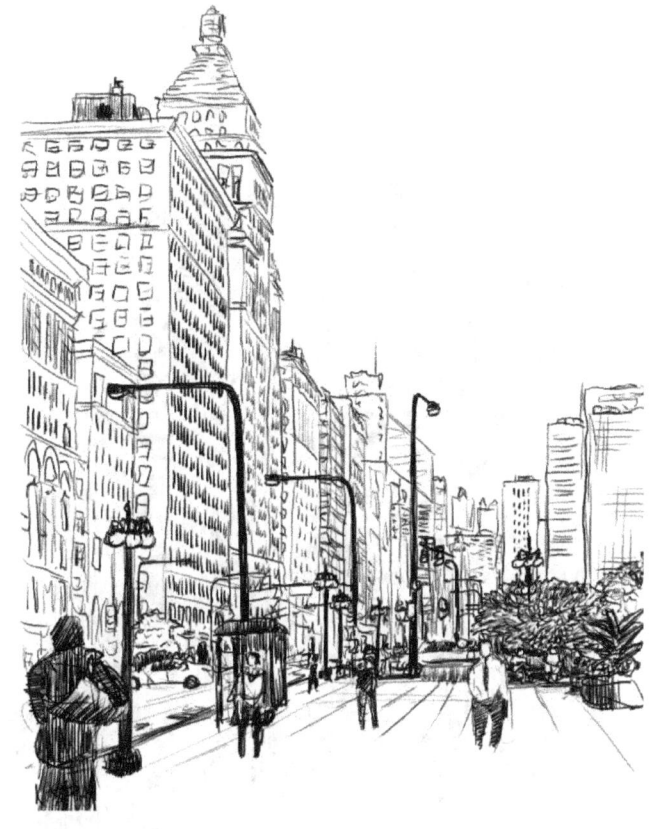

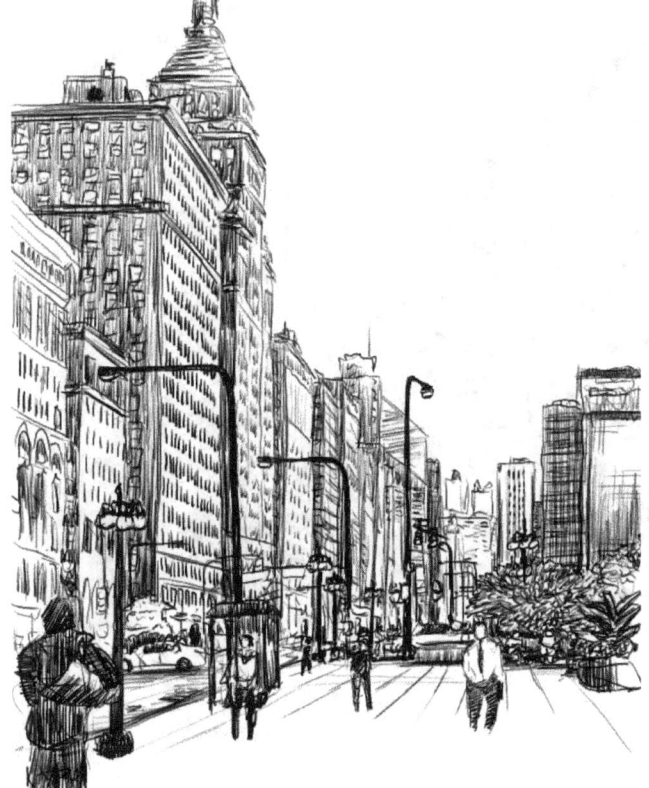

Then we fill in the background. Make sure that one side of the skyscrapers is in the shade and the other side is illuminated by the sun.

The last step we take now is to draw the shadows. This involves the people, the street lamps, the bus stop and the plants. The shadows add the finishing touches to the drawing.

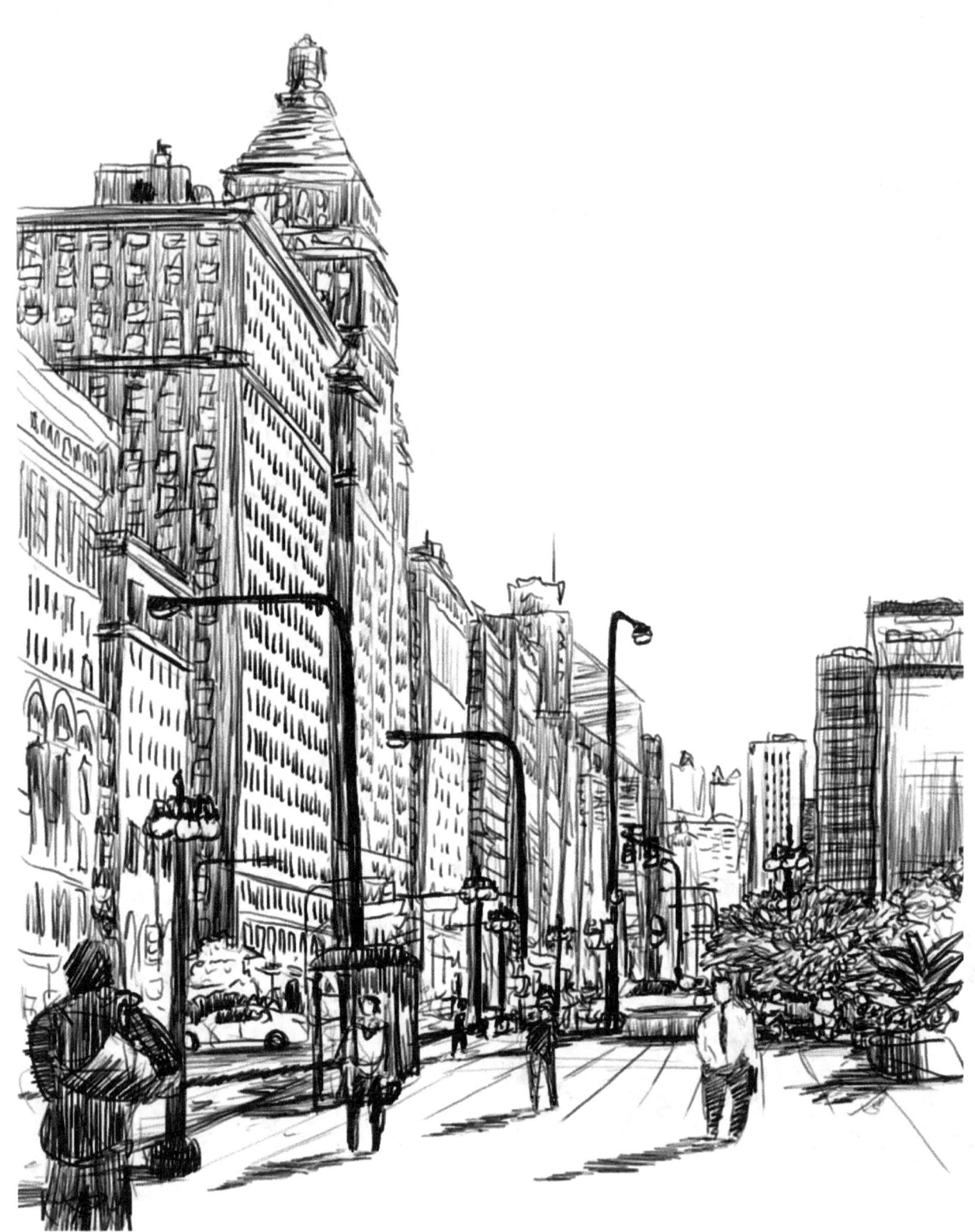

Closing Remarks

» The old saying "The first step is always the hardest." is only valid for skills. In art, nothing is more difficult than ending – which at the same time means perfecting. «

- Marie Freifrau von Ebner-Eschenbach -

7 Closing Remarks

With the concluding chapter of exercises we have reached the end of this book. I hope that you have enjoyed it and, above all, that it has helped you. Certainly, reading and working through the book does not make you an ingenious artist in the field of landscape representation, but the book should convey the most important basic knowledge. Through the exercises, I have tried to convey many more tips and to increase the level of difficulty without overwhelming beginners from the beginning.

In order to further improve one's own drawing skills, a lot of practice is required. Let yourself be inspired by your surroundings to create your own landscape drawings. You can also practice perspective drawing and gain experience in creating appealing picture compositions.

As you have seen, landscape paintings are very versatile and include several visual arts themes. They already belong to the more complex subjects in the world of drawing, but offer almost infinite possibilities. In addition, landscapes can also be used as a background for a portrait, an animal motif, a comic drawing or the like. So it can happen that sooner or later you can fall back on the knowledge of landscape representation, if you also enter into other subjects of the visual arts.

And if you have enjoyed this book, I would also be very happy if you would recommend it to friends, acquaintances or on the net.

You can also visit me on my website! There you will find more instructions on how to learn to paint and draw and many of my own pictures:

    www.art-class.net

Thanks and greetings to all readers and all who have supported me in creating my book!

Markus S. Agerer

Book Recommendation

Drawing Perspective & Space:
Basic Principles of Drawing in Perspective
von Markus S. Agerer

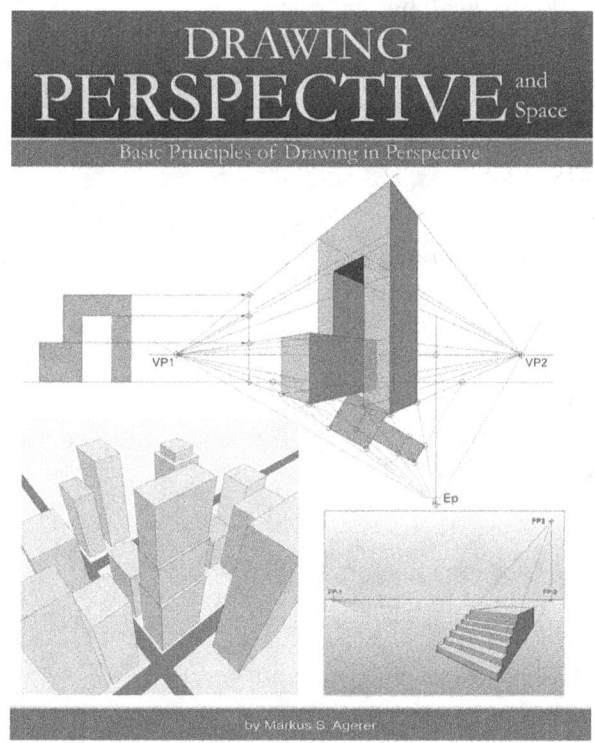

8 Source

Books:

„Perspektivisch Zeichnen"
Grundlagen zur Darstellung des dreidimensionalen Raums
Autor: Gernot Störzbach;
Verlag: Christophorus Verlag GmbH & Co. KG., Freiburg

"Underweysung der Messung mit dem Zirckel und Richtscheyt"
Albrecht Dürer der Jüngere; Nürnberg 1525

„Leonardo da Vinci. Sämtliche Gemälde und Zeichnungen"
Autor: von Johannes Nathan (Autor), Frank Zöllner (Autor);
Verlag: TASCHEN Deutschland GmbH

„Der fotografische Blick - Bildkomposition und Gestaltung"
Autor: Michael Freeman;
Verlag: Markt+Technik Verlag; Auflage: 1 (1. Juli 2007)

„Meisterwerke 41 – Caravaggio"
Autor: Gaspare de Fiore, Luisa Cogorno, Giovanna Bergamaschi, Gianni Robba
Verlag: Fabbri Verlag (1991)

„How to Draw: Drawing and Sketching Objects and Environments"
Autor: Scott Robertson
Verlag: Design Studio Press

Internet:

http://www.kunstkurs-online.de

http://zeichnen-lernen.markus-agerer.de

http://www.wikipedia.org

Kunstgeschichte - 20. Vorlesung - DIE MALEREI IN HOLLAND UND FLANDERN IM 17. JAHRHUNDERT
https://www.youtube.com/watch?v=hy-_259eRYs

How Dutch Painters Invented Atmosphere – YouTube Yale – University Art Gallery
https://www.youtube.com/watch?v=MZyr4cLgS5E

www.ingramcontent.com/pod-product-compliance
Lightning Source LLC
Chambersburg PA
CBHW080456220526
45465CB00006B/2287